Compet[illegible] Human Resource Management

A Complete Text with Case Studies on Competency Mapping, Modelling, Assessing and Applying

SRINIVAS R. KANDULA
Executive Vice President and Global Head—HR
iGATE Corporation
Bangalore

PHI Learning Private Limited
Delhi-110092
2013

₹ 350.00

COMPETENCY-BASED HUMAN RESOURCE MANAGEMENT
Srinivas R. Kandula

ISBN-978-81-203-4705-2

The export rights of this book are vested solely with the publisher.

Published by Asoke K. Ghosh, PHI Learning Private Limited, Rimjhim House, 111, Patparganj Industrial Estate, Delhi-110092 and Printed by Mudrak, 30-A, Patparganj, Delhi-110091.

Contents

Preface

I believe applying competency approach to the theory and practice of Human Resource Management has been watershed in the evolution of people management, ever since it came into existence as a managerial function. The end objective of Human Resource Management has been enabling people and institutions to accomplish their goals, but the means to attain them have never adopted such a scientific approach till the origin of competency orientation in human resource applications. Competency-based human resource management can provide optimization of human talent, and extend the benefit of prediction to businesses. Often competency approaches have been discussed more from a conceptual point of view rather than from a perspective of practice. This book is an attempt to bridge that gap in a fundamental way. I have made attempts to present the competency-based human resource management as an art and science in a simple and lucid manner.

The book consists of five key chapters. The first chapter deals with competency definitions and contrast competency with core competence, intelligence, multi rater inventories, performance assessment, and potential assessments. The chapter also tracks historical background of competency movement and how it had exploded the myth of intelligence as factor of effectiveness, and why human resource application ought to be competency-based. Mapping methods and techniques such as Repertory Grid, DACUM, Competency Card Sort Activity, Focus Group Discussions, Critical Incident Technique, Behavioural Event Interview (BEI) Survey methodologies and so on are discussed in the second chapter titled as Competency Mapping. The expected outcome of this chapter is to equip students and practitioners to identify the threshold and distinguishing competencies associated with successful performance of incumbents of different roles. Analytical tools to build competency models and establish reliability and validity are vividly presented in the third chapter of the book titled Competency Modelling. The chapter also discusses classification and types of competencies and model competency dictionaries and variety of sample competency ladders for wider benefit of readers. Benchmarking competency models as assessment tools are dealt in the fourth chapter: competency assessments. Topics such as assessment centers vs development centers vs 360 degree technique, Delphi technique, self-concept, launching an assessment center and their pre-requisites are included in the said chapter. The fifth and final chapter is dedicated to the discussion on competency applications to Human Resource Management in the functional areas of recruitment, training and development, compensation, performance appraisal, employee engagement and satisfaction.

This book could not have been what is now without the encouragement and support of my family, friends and colleagues. I thank all of them, and especially thank PHI Learning editorial and production departments, whose efforts have made this work as worthy of publication.

Srinivas R. Kandula

CHAPTER 1

Competency-Based Human Resource Management An Overview

Practice of identifying and utilizing human resource competencies, though existed in some or other form for ages; the credit for resurgence of competency movement goes to two eminent researchers of organizational behaviour and psychology—Robert White and David McClelland. Both the scholars have contributed in their own way for development of competency as a strategic business tool. Robert White, through his paper titled as 'Human Motivation Reconsidered: The Concept of Human Competence' published in *Psychological Review* in 1959, had introduced the concept of competence in a scientific manner. David McClelland (1973), who while working on the motivational behaviour, especially achievement motivation, had found that the real performance of an individual do not necessarily come from intelligence (knowledge and skills) but mainly from the need for achievement. McClelland based on his study of US State Department Foreign Service Information Officers and Massachusetts human service workers found that selection tests were designed to test the intelligence rather than competence. Further, research on this issue led McClelland to identify that competence is different from intelligence, and also competence is far more reliable factor than intelligence for predicting job success. Ever since this revelation came into light, a movement to identify the relevant human resource competencies has begun across organizations around the world.

Richard Boyatzis (1982) and Spencer & Spencer (1993) through their research and consultancy projects have spread the competency movement to the ground level of human resource management practice. Several organizations have realized the advantages of pursuing competency-driven human resource applications. Though, this trend is significant in the countries like USA and UK, many organizations in India also have joined the bandwagon of competency movement with the prospect of winning global business competition. Recognition of competencies as formidable performance tools, influenced the course of human resource management since it has implications for the way people are selected, trained and rewarded in organizations. Competency framework can be applied as foundation for the practice of human resource management to obtain greater business results. Recent publications on human resource management literature held the similar view. For example, Rodriguez, Patel, Gregory and Gowing (2002), based on their exhaustive study, argued that competency models can be effectively tapped to promote integrated human resource practice in organizations. There is ample survey evidence in support of growing allocation of resources and investment for pursuing competency-driven human resource practices in organizations running into several million dollars.

Defining Competency

Many definitions are advanced during the last ten years explaining competency and what it constitutes of. Despite this, the precise meaning of competency is not free from confusion. A few well-acknowledged definitions are given in Table 1.1. In a more general sense, competency is understood as the quality of being adequately or well-qualified physically, psychologically and intellectually to perform a role/job/task/ activity. Universally accepted definition of competency is a cluster of knowledge, skills and personal attributes that affects a major part of one's job that—correlates with performance on the job; can be measured against well-accepted standards; and can be improved via training and development (Parry, 1998). The pictorial presentation of competency definition is shown in Figure 1.1. As may be seen from this figure, knowledge refers to the information a person possesses in a specific subject/discipline

TABLE 1.1 Selective Definitions of Competency

Klemp (1980)	An underlying characteristic of a person which results in effective and/or superior performance in a job.
Boyatzis (1982)	An underlying characteristic of an employee (that is, a motive, trait, skill, aspect of one's self-image, social role, or a body of knowledge) that results in effective and/or superior performance.
Guion (1991)	Competencies are underlying characteristics of people and indicate 'ways of behaving or thinking, generalizing across situations, and enduring for a reasonably long period of time'.
Spencer and Spencer (1993)	An underlying characteristic of an individual that is causally related to criterion-referenced effective and/or superior performance in a job or situation. They further clarified each of the terms as under: Underlying characteristic means the competency is a fairly deep and enduring part of a person's personality, and can predict behaviour in a wide variety of situations and job tasks. Causally related means that a competency causes or predicts behaviour and performance. Criterion-referenced means that the competency actually predicts who does something well or poorly, as measured on a specific criterion or standard.
Rodriguez et al., (2002)	Competency is a measurable pattern of knowledge, skills, abilities, behaviours and other characteristics that an individual needs to perform work roles or occupational functions successfully.
UNIDCO (2002)	A set of skills, related knowledge and attributes that allow an individual to perform a task or an activity within a specific function or job.

and skill means the ability to perform certain physical and mental activities/tasks, whereas personal attributes represent motives, self concept (attitude, values and self image) and traits.

It is widely believed that knowledge and skills are relatively easy to modify and impart to a person while it is extremely difficult to bring about a change in personal attributes. All these three domains—knowledge, skills and attributes affect the performance of an individual. However, McClelland's research on competency reveals that personal attributes are more influential factors in predicting job success rather than knowledge and skills. In effect, he argues that personal attributes decides who performs on the job well, whereas knowledge and skill merely contributes for a minimum acceptable performance on a job.

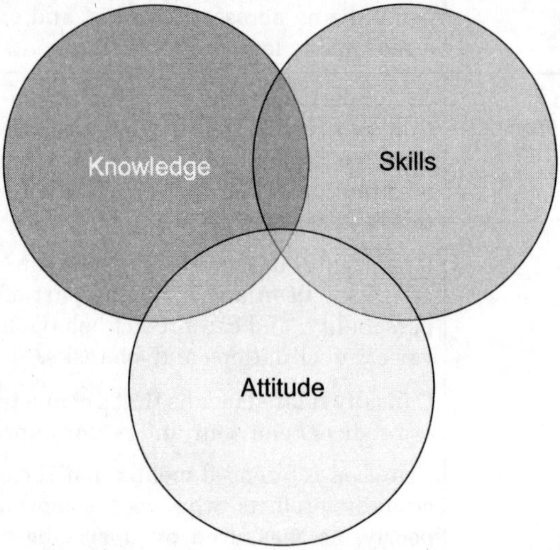

FIGURE 1.1 Definition of competency.

All these definitions of competency have common elements in them as illustrated here:

1. Competencies are a cluster of knowledge, skills and personal attributes such as motives, traits and self image.
2. Competencies are underlying characteristics of a person.
3. Competencies correlate with performance on a job.
4. Competencies can predict the behaviour/performance.

In this context, we must understand the precise meaning of various words used in these definitions for better grasp of them:

Knowledge

It refers to information retention. For example, how informative a company secretary is about Companies Act, Income Tax Act, and so on. This competency is primarily concerned with content part.

Skills

It refers to application capability comprising a series of actions. For example, a company secretary though possesses adequate information on Companies Act, but he/she may or may not be able to demonstrate the same in order to influence and guide the course of action. Ability to demonstrate, influence and guide the course of action in achieving an objective is called skill. Being knowledgeable does not automatically mean skillful. An individual may be very knowledgeable about planning management, but may not know how to plan the activities and implement them in attainment of a goal. Skill is personal to an individual that enables situations, and support people to reach the goals. Skills are not same that of tasks, functions and activities associated with a job, but distinct characteristics associated with people.

Motives

McClelland (1971) defines motive as a recurrent concern for a goal state, or condition, appearing in fantasy, which drives, directs, and selects behaviour of the individual. Motive in the context of competency represents achievement need. A constant urge to exceed the normal performance standards and maximize one's potential. Self-motivation, consistent attempts to stretch one's goals, etc., fall into this definition.

Traits

Trait is typical to a person, for example, leaving achievement of a goal to the external conditions like luck without making adequate efforts. Trait produces similar or same behaviour in a variety of situations. For example, a person tend to leave achievement of every goal to the factor of luck rather than to own effort.

Self-image

This is an important element in the personal attributes. Self image as the term represents one's own opinion/understanding/ belief about the self. This also includes self-esteem and self-worth in one's own perception. Self-image also embodies personal values.

Behavioural Competencies over Knowledge and Skills

Personality traits such as motives, traits and self-image (self concept, esteem, and values) can influence as well as predict the actions associated with acquisition and application of knowledge and skills for effective performance. Research conducted by Daniel Goleman that culminated into development of emotional competency framework proves beyond doubt that behavioural competencies hold the key for superior performance on a job. McClelland found that it is the achievement motivation that determines the actual performance rather than knowledge and skills themselves. In fact, this learning contributed for competency movement. However, none of these works emphasizing the importance of behavioural competencies does undermine the significance, relevance and contribution of knowledge and skills. These studies, however only point out that they only account for normal performance in any job/activity/task. As discussed earlier in this chapter, it is difficult to alter and bring change in personal attributes in comparison to knowledge and skills. Further, personal attributes form as a basis for actual performance on a job, and can be called pivotal competencies. As depicted in Figure 1.2 (competency tree), personal attributes are akin to roots, knowledge is like stem and skills are similar branches of a tree.

Are all personal attributes/characteristics competencies?

The term personal attributes has been used somewhat lavishly in the competency literature. Hence, it must be noted that all personal attributes/characteristics not necessarily are competencies. A characteristic should lead to effective performance and contribute for success on a job in order to qualify as competency. Further competencies in the context of competency management must bear the following elements:

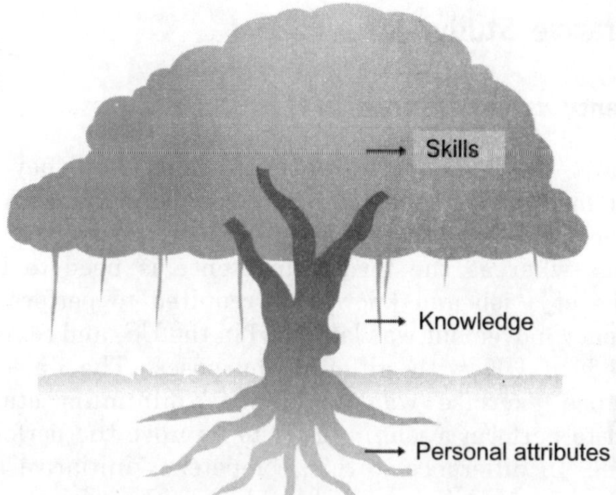

FIGURE 1.2 Competency tree.

1. Competencies must be demonstrable, for example, communication effectiveness. The features of effectiveness in communication must be clear, observable, assessable and evident for the professional eye.
2. Competencies must be transferable. For example, the customer care competency can be used in different situations and in various jobs. Hence, it must be transferable.
3. Competencies must be relevant to the positions, job families and to organization. In the absence of such relevance, competencies lose value. Therefore, may not qualify the definition of competency.
4. Competencies must be characteristics of employees that are responsible for effective performance on a job.
5. Competencies should have the virtue of predictability. It does mean, competency must predict the level of performance of a person.
6. Competencies must be measurable and can be standardized. It is the fact that some competencies are easily measurable and some are tough to quantify and qualify. The principle is finally they must be measurable. The second issue is standardization of competencies. Standardization helps for a meaningful understanding of competencies and their management.
7. Competencies can be developed, imparted and nurtured.

Comparative Study

Competency vs Competence

Both these terms, though are synonymous, but they convey different meanings in the context of competency management. Competency is used to identify and assess a person's personal attributes whereas the term competence is used to identify the tasks of a job and knowledge required to perform a job. Competency movement was launched in the US, and competence was used in UK with different purposes. The objective of competence exercise was to identify minimum standards required to perform a job, in order to improve the performance standards. In difference to this, competency initiative is more comprehensive that is intended to identify the critical personal characteristics of superior performers in order to multiply such superior performance in organizations through standardizing and applying these personal characteristics of superior performance for various human resource management applications such as recruitment, talent development, career planning and reward. Job is center of focus in competence and person in competency. Historically, competence is used for shop floor positions and competency for managerial personnel. However, there is a change in this scenario since more and more organizations are extending the competency intervention to non-managers too.

Competency vs Psychometry

Psychological assessment is different from competency mapping and assessment. In psychological assessment, the focus is more on psychology of a person such as type of personality, motivational behaviour and attitudinal framework. Such an assessment of psychological framework of an individual would not lead to identify the competencies responsible for superior performance. In competency mapping, the focus is on competencies alone; precisely what personal attributes of a person contribute for star performance and success on a job. For example, psychological assessment mere leads to identify the type of personality. In competency assessment, the assessment is to understand how a particular type of personality facilitates to behave in a particular way in a situation that may be responsible for superior performance. To put it briefly, psychological assessment helps in identifying the broad characteristics and competency leads to identify the superior performance characteristics by travelling more deep into these broad psychological characteristics. However, the wisdom and advances made in psychometry are widely used in competency management especially in competency mapping and assessment.

Competency vs Core Competence

Both these terms also tend to create confusion. Core competence is used at organizational level, as an organizational strategic tool for growth, for example, miniaturization of products is core competence of Sony. Competency is referred in reference to employee's knowledge, skills and personal attributes that cause superior performance. In that sense, core competence can be understood as an organizational level factor and competency as at employee level factor.

Competency vs Performance

There is always a debate surrounding what is the difference and similarity between performance and competency. Whether performance is the same that of competency or is it an indicator of competency or competency is an indicator of performance. Competency is what a person possess as knowledge, skills and attitude, whereas performance is what a person delivers. Of course it is widely believed that competency is a reliable indicator of how a person can perform and probability of success, and also performance can be a medium for understanding the play of competency and it's relation to outcomes of a person in a job. Also, one of the purposes of creating and implementing competency-based human resource management is to institutionalize performance behaviour in organizations. Therefore, both of these are highly interrelated, yet very distinguishable.

Competency vs Potential

Potential is defined as to what extent and in what area; a person can be developed to perform to a particular standard where as competency deals with what a person possess as core strengths and limitations. Both of these are closely interrelated concepts. Competency deals with both performance and potential since competency focuses not only what currently a person is demonstrating but also what the said person possibly can demonstrate in future. In that sense, competency can significantly help to gauge a person's potential, so competency is very useful in understanding the potential. Similarly, potential is an important instrument for understanding competency profile of a person, and both are very important to each other, but not the same or substitutable to each other, because their purpose, meaning and scope are different.

Competencies

Competencies can be classified into different categories based on their nature, importance, relevance and job performance criteria they predict. Categorization provides easy understanding of competencies and what they predict of a job success. Also, suitable assessment tools can be developed to measure these competencies. Existing literature on competency suggest different methods for classifying the competencies. These classifications are as follow:

Threshold and differentiating competencies

Threshold competencies represent knowledge and skills related to a job where as differentiating skills are those that distinguish superior performance from average performance. Attitude, values and self image, achievement orientation are examples of differentiating competencies. Threshold competencies are like basic necessities to perform on a job but not sufficient to obtain superior performance and real success on the job.

Generic and specific competencies

As the title suggests generic competencies mean every employee should possess certain competencies that are common across the organization/job families. For example, every employee must possess good communication and interpersonal skills. Whereas, some skills are specific to the job a person holds. For example, finance executives need to have finance-related skills and operations manager must own skills specific to his/her field. Generic skills can be referred to as general managerial skills and behavioural skills and specific as technical/functional skills.

Higher and lower order competencies

Competencies can also be classified into either higher or lower order or advanced and fundamental-based on their importance to a job/function/organization. For example, problem-solving, ability to face uncertain situations, ability to perform on the face of resource constraint can be referred to higher order competencies and performing routine tasks under supervision can be called lower order competency.

Similarly, tasks that call for fine thinking and mastery in a field can be classified as advanced, and activities those can be performed with minimum skills as fundamental.

Types of Competencies

Competencies also can be classified based on their type. For example, psychomotor skills, intellectual skills, analytical skills, communication skills, etc. Types of competencies involve various domains of human behaviour. Understanding competencies based on their type helps to apply and develop such competencies in a scientific manner targeting at appropriate domains of human behaviour.

Levels of Competencies

This is similar to arranging competencies in hierarchical order depending on their intensity and complexity. Typically, competencies can be levelled as primary, proficient and advanced. For example, the competency of interpersonal communication can be classified into three levels—primary, proficient and advanced—based on its effectiveness and causal relation to the superior performance. Same person may possess different levels of competency since the demonstration of competency is moderated by several factors such as motivation.

Macro View of Competency Approach/Framework

Competency framework should be given a strategic orientation for broader results. Such an orientation involves attempting competency framework development and approach from macro perspective. The macro perspective encompasses the following steps:

Step 1: Study of Company's Vision, Mission and Business Goals

First step in building macro competency framework ought to start from understating company's vision, mission and business goals. It is also important for competency managers to interview and hold discussions with key leaders of the company to understand organizational plans in more detailed fashion. The business plans, in short, medium, and long-term have significant implications for the kind of employee competencies those needed to be built in an organization.

A competency framework that has no linkage or weak linkage with company vision, mission and business values will not contribute to the desired results.

Step 2: Study of the Organizational Macro Competencies

Ideally, an organization should draw and clearly articulate the macro competencies that an organization possess or is trying to build, in order to further the organizational vision, mission and business goals. The macro competencies are the vehicles of an organization to achieve the growth. When such competencies are evolved into a matured stage they are called core competence. Though every organization definitely will have macro competencies built into it but very few organizations are found to have well-documented macro competency approach. Therefore sometimes, competency managers have to take up this responsibility to develop a tangible macro competency document and approach. This is critical for building employee macro competency framework, and whose absence or lack of articulation would create challenges.

Step 3: Development of Employee Macro Competency Framework

Based on organizational macro competencies, the employee macro competency framework shall be developed. For example, if in an organization, customer service is a macro organizational competency, then the employee competencies such as customer orientation, service attitude, customer management, so on and so forth, must be flown. Similarly, employee macro competencies need to be defined and the linkage need to be direct, sharp and immensely meaningful among all such macro competencies. The macro employee competencies should contribute for building organizational macro competencies in a robust and systematic manner. Therefore, the employee macro competency framework must be detailed and well-defined.

Step 4: Development of Employee Micro Competency Framework

This is the most operational element of competency framework. Based on employee macro competency framework, the micro competencies shall be drawn. For example, leadership can be an organizational macro competency. Similarly, visioning, leading, inspiring and so on can be defined as micro competencies. The micro competency framework must encompass all categories of employee competencies with operational definitions, behavioural indicators and proficiency levels. The micro competencies becomes a basis for all competency-based human resource management practices like hiring, training, performance and career planning systems and compensation management. The micro competency framework shall be understood as integral part of macro competency framework, because micro framework, essentially is meant to realize the macro competencies in an organization.

Step 5: Socialization and Feedback on Macro Competency Framework

For successful deployment and execution of framework, it is important that the macro competency framework is socialized and the feedback is obtained. Frequent meetings and educational sessions and debates are ideal platforms, which should be used for generating awareness of the competency framework as well as validating benefits from all the stakeholders. In the absence of awareness, understanding of the competency framework may not be at an appreciable level. Further, effectiveness of the competency framework is largely dependent on awareness and appreciation of the framework. So, it is important step and also this shall be done in a way that all stakeholders own the competency framework. The feedback must be used to validate and if required renew the framework. Such renewals can happen at regular intervals.

Challenges of Competency-based HRM

Driving competency management in organizations is a formidable task which is fraught with many challenges. Adequate understanding of these challenges and their implications is a basic necessity for tactful and systematic implementation of competency-based approach. A few prominent challenges are discussed as follows:

Gaining Top Management/Organization's Support

In an era of fast changing fads, it is not easy to buy the top management support for launching competency-based management approach. Unless top management representatives understand the competency as a valuable instrument of business growth, their support may not come forth. Therefore, competency manager's first task must be to present the advantages and essence of competency management in a way that top managers receive it in right earnest. Further, the actual implementation of competency based management can happen only when line managers take keen interest in it, and become partners of such movement. So, buying line managers' support is also of significant importance for successful adoption of competency management. Competency management is not a simple technique that can be launched over night in organizations. This involves organization wide revolution since competency approach literally can impact every system, process and practice of people management, and gradually, the way organization is managed. In view of this, ensuring greater awareness about competency approach is critical. A competency manager requires to devote considerable time and effort. There is a fair possibility that the initial effort may not evoke a positive response due to two factors. One is when top management representatives and line managers are yet to appreciate the real advantages of competency management, and second when they really understand the scale and intensity of efforts involved and resources required. In either case, competency managers must manifest perseverance and pursue the 'educational programme on competency', highlighting it's advantages for employees and organization in their growth plan.

Capital Intensive

As of now, transforming organizations as competency-based, calls for substantial investment in terms of money, time and man hours. This may differ from organization to organization depending on the size, occupations, number of people and business environment. Conducting organizational and employee diagnosis, mapping competencies, developing models and applying them as standards for improving the performance is a long drawn assignment for any organization. However, the investment is fully justified when results are considered in the post competency era. The challenge is, organization and top managers may withdraw, especially when they analyze the cost factor. Therefore, competency managers must conduct a systematic audit, showing the net benefits to organization when competency approach is followed. Competency management must be approached as a business case that helps an organization to gain strategic advantage.

Rigorous Process

Competency management is a complex, intensive, rigorous and soft technology-laden practice. Reliability and validity of various tools, techniques and methods used for competency mapping, modelling and assessment is very important. Utmost diligence is ought to be taken since traps are aplenty in the journey of competency management. History of competency mapping and modelling is not free from failures and mismanagement. Ensuring rigor is fundamental for competency management, and it is a major challenge.

Launching Organizationally Sensitive Competency Management

Competencies are organizational sensitive even in the case of organizations in the same industry. Therefore, competencies need to be identified in the context of an organization. Competencies that are valuable for one organization may not be so for some other organization. Likelihood of goofing up competency initiative is bright when organizations are in a hurry to implement some kind of competency initiative. They tend to opt for off-the-shelve commercial competency tools that may not be of much use.

Identifying organizationally relevant competencies is a comprehensive exercise, and requires professional support. Identifying and developing organizationally appropriate competency models are one of the professional challenges in competency management.

Competency Management is a Continuous Activity

Identifying, mapping and modelling competency models is not one time but a continuous affair. Competencies tend to change with the changing environment. Therefore, competency models need to be revisited at regular intervals in order to make them contemporary and valuable. The challenge is, there must be readiness to identify new competencies and model them for widespread application in organization.

ROI of Competency Management

Proving return on the investment of competency initiative is one of the biggest challenges that competency managers are likely to encounter. At this point of time, it is difficult to establish ROI of competency in definite terms as the subject is still evolving and currently there is no scientific model.

However, it can be established how a competency initiative can resolve an existing organizational problem and or how it can support attempts of achieving organizational change/growth programmes.

Advantages of Competency-based HRM

There are several attractive reasons why organizations must opt for competency-based human resource applications. Certainly, competency approach can improve performance of organizations through building organizationally relevant competencies. The following are the examples of how competency approach helps organizations, especially in their management of human resource:

Hiring right competencies: Competency-based approach supports in drafting selection tests that measure competencies. In a sense, competency-centric recruitment and selection ensures recruiting right people to right positions. This position-person fit have positive implications for organizations since the attrition rate tend to be negligible, and chances of person being happy with the selection and placement to a suitable position/assignment are fair.

Training effectiveness: Traditional approach of training employees, based on general training needs and based on the position and department they are working for, proved to be less useful. Competency-based approach has enormous potential in identifying employee-wise competency development needs and guides training initiative to build these competencies in a meaningful manner. Competency-based approach can bring transformation in the training system in order to make it more effective, both from organizational and employee point of view.

Skill-based compensation: Competency-based approach can facilitate in ensuring rationality in skills-based compensation. Several organizations though are inclined towards skill-based compensation, but wary in implementing in the absence of measures to assess the competency of employees. This void can be filled with competency management.

Career and succession planning: Competency assessment of employees provides a rich data on the competency profile of employees. This data can be gainfully used for career and succession planning of employees. Such planning drawn from the competency profile of employees can help an organization to create able leadership at all levels.

Performance improvement: Competency management can contribute for raising the overall performance of employees and organization. Competency-based approach helps in recruiting right people, training on right competencies and implementing right career planning method for building able leadership.

Views against Competency-based HRM

There is a school of thought that discourages and critical about competency-based practice. The argument here is no matter how systematically we want to capture, it is just not possible to build a competency approach that is realistic, and that has the capability which can drive meaningful understanding. Such views can encompass the following:

Not possible to capture realistic competencies

Often the competencies and behavioural traits which drive successful behaviours are not possible to understand and capture. It is possible to capture knowledge and skills part of competency, but not behavioural dimension of competency, because it is highly dynamic and invisible. For example, it is easy to capture the definition of a competency like communication stating vocabulary, pronunciation, body language, listening, articulation, content, voice and so on, but still that cannot capture what would make someone as a good communicator. The real connect that can happen cannot be captured through some standard definitions. Therefore, the view is that competency definitions always are highly bounded and they are not entirely realistic.

Competency approach is merely intellectual

Competency approach is more of theory and less of practice. Critics analyze competency approach is nothing new. It has been there in some form or the other, and what is new is only its title. Competency definitions and indicators are highly conceptual, and they lack practical orientation. In reality, no two people can be evaluated using the same definition since their demonstration can have huge variation, yet both of them may be having same level of proficiency in a competency. Further, the skeptics of competency approach believe that the competency approach is made popular by consultants more for meeting their own ends rather than helping people and organizations. Competency approach can be more for intellectual discussions and conceptual expressions rather than for managerial decisions and applications.

Competency is not a reliable indicator

It is also felt by a few mangers and competency critics that competency modelling and eventual assessment exercise are not a reliable indicator of actual performance. Even in competency like in intelligence quotient tests can be faked and someone can score very high and still be a poor performer. Therefore, the argument of skill can be only faked but attitude cannot be faked is not logical.

Time irrelevance

Competency approach always captures precedence, because it studies what succeeded in the past, and tries to suggest the same for the future. The approach conveniently excludes the fact that what might have worked in one context and occasion will not necessarily work in other context or the situation even when there is a significant similarity. Further, such an approach can run into severe impairment given fast changing managerial profile of work.

Competency approach undermines hard skills

Competency though is defined as inclusive of both hard and soft skills, however in actual practice the same is driven as mere soft skills undermining the importance of hard skills. It is fundamental for any success on the job it is hard skills those qualify and contribute for success but competency advocates have chosen to spread the idea that competency is nothing but soft skills.

Competency causes shift of focus

Since competency assumes that learning is only aspect that is important and not actual application can cause loss of focus from performance enhancement. Employees tend to believe that they merely need to demonstrate their competencies and proficiencies and they need not actually apply them at work performing on a task. Hence, competency approach can create a situation where there is more learning and less of performance and productivity.

Competency is capital intensive

Competency mapping, modelling and assessments involve huge expenses and budgetary requirements. Only those organizations which reap large profits only can afford to implement such an approach, and organizations whose financial condition is not very healthy will not be able afford. Therefore, competency approach restricts its usage and application to few financially rich organizations, limiting its utility and presence to a few organizations.

Competency ROI is questionable

Whether competency-based HRM will yield employee and organizational results in tune with the investment to be made is questionable according to a few experts. Especially the tangible benefits and their evidence is yet to emerge clearly. So one need to proceed with a faith that competency approach and budgets spent may give benefits but not sure.

Competency breeds homogeneity

One of the major drawbacks of competency approach is it seeks to kill diversity and heterogeneity and promotes everybody being identical in their behaviour. This identical behaviour deprives an organization of creativity and innovation. Organizations can thrive only when it has employees with divergent behaviour and views.

Setting Objectives of Competency-based HRM

Competency-based HRM must begin with formulating specific objectives for itself. In this stage, questions must be raised why an organization want to implement competency-based HRM. Precise expectations out of such competency management initiative need to be dealt in detail. There must be a clear need at organization and employee level for such an initiative. Need can be different from organization to organization. Expectation of organizations can be primarily classified into three types:

1. To identify the Human Resource competencies required to achieve organizational vision, mission and business goals,
2. To achieve and attain high quality and competent human resource,
3. To apply competency-based approach to Human Resource Management applications like recruitment and selection, training and development, compensation, performance management and career management so on and so forth.

Design of the Book

The concept of competency-based HRM is explained in four parts as shown in Figure 1.3.

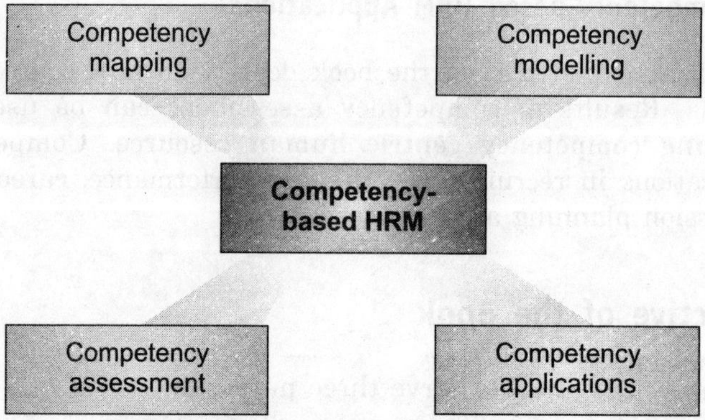

FIGURE 1.3 Design of the book.

1. HRM: Competency Mapping

The first part of the book is devoted to competency mapping. Process followed for competency mapping together with methods, tools and techniques are presented here. Selective experiences and case studies of organizations which have mapped the competencies are also discussed in detail.

2. HRM: Competency Modelling

The objective of this part is to present the process involved in competency modelling, step-by-step. In addition, selective competency frameworks are also illustrated to ensure greater understanding of the subject of competency modelling and how it is different from the activity of competency mapping.

3. HRM: Competency Assessing

Competency models can be used as standards against which employees can be assessed in order to profile their competency. structure. Methods such as assessment center, development center, 360 degree feedback system and multi rater approaches are discussed. Here also, attempt is made to briefly introduce experiences of organizations with competency assessing.

4. Competency-based HRM Applications

Fourth and final part of the book deals with how competency models. Results of competency assessment can be used for ensuring competency centric human resource. Competency applications in recruitment, training, performance, career and succession planning are discussed.

Objective of the Book

The book is written to serve three purposes:

1. To present the competency management in a simple yet comprehensive manner covering all the vital topics such as competency mapping, modelling, assessing and applying the competency approach to Human Resource Management.
2. To enable professionals to design and in implement competency system by providing a practical step-by-step approach to competency management.

3. To provide a standard textbook to postgraduate students of management, as currently there is a gap/scarcity of well-structured books on competency management.

BOX 1.1 Resources Needed to Launch Competency-based HRM

Committing adequate resources is key to successful adoption of competency management. Many of the resources must be already available in organization and some may have to be created specifically for implementation of competency management. The following are resources that will be enormously helpful in initiating competency management according to Dubois and Rothwell (2000).

1. *Organization sponsor for the project:* The support of top management and key executives in the company is essential for introduction, implementation and institutionalization of competency management.
2. *Constitution of project steering committee:* The sponsor of competency initiative must be followed up with constitution of a competency project steering committee comprising of members from line, top management and support functions. Steering committee would be responsible to the project manager.
3. *Project manager:* There must be a dedicated manager handling the competency initiative. Project manager must be given adequate authority and responsibility to decide all the issues connected with competency initiative.
4. *Adhoc project team members:* There would be many stages, phases and assignments in competency project for which different project teams may have to be formed to serve a specific purpose.
5. *Involvement of human resource department:* Much of the work is usually completed by executives of human resource department. It is ideal if the project manager is selected from HR area. Coordination can be effective if HR executive becomes project manager since large portion of work is to be done by the HR department.
6. *Equipment:* Computer hardware, software, stationary, etc., need to be exclusively provided for the competency project.

Summary

In this chapter, the basic concepts like what is competency definition, difference between competency and competence and difference between psychometric and intelligence concepts has been explored. The chapter also has dealt with managerial issues like types of competencies and categorization of competencies and raises important questions like whether all personal attributes are competencies and answers them in a vivid manner. Objectives' of competency-based HRM and challenges with such an approach are discussed. As a part of introduction topics like what precautions an organization need to take for launching competency-based HRM and design of the book are presented towards end of this chapter.

Questions for Discussion

1.1 What is competency and what is the difference between competence and competency?

1.2 What is the role of psychometric and intelligence tests in competency-based HRM?

1.3 What are advantages with competency-based approach to organizations? Whether will it improve the bottom-line? Will it result in more employee satisfaction?

1.4 Discuss the challenges with competency-based HRM?

1.5 Write brief note on categorization and type of competencies?

1.6 Establish ROI of competency-based HRM?

Case Study for Discussion

Belver is a financial company mainly interested in institutional financing. It employs over 6500 financial professional working in over 12 countries. All of them are qualified resources chiefly in competencies like financial management, audit, treasury, taxation, financial analysis, accounting, investment management and equity market management. The management of the company had invited human resource head for a discussion on the human resource model that company should drive in order to create differentiation mainly through the quality of human resources they employ. Human resource head came up with this suggestion that organization must move towards creating a competency-based Human Resource Management for which the management board has agreed and wanted human resource head to come up with budget estimates and assessment of what resources are required to create this competency-based HRM. Discuss and substantiate the resources required to create a competency-based HRM model especially keeping in view the nature of organization and its business.

References

Boyatzis, Richard (1982): *The Competent Manager: A Model for Effective Performance*, New York: John Wiley.

Guion, R.M. (1991): "Personnel Assessment, Selection and Placement," *in* Dunnette, M.D. and Hough, L.M. (Eds), *Handbook of Industrial and Organizational Psychology*, Palo Alto, CA: Consulting Psychologists Press, p. 335.

Klemp, G.O. Jr. (Ed.) (1980): *The Assessment of Occupational Competence*, Washington D.C.: Report to the National Institute of Education.

McClelland, D.C. (1971): *Assessing Human Motivation*, New York: General Learning Press.

McClelland, David (1973), "Testing for Competence rather than for 'Intelligence'," *American Psychologist*, **28**, pp. 1–14.

Parry, Scott, B. (1998): Just What is a Competency (and why you should care), *Training*, June, pp. 58–64.

Rodriguez, D., Patel, R., Gregory, D. and Gowing, M.K. (2002): "Developing Competency Models to Promote Integrated Human Resource Practices," *Human Resource Management*, **43**, pp. 309–324.

Spencer, Lyle, M. and Spencer, Signe M. (1993): *Competence at Work: Model for Superior Performance*, New York: John Wiley.

White, Robert (1959): "Motivation Reconsidered: The Concept of Competence," *Psychological Review*, **66**, pp. 279–283.

CHAPTER 2

Competency Mapping

This chapter presents the salient features of competency mapping. Study of this chapter enables readers to understand and practice competency mapping. The chapter deals with the following major topics:

- Approaches to competency mapping (including limitations)
- Process of competency mapping
- Preparing organization for competency mapping
- Identifying jobs/functions for competency mapping
- Setting performance effectiveness criteria
- Data collection methods for competencies identification
- Listing, classifying and arranging identified competencies in a hierarchy based on their significance to a job.

The presentation is supported by examples and practical demonstrations, wherever required. In addition, questions for discussion and exercises are also given in order to facilitate readers to get hands-on-experience with competency mapping.

First major step in pursuing competency management is launching competency mapping process. Competency mapping is a process of studying the job behaviour of employees in order to identify the knowledge, skills and personal attributes that result in superior performance. Various methods, techniques and tools are used in identifying the competencies that lead to job success. Effectiveness of competency initiative is largely dependent on the quality of competency mapping process. Therefore, utmost care must be exercised in developing a plan for competency mapping process. Currently, organizations follow different processes for mapping the competencies suiting their internal, external environment and business requirements. The most commonly used and popular competency mapping methods are discussed in this chapter.

Approaches of Competency Mapping

How to approach the competency mapping process is a genuine problem many organizations face once it has been decided to adopt competency management. The approaches to competency mapping can be classified into following types:

Top-down Approach

This approach is basically guided by competence, rather than competency. However, organizations that employ this approach argue that this is a competency and not competence approach since mapping is done using and with the help of job incumbents of various positions in the company spanning from CEO to junior most employee and by observing the job behaviour of employees at all levels. In this approach, competency mapping is driven from the organizational level as shown at Figure 2.1. In the first step, vision, mission, objectives, goals and strategic plans of organization in the long, medium and short terms are studied. Based on this study, competencies required to attain such organizational vision, mission goals, plans, etc. are mapped. This exercise would generate a long list of competencies that are essential for superior performance of organization.

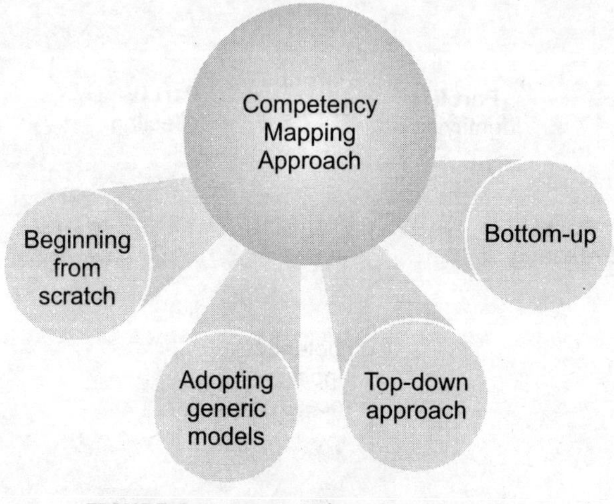

FIGURE 2.1 Approaches to competence.

Generally, it is a long drawn process that involves use of variety of data collection techniques, active participation of all employees and support of expert guidance. The competencies mapped at organizational level are cascaded down to functional/departmental/group level in the second step. Based on the nature of competencies, functional departments and work groups are formed. In the third step, competencies identified at departmental/work group level are cascaded down to jobs and positions. These jobs/positions are formed comprising the competencies required to perform in a given department/work group.

Bottom-up Approach

Process involved in this approach is reversal to top-down approach as shown in Figure 2.2. This is the most popular approach in the competency mapping. It is a person specific too qualifying the definition of competency mapping, i.e., studying the job behavior of employee that causes superior performance. In bottom-up approach, firstly key positions/job families are identified for studying the competencies required to perform those positions effectively. Here also, a variety of data collection tools are employed to map the competency profile of key persons holding these key positions. These individual competencies as identified are consolidated at the level of job families/work

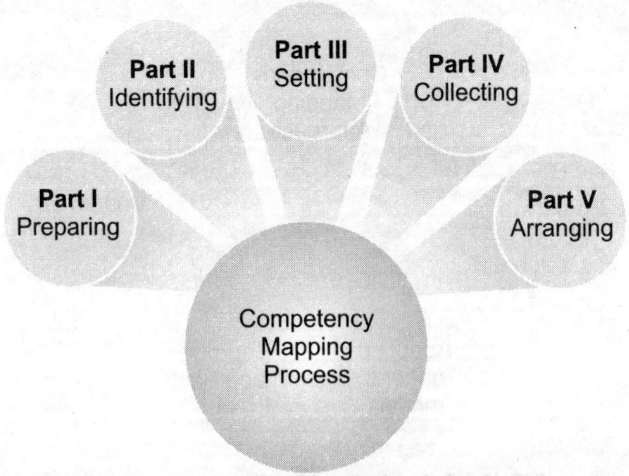

FIGURE 2.2 Process of competency mapping.

groups and in some cases at functional/departmental levels in the second stage. In the final stage, based on the competencies identified at person holding a position level and functional level are consolidated at organizational level. This can also be referred to as grouping of the competencies.

Beginning from Scratch Approach

Some organizations opt for initiating the competency mapping from scratch instead of adopting the generic competency frameworks. In this approach, organizations would need to form the competency management objectives, plan the competency mapping process, engage a competency project team and train them on competency mapping process, develop competency identification and data collection tools for identifying the competencies and map the competencies of target jobs.

Adopting Generic Competency Models Approach

In contrast to the scratch approach, some organizations adopt the generic competency approach. Here, organizations adopt the relevant competency models after validating and establishing their appropriateness. However, due to the increasing uniqueness of organizations even when they belong to the same industry, driving organization specific competency programme from the scratch instead of adopting the generic competency models has become order of the day.

Process of Competency Mapping

The objectives of competency mapping process are manifolds (see Figure 2.2). The principal objective is to facilitate building the most relevant competencies that enable an organization and its employees to create and achieve significant growth. Equally important is to help employees to identify their competency profile so that they can undertake efforts to develop themselves, plan careers suiting their competency base and to lead a meaningful work-life. As discussed above, broadly organizations have two choices in competency mapping initiative—either to launch competency mapping exercise right from the scratch or to adopt a successful competency model developed and practice in related organizations with suitable modifications and validation. As discussed in Chapter 1, it is advantageous as well as a basic necessity that each organization develop its own competency mapping framework from the scratch. This is due to the fact that launching competency initiative from the beginning can contribute for infusing competency culture in the organization. Secondly, any amount of modification and validation may not create the kind of impact the original mapping process can do to organizations. However, it is always prudent to learn lessons from the experience of other organizations and also to consider actively the competency frameworks while building one's own competency mapping framework.

It is also an undeniable fact that building own competency framework by launching an organization specific competency mapping initiative is resource intensive. However, when executed diligently and professionally, competency mapping can contribute for employee and organizational results superseding the costs. Competency mapping though is a practical and action-oriented process with significant results has its own limitations. Few of such limitations are illustrated in Box 2.1.

An attempt is made here to present the competency mapping process suitable for organizations intending to pursue competency mapping intervention. The approach followed here is neither top-down nor bottom-up, but a mixed simultaneous action. Managers intending to follow this framework can adopt as it is or can adopt with suitable alterations. The following framework captures a variety competency mapping techniques and in comprehensive manner. The competency mapping process that should be followed in organizations is contingent upon its history, human resource practices, business imperatives and internal and external environments. Due to this fact, today there are dizzying array of frameworks that are in circulation in several organizations with mixed experience of success and failure. A model competency mapping framework implemented in Anheuser-Busch Learning Center for sales personnel is described in Box 2.2 to serve as an example.

BOX 2.1 Limitations of Competency Mapping*

1. *Living in the past:* Techniques employed in competency mapping such as critical incident technique, repertory grid, interviews, observation methods, etc., help in identifying the characteristics that cause superior performance presently. They do not predict what competencies would be appropriate in the future to obtain effective performance. This is a serious flaw since competency frameworks developed based on present studies are meant to use in the future. In most of the cases, competency frameworks that are built based on the past may not meet future requirement.
2. *Irreconcilable differences:* In few of the cases, the methods adopted for competency mapping may be misleading and in many cases, the methods may not be wholesome capable of collecting all the data. For example, comparing highly performing employees from that of averagely performing employees in order to identify the differentiating characteristics is one of the popular methods in competency mapping process. It may happen that, even the highly performing employees may not possess some characteristics which are essential for effective performance on the job. Similarly, the indicators/dimensions/measures adopted by the organizations to identify competencies may not be fool proof and may be biased or favoured to the advantage and disadvantage of some people.
3. *A shoddy job:* It is the fact that several organizations that have attempted competency mapping have not been successful. Lack of professional approach and inadequate knowledge in competency mapping process is one of the major reasons for such failure. When professional treatment is absent, organizations tend to identify competencies that are too large to handle and adopt/develop competency measures and data collection instruments without establishing their reliability and validity.
4. *Cloning:* Method of identifying high performers and trying to create more such people based on the characteristics of high performers is against the fundamental principles of innovation and workforce diversity. Apart from this, it is difficult to create cloning since some of the characteristics that are responsible for superior performance of a person can be very unique to that person. Cloning may be a highly possible mechanism as a concept and difficult nearing to impossible as a practice.
5. *Short life cycles:* The competency frameworks that are developed spending months of effort, valuable resources and labour may become irrelevant in one or two years of time with changing technology, work culture and performance effectiveness standards. When competency frameworks are not reviewed at regular and frequent intervals, there is a danger that they may become counterproductive.

---

*Based on: Wood, Robert and Tim Payne (1998). *Competency-Based Recruitment and Selection*. New York: John Wiley & Sons.

BOX 2.2 Competency Mapping Model of Anheuser-Busch Learning Center

Anheuser-Busch Learning Center (ABLC), a US-based company was successful in competency mapping project for its sales personnel consisting of sales supervisors and frontline personnel deployed in various offices. ABCL initially had identified about 3000 competencies which were filtered down to 72. Competency mapping process followed by BUL comprised of 17 critical elements. These are:

1. *Organizational commitment:* Commitment of organization to competency mapping project is manifested by the active involvement of the head of sales and by extending significant budgetary support and deployment of personnel.
2. *Ownership/administration center for the project:* All employees in the sales department were encouraged to own the process and the administration of the exercise was kept with head of sales. However, the administration was later shifted to the development department when the project attained a matured state.
3. *Execution of the project:* The project was executed drafting help from various resource persons in the sales department. Outside help was sought by hiring consultant for development of data collection instruments. A manager working in human resource department engaged on job analysis assignment was actively involved in the design of the project.
4. *Kickstart of the project:* The project was initiated by launching a large scale communication on the nature of competency mapping initiative and disseminating its benefits and challenges to all employees. Head of the sales project took this responsibility on himself in sharing the aspects of competency mapping project to all employees.
5. *Helping employees to meet position standards:* BUL model designed to help every individual employee to assess own competencies and compare such self competency profile with position standards of competency.
6. *Periodic development effort:* Based on the step 2 above, developmental plans are developed on individual employee basis to plug the gap between existing competency profiles and desirable competency standards. These developmental plans are reviewed periodically.
7. *Periodic assessment:* The assessment of competencies is also done on periodical basis like once in a year towards end of the calendar year. The assessment results are formed as basis for designing developmental plans.
8. *Target of competency exercise:* Competency mapping in ABLC is targeted at mapping competencies to understand what competencies exist instead of what competencies should exist.

9. *Duration of competency project:* The initial competency project took about 18 months that include conceptualization, design of data collection instruments, implementation and writing of reports.
10. *Mapping results for developmental purposes alone:* ABLC restricted use of assessment results to developmental purposes. Results are not allowed to affect the management of performance appraisal, compensation and benefits and career related issues.
11. *Expected competency mapping results to organization:* ABLC anticipated that competency mapping exercise would help to eliminate wastage of training investment and effort, and lead to overall effectiveness of employees developmental efforts.
12. *Expected competency results to employees:* It was expected that competency mapping would help employees to identify their competency profile, prepare self developmental plans to meet the position standards, understand the competency requirements at different levels and positions in the organization and prepare themselves to acquire them in order to progress in the career.
13. *Measurement of competency mapping project effectives:* The effectives and overall usefulness of competency mapping project was assessed using feedback system and auditing the competency mapping process, especially evaluating how far the competency mapping project fulfilled its own objectives of building competencies.
14. *Target group:* All employees working in sales department with very few exceptions were covered under the project. There were 11 different working, professional and operational positions in the sales department for which specific competency mapping profiles were developed covering all the employees.
15. *Assessment instruments:* ABLC employed paper based and electronic form of tests, questionnaires and case study material using organization's intranet.
16. *Assessors:* ABLC had trained few of its managers who were found to be possessing requisite orientation for assessment activity. They were used as assessors and facilitators in competency mapping.
17. *Validation of competencies:* Competencies as generated using various instruments were classified into clusters. These clusters using charts with explanation were circulated among employees and opinions were sought. Based on the feedback and focus group discussions, the final list of competencies for each of the job families were decided.

Competency mapping is to be approached in an evolutionary manner with a professional acumen for real results. Competency mapping is a long drawn process involving a series of connected actions as illustrated in Figure 2.1.

Preparing Organization for Competency Mapping

Buying top management support and obtaining approval for competency project action plan, forming project team and training them constitutes the critical steps in phase 1 of competency mapping process. The objective of this phase is to lay the administrative ground work for competency mapping. This phase also must be leveraged for inducting competency culture in the organization as most of the actions in this step are meant for creating awareness of competency management. These steps are elaborated as follows:

Step 1: Apprising Top Management and Key Persons

The core objective of this step is to obtain the support of top management and also key persons in an organization for implementation of competency mapping initiative. It is possible that any line executive or representative of top management who is aware or know about competency mapping may initially discuss about desirability of rolling out a competency plan in the company. However, the responsibility for creating awareness, communicating the salient features, and analyzing and appraising benefits of implementing competency mapping lies with human resource management department. In many cases, people in the senior level though understand what a competency initiative means may not have been well-informed about the process and its outcomes to organization and employees. Therefore, in the first stage of competency mapping process, head of human resource management must either take up this responsibility himself/herself or identify a fairly experienced manager in human resource department to be responsible for spreading the awareness of competency mapping initiative. At this stage, efforts must be centered on communicating top management and key resource persons in the company about the following:

- Salient features of competency management in general and mapping in particular
- Process of competency mapping
- Case studies of competency mapping, preferably of related organizations if available
- Benefits of competency to organization and employees
- Challenges of competency mapping

It must be noted that this should not be a mere general briefing about competency mapping. Briefing and presentation must be done in the context of one's own organization. Issues involved in the process are:

- Why competency mapping is highly desirable in the organization?
- What will be the outcomes of such initiative to an organization? It is preferable that if presentation touches upon how competency mapping helps to resolve an existing organizational problem, how it can support an organizational plan of growth and strategic plans.
- What are the possible disadvantages the organization has to face in the absence of competency-based systems?
- What resources organization possibly needs to allocate for competency initiative?
- What are the minor and major problems the organization may encounter in implementation of competency mapping?
- Who can be the target group for competency mapping?
- What will be the possible time frame for completion of competency mapping project?

It is a prerequisite that human resource department must be clear and possess all the related information before embarking upon the briefing sessions. Not only thoroughly understanding/possessing the information on competency mapping process, but also how competency mapping augments the efforts for:

- Achievement of vision, mission, strategic plans and objectives of the organization.
- How it can address various human resource related problems like attracting and retaining talent, building competency centric culture and motivating employees for higher performance.

Presentation on competency mapping initiative should not be approached as if the objective of competency mapping is identifying the competencies alone. The objective of competency mapping is to enable business process, and enable human resource to optimize their abilities. It is prudent that human resource managers must ask the above illustrated questions, and seek answers themselves before attempting to create awareness in the organization. Unless, human resource managers are convinced themselves about the desirability of adopting competency management, it does not make professional sense in trying to embrace competency management just for the sake of it or for reasons not genuine.

The briefing sessions can be implemented in a manner appropriate to the context of an organization. Either, a meeting scheduled for some other purpose can be utilized for presentation on competency mapping project, or an exclusive meeting can be called for. In addition to it, intensive discussion can be held on one-to-one basis with a few senior level managers whose consent holds the key. It is important that head of human resource to take a few people in the top into confidence before making the presentation for gaining overall support of the top management team. Making more than one presentation also can be considered if the size of an organization is large and in some cases, two types of presentations can be done: one to spread basic awareness, and the second in order to influence the group for agreeing for rolling out a competency mapping project.

This stage typically puts convincing ability of human resource managers to the test. Therefore, adequate preparation and dry run of presentation can be done within the human resource management department before the actual briefing session. Efforts must be made to avoid using jargon not understandable to line managers. Presentation, content and explanations during the discussion must be straight, honest and based on substantive points. The briefing session ultimately must result in gaining the critical resources such as:

- Approval for implementing competency mapping project in principle.
- Identifying the principal sponsor of the project (one of the members of top management team as project chief).
- Approval for installing a separate group/department for competency management initiatives.

Step 2: Planning Competency Mapping Project

The deliverable at the first step is obtaining approval of top management and key resource persons in the organization for possible implementation of competency mapping project in principle. Once, the first step is completed successfully, the next step involves development of detailed plans for implementation of competency mapping. Issues such as 'how to do it' need to be addressed. Planning plays a significant role as this process enables us to foresee many of the issues and events. The plan must comprise:

- Identifying the target population/departments/functions to be covered under competency mapping
- Identifying exact resources required such as budget (money), infrastructure like computer, software, office paraphernalia
- Formation of team and their training on competency mapping
- Involvement of outside help like hiring consultants
- Methods to be used for competency mapping
- Nature of competency reports to be generated
- Types of uses of competency reports
- Post-competency mapping scenario
- Role of top management (where their intervention and support is precisely required)
- Zones/people of possible resistance and remedies
- Strategy for spreading the awareness of competency management to the bottom level of organization

The remaining text in this chapter deals with the above-mentioned steps in detail. Therefore, an explanation of these steps is not given here.

On successful completion of the first step, i.e., gaining consent of top management for rolling out competency mapping project, the first action that should be in place is identifying a project manager wholly responsible for competency mapping. It is preferable that head of human resource management or human resource manager who took the lead during the first stage be identified as project manager. Many of the issues involved during the competency mapping process are principally employee-centric, having relation with human resource management. Therefore, it can be beneficial if a human resource manager is handed over this responsibility. Project manager will have the primary responsibility for developing the competency mapping planning report as discussed above. Project manager must be made reportable to project sponsor chosen at the Stage 1 for the purpose of this project. Project manager and project sponsor should be responsible for identifying the rest of the team for competency mapping.

The planning report must be circulated among the departmental heads such as head of marketing, production, operation services, customer services, and other technical and managerial functions. Based on their response and suggestions, the planning report must be reviewed. As much as possible, the views of all stakeholders like head of the departments must be incorporated in the report. It is advisable that views of trade union representatives are also sought in unionized environment. In order to gain the exclusive attention of departmental heads, possibility of conducting a full-fledged meeting on planning of competency mapping project can be explored into. Such meeting essentially helps to deal with all the issues at a single stretch.

Once, the planning report receives the support of all departmental heads through the means of expressing their views, the same shall be presented to top management for approval. On approval, the planning report must be printed in multiple copies and circulated amongst all the concerned.

Step 3: Forming and Training of Competency Mapping Project Team

Project sponsor and project manager in active collaboration of various stakeholders in the organization like departmental heads, must identify the project team members. The project team must be heterogeneous consisting members from different departments/disciplines and locations. Members must be chosen on voluntary basis rather than forcing upon the responsibility or making it as a part of routine job responsibilities. Utmost care must be taken while forming the project team since success of competency mapping depends on the team quality to a large extent. There should not be any scope for politicization or discriminatory approach in selection of project team members. It must be made clear that the role of project team members is more of responsibility rather than any privilege. Any grouse and ill feelings during formation of project team can lead to dilution in the credibility of competency mapping process. Therefore, identification of team members must be transparent and objective process.

Project manager in association with project sponsor must make arrangements for training of members of project team on competency mapping, methods, reporting and code of conduct of assessors. This can be training at fundamental level. Wherever feasible, departmental heads and other line managers can also be invited for participating in the training. Ideally, training must be arranged in-house, drawing the expert faculty/trainers from outside. Project team members must be given sufficient literature and hand book on the competency management. They also needed to be exposed to sensitivity training since most of their work involves human process skills. The volume of team depends on the size of target population to be covered under competency mapping process. The objective of the training need to be to make members as experts on competency mapping, and, also as efficient users of the system as well as assessors of competencies. The training can span for three to four days addressing all the fundamental issues of competency mapping, especially at practical level. This forum also can be used to discuss implementation related issues. Care must be taken that the general responsibilities and positions of project team members are disrupted least for participating in competency training.

Step 4: Defining Expectations out of Competency Project Team

On successful completion of training sessions, preferably towards end of the training, project team members must be apprised of management expectations from them. Project manager ideally must handover them a written description of their role and performance expectations. Views of project members also must be taken into account while finalizing the performance expectations. Project manager must discuss the planning report of competency project approved by the management for the benefit of team members. Project manager specifically must deal the issues, such as deliverables of competency project for employees and organization as dealt in the planning report indicated Chapter 1.

Identifying Jobs/Functions for Competency Mapping

The objective of this phase is to identify what jobs, job families and functional areas are to be covered under competency mapping project and what methods (methodological issues) should be adopted for competency mapping. The coverage depends on the target population size, i.e., number of employees to be brought under competency mapping project. It is preferable that if all jobs are targeted, selective jobs can be identified initially wherever the variety of jobs is large in the organization. The mapping process can be extended to other jobs once the initial mapping process is consolidated. Project team members can be involved in this exercise wherever required. Following steps are illustrative of actions to be arrived on at this phase.

Step 1: Identifying Target Jobs for Competency Mapping

This is a critical step since precisely identifying target jobs for competency mapping is challenging. Action to be taken here must be consistent with planning report approved at phase 1 causing no or insignificant deviation. It may not be possible to select all the jobs in the organization for competency mapping since it is not feasible to perfectly map competency for all the jobs and in some cases the number of jobs may be too large to address. Therefore, a choice must be exercised in identifying the target jobs. Such choice needs to be exercised on the basis of a rational criterion like:

- Jobs/functional areas that are of strategic importance to the organization. For example, marketing jobs can be critical for an FMCG company.
- Jobs/functional areas where performance is not upto the mark and competency mapping most probably can bring significant improvement.
- Jobs/functional areas which can be studied easily.

- Jobs/functional areas in which if competency mapping is done can enhance the performance of organization.
- Jobs/functional areas that have the high visibility in the organization.
- Jobs/functional areas which are considered to be problematic and optimization is sub normal due to variety of challenges, like employee attrition, absenteeism, etc.
- Job/functional areas where resistance to competency mapping study can be least and encouragement is high.

Identification of job must be done logically and with substantive reasoning/criteria. Project team members, senior managers and departmental heads can be consulted for identifying the jobs based on the above questions. Option of developing a written questionnaire incorporating the said questions also can be explored wherever number of such senior managers is large. Data obtained from these resource persons must be tabulated and analyzed. Jobs/job families/functional areas as identified must be listed out.

Step 2: Determining Competency Mapping Methods

A few approaches to competency mapping are discussed in the beginning of this chapter. This step involves determining which of the competency mapping methods are most suitable for the project. Currently, a variety of methods are being used in organizations as shown in Box 2.3 Deep thinking need to go while deciding the method. Expert advice can be solicited in this respect. The appropriateness of the method depends on the overall objective of competency mapping.

The methods can be basically classified into two:

Adopting generic competency models after validation

The existing body of literature presents number of competencies. The competencies list is exhaustive and offers wide range. Based on the requirement and preference, an organization can choose a set of competencies for a job or a group of jobs. For example, customer satisfaction related competencies can be identified for employees working in hospitality industry. Competencies as identified for a job or group of jobs can be validated and

BOX 2.3 Competency Mapping Methods*

The following competency mapping methods are in vogue. They are widely used for identifying the competencies responsible for superior performance on a job. Though their purpose is same i.e. identifying competencies that distinguish superior performers from the average performers, the route they follow in identifying such competencies are different.

1. *The job competence assessment method:* Techniques such as interviews, critical incident and comparing superior and average performers is used to identify the performance oriented competencies here.
2. *The modified job competence assessment method:* As the title suggests, it is basically similar to the job competence method. The difference is instead of engaging assessors for making observations of critical incidents; employees themselves provide the descriptive account of such incidents.
3. *Generic model overlay method:* Organizations once identify the target jobs for competency mapping, opt to purchase commercially available competencies list applicable to such jobs or simply adopt generic competencies described in the competency management literature.
4. *Customized generic model method:* Two major steps are followed in this method. Firstly, competencies required at organizational level are identified. In the second step such competencies are tested and validated at the level of each job and modifications are carried out.
5. *Flexible job competency model method:* This method recognizes the unique nature of jobs and variety of competencies required in performing the job tasks. Therefore, a number of techniques are used to identify the type of competencies required to perform the job under different conditions and in different situations.
6. *Systems method:* Similar to flexible method, here competency identification exercise is centered on mapping the competencies required to perform exemplarily not only for now but also in future.
7. *Accelerated competency systems method:* This method is widely used in identifying competencies of jobs connected to production and services.

Adapted from Lucia, A.D. and R. Lepstinger (1999): *The Art and Science of Competency Models: Pinpointing Critical Success Factors in Organizations*, San Francisco: Jossey-Bass.

adopted. The process of validation is discussed in detail in the third chapter. Advantages and disadvantages of choosing generic competency method are as follows:

Advantages

- *Cost-effective:* Adopting generic competencies is cost-effective as this process helps in skipping a few resource intensive actions such as data collection for identifying the competencies and using techniques like criterion reference, critical incident technique etc. Generally, services of outside consultants are drawn to develop the data collection tools and in analysis of the data. This can be done away with in a significant number of cases.
- *Time effective:* This is corollary to the first advantage. Time that is generally spent on developing data collection tools, applying these tools and analysis of data for identifying the competencies can be saved. Substantial time can be saved by adopting generic competencies in comparison to the method of implementing competency mapping project from the scratch.
- *Roadmap:* Generic competencies, with their large scope, provide a road map for organizations. Generic competencies present a kind of ideas which organizations might have not thought of. Similarly, generic models lead organizations to progress in a well laid down direction in their journey of competency mapping.
- *Choice and range:* A wide range of competencies are available with good choice. This range and choice gives a good idea of the type and group of competencies required for superior performance. Even an original study sometimes would not come up with such a large list of competencies. An organization based on its performance criteria and business environment and demands of job can chose suitable competencies.
- *Tested and validated:* Competencies identified as a generic package are tested and validated. Therefore, they are reliable and effective predictors of good performance on a job. Further, experience of organization where these competencies are identified and used to promote can be of substantive support.

- *Improvements and advancements:* In a generic competency method, organizations could save efforts and focus on post preliminary work. Focus can be accorded for improving the generic competencies as identified and advancements can be made to them on terms of bringing fineness in those competencies.
- *Avoidance of duplication:* In a general and macro perspective, adoption of generic competencies averts duplication of efforts. For example, competencies required for front line staff in a banking organization are greatly similar across the banking industry. Therefore, it makes absolute sense to adopt all ready existing competency frameworks from organizations instead of launching a fresh effort.

Disadvantages

- *Too generic:* There is a danger that generic competency method offer too general competencies that finally may not be the competencies that cause superior performance. Generic competencies may mislead organizations by adopting them as suitable whereas in reality they may not be productive to an organization.
- *Culture incompatibility:* Competencies are culture specific. It is difficult to find two organizations with identical culture. Therefore, every organization has to identify competencies specific to its culture. Adoption of generic competencies tend to cause cultural misfit causing performance catastrophe.
- *Adoption can never be original:* Generic competency method can never enable an organization to feel confident with its competency management because after all they are not original. Practically speaking, competencies identified in some other context can never be suitable to any organization. This is like treating X organization based on the symptoms and diagnosis of Y organization.
- *Cost and time saving can be unreal:* Generic competencies need to be validated before their adoption. The process to be adopted for validation can set off all the savings accrued since the validation exercise starts from the scratch in the absence of any prior work on competencies.

In contrast, basic work that offer support to validation would be available in a job competence assessment method.

- *Weak competency movement:* Competency mapping process is not only expected to enable an organization to identify the distinguishable competencies of superior performance, but also to usher an organization into competency movement. This can be true with organizations where competency identification exercise is launched from the scratch. As opposed to this, organizations that follow the adoption model may not be successful in institutionalization of competency culture in the organization. The prime reason for this is, employees are involved and feel ownership in job competence assessment method and such ownership and involvement does not quite happen in generic competency model since competencies are adopted.
- *Counter productive results:* Generic competencies can cause performance dwindling rather than helping. Competencies identified in a particular job and organizational context cannot be the most suitable to some other job and organization though both are similar. The surrounding environment, culture and value system of organization have enormous influence on the kind competencies required for superior performance. Therefore, adopting competencies of some other organization or commercially available list of competencies cannot assure success of organizations. Further, the basic purpose of competency management is to obtain strategic advantage over other organizations through building organizationally relevant and unique competency framework. Such an objective gets nullified, if generic competency model is followed. In a few cases, adopted competency framework may destroy an organization's true character culminating into poor performance of its employees.

Initiating competency mapping project from scratch

The second most popular method of competency mapping is to initiate the competency identification from the scratch. It implies that an organization has to pass through the critical stages as explained in this chapter from part 1 to part 2. The greatest advantage with this method is organizations can identify and model the most pertinent competencies that contribute for superior performance. Such identified competencies can be used to revamp the total human resource management system from recruitment to separation, based on the competency approach.

Setting Performance Effectiveness Criteria

This is one of the basic yet challenging phases in implementation of competency mapping project. Once, identification of jobs/job families is done as target of competency mapping, their performance effectiveness criteria should be defined. Unless, there is well-defined performance effectiveness criteria, identifying the competencies of performance becomes hazy. There is also a view that such setting up of performance effectiveness criteria is not a basic necessity since competencies that contribute for superior performance are only to be identified. This school of thought also do emphasize that defining such performance effectiveness criteria only results in duplication of effort since many of the data collection instruments used for the purpose of identifying competencies do collect data similar to performance effectiveness criteria.

Therefore, there is a choice whether to define performance effectiveness criteria or skip it to address later during data collection phase. However, a brief description is given here. Following steps are indicative of actions to be taken as a part of setting up performance effectiveness criteria:

Step 1: Defining Performance Effectiveness Criteria Based on Secondary Data

With a few exceptions, all organizations follow setting key result areas/performance targets as a part of performance management/appraisal. In these documents, what outcomes/deliverables are expected from each job is defined. Further, these documents also contain operational definition/meaning of superior performance, generally termed as outstanding or exemplary performance. Data of outstanding performance can be obtained with the help of these documents. It is undeniable fact that, it is difficult to gain such quantified performance targets in respect of many jobs especially in service and research-oriented organizations. However, even in such cases, some indicators of performance do exist. The performance targets, at outstanding level, can be used to define performance effectiveness criteria for the jobs so identified for competency mapping.

Step 2: Collecting Primary Data on Performance Effectiveness Criteria

Data obtained with the support of secondary sources can be complimented with primary data. The primary data can be obtained using survey method. Employees performing the jobs identified for competency mapping, their superiors, subordinates and customers can be surveyed collecting their expectations of such jobs at outstanding level. All these data can be consolidated for defining the performance effectiveness criteria. Alternatively, experts can be consulted to understand what can be the performance criteria for a particular job/job families.

Data Collection for Identification of Competencies

The objective of this phase is to collect all the relevant information for identifying the competencies of superior performance. At the end, this phase is expected to generate comprehensive data on technical, functional and behavioural competencies. Currently, a number of data collection methods are in circulation. Based on the requirement, an organization can chose all the methods or some of them. Cost-effectiveness, user-friendliness, reliability and applicability are the issues those must be carefully evaluated while choosing a particular data collection method over others. Every data collection method has its own merits and advantages. However, various factors influence their actual utility.

Factors Influencing Data Collection Method

- *Type of jobs:* Firstly, the appropriateness and effectiveness of data collection methods depends on the type of jobs to be studied. For example, critical incident technique may be appropriate in case of administrative positions, because competencies in such positions are contextual sensitive. Similarly, card sort out method can be immensely useful for identifying competencies for a group of jobs/job families. For example, using this method, competency can be identified for people working in front office and sales in a hotel industry. Therefore, the first consideration should be, there must be compatibility between the type of data collection method to be used and nature of the job.

- *Operating organizational culture:* Prevailing culture of an organization also plays a vital role in choosing a data collection method. It has been the experience with some organizations that though data collection method they have chosen was highly valuable but did not yield factual information due to non support of organizational culture. For example, interviews can't obtain valuable information in case of some organization where an element of distrust exists. On the other hand, interview may result in collecting some information which may work against the interest of identifying competencies. Therefore, data collection method must be adopted keeping in view the type of organizational culture.
- *Type of organization:* Some methods can be most suited to manufacturing organizations and some other for service oriented organizations. Similarly, geographical spread of employees/operations and technology, demographics and educational profile of employees can have implications for the type of data collection methods to be employed.
- *Cost-effectiveness:* Cost in consonance with overall budget sanction for implementation of competency management must be ensured. Some of the data collection methods can be cost-intensive since an organization may have to hire services of experts. For example, hiring case study writers can cost, whereas the same can be dealt by asking employees to write case studies themselves incorporating the critical experiences. However, the cost consideration should not override the concern for quality and reliability of information. Unilateral focus and consideration on the

cost factor can defeat the basic purpose of competency mapping initiative.

- *Reliability:* This is the most important factor. Unless, method is employed reliable, there is a chance of identifying incorrect indicators of competencies culminating in identifying wrong competencies. Data collection methods tend to be more reliable in some organizational contexts independent to their own reliability. Therefore, reliability must be given due importance in selection of data collection method.
- *Resources:* Adequate infrastructure and availability of trained assessors is also a factor to be reckoned with while deciding on data collection method. It doesn't result in collecting valuable information if trained assessors are scarce, though the data collection method itself is valuable. Therefore, data collection method must be chosen in tune with the resource availability.

The most popular data collection methods are discussed in the following text, in detail, keeping in view their significance in competency mapping. In practice, an organization can chose few or more of these methods while considering the factors discussed above.

Classification of Data Collection Methods

Data collection methods used in competency identification can be classified into two types. Apart from these two methods, general sources such as studying generic competency models and competency card sort out methods are also used to gather the information.

Person-based data collection methods

Data collection methods here focus on the characteristics of the person performing exemplarily on a job and amassing the data on desirable characteristics of a person to perform a job well. Behavioural Event Interviews (BEI), expert/focus group discussions, interviews, observation, critical incident technique, survey technique, 360 degree feedback, etc., are examples of person-based data collection methods. Objective of data collection here is to gather the information about the characteristics of a person enabling to perform exceedingly well in particular job or job families.

Job based data collection methods

Focus here is on job. The objective is to understand what kind of competencies are required to perform the job well. Information collected in this type is essentially is used to compliment the person-based information. Position description, job analysis reports, job descriptions, job specifications, performance plans, appraisals, training curriculum, daily logs, etc. are used to collect the job-related data.

Data collection methods play a central role in competency mapping as discussed above. Other methods of data collection methods are discussed as follows:

Position-based data collection methods

Overriding concern of any data collection exercise is to collect the data in a meaningful manner so that it can be classified, analyzed, interpreted and used purposefully. Therefore, data collection techniques should be used in a manner that avoid wastage of efforts and focus on the real issues. There is a misconception that all persons holding a particular job and job families will be interviewed, their job behaviour is observed, and all such data collection methods will be used to gather the information in order to identify the competencies. Such an exercise can become never-ending and can present a confused picture on competencies. Therefore, the first task in using position-based data collection method is to follow scientific criteria to collect the data. This criterion must lead to identify and select a sample that result in collecting valuable data for identification of competencies of superior performance.

The most widely practised criterion sample is further explained in steps:

Collecting person based data: Popularly used criterion for identi-fying competencies using person based data collection methods is studying and comparing the following categories of employees:

(a) *Outstandingly performing employees:* Employees whose performance is found to be (exemplary: exemplary means performance must be far superior to expected level and consistent).
(b) *Poorly performing employees:* Employees whose performance is appraised to be below than normal.
(c) *Averagely performing employees*: Employees whose performance meets average standards.

However, classifying employees on the parameters explained above is easier said than done especially in organizations where there is no systematic performance management system. In the absence of objective performance criteria, organizations tend to classify the employees based on 'feel' factor or based on popularity of employees. This can be quite misleading and can lead to identifying competencies on wrong criteria. Therefore, organizations must resolve this issue in rational and objective manner before data collection phase is launched.

Results obtained in setting performance effectiveness criteria for jobs/job families can be used as the basis for identifying superior, poor and averagely performing employees. The other available sources such as performance appraisal ratings, reward management schemes data and star performers data can be utilized for this purpose. It is not necessary that an organization has to identify all the employees working on a particular job/job families. About 12 to 15 employees for each category, i.e., highly, poorly and averagely performing can be identified. This size of sample is suggested since it can permit the use of statistical methods for data analysis, and also it can be the ideal size to understand the performance behaviour. Where the total number of employees working in a particular job is less than 100, about 5 persons in each category can be chosen. Despite all these sources, precisely selecting the employees for competency identification exercise can still be tricky. Reasons can be organization-specific, and it is difficult to provide readymade solutions to all of them. The cardinal principle in such situations is whatever may be the solution arrived at, it must be objective, transparent and rational. In some cases, the number of employees in a category is so large that selecting 15 out of the total strength can be a problem. In such cases, random sampling or stratified sampling methods can be used.

Further, the sample must be identified in a way that represents the universe. The variables such as age, gender, level, tenure and location must be equally represented to avoid any imbalance and represent the universe properly.

Data Collection Methods for Competency Indentification

Once, employees (sample) are identified on the above described three-tier criteria, data collection can be commenced with the help of suitable methods. These data collection methods are:

Data Collection Method 1: Interview in Competency Mapping

Interview is probably one of the commonly used methods in all competency mapping projects. Using interview method for competency identification involves the following steps:

- Identifying interviewers
- Training/orienting interviewers
- Allocating interviewers for specific job/job families together with particular interviewees
- Developing the interview format
- Developing guidelines for conduct of interview and documentation
- Schedule for conduct of interviews
- Communicating the schedule and details of interviewers to all concerned
- Implementation of interviews
- Group meeting of interviewers
- Submission of interview reports on competency identification for each jib/jib families

These issues are discussed in the following text:

There is also a tendency to over use this method due to its simplicity. The fact is interview may appear as a simple process in administrative terms, but a complex issue from content point of view. Interview method when used objectively can obtain very valuable data, but can lead to gather wrong information and overlook vital information when bias creep into it or interview is implemented in an unprofessional fashion. Therefore, interview method must be used in a structured manner without losing the value of flexibility it gives. There are advantages and disadvantages using this method. The advantages are:

- Information from the job incumbent can be gathered first handed
- Depending on the situation and context, lead questions can be asked which provide additional and vital information
- Interviewee may find it easy to provide information in interview rather than some other methods where written scripts are involved
- Interviewee tend to share information freely
- Facilitates direct observation
- Generates exhaustive data
- Information which exists as confidential also can be gathered
- Allows flexibility

The disadvantages are:

- Interviewee tend to be subjective
- Bias can occur
- Time consuming
- Generates lot of low value and irrelevant information
- Expensive to conduct the process especially when expert interviewers are engaged

Interview technique by nature is subjective. This is both advantageous and disadvantageous (see Box 2.4). Subjectivity when used properly facilitates identification of right competencies, whereas improper use can cause severe problems. Improper use of subjectivity supersedes proper use for a good number of reasons. Therefore, limiting subjectivity in interview process is important in ensuring its reliability. With careful planning, training of interviewers, structuring of the interview process and by adopting the latest procedures/aids, the disadvantages of interview method in competency mapping can be tackled. Among all these, structuring the interview process helps greatly in ensuring the systematic approach and uniformity in interview.

BOX 2.4 Challenges of Interview Method in Competency Mapping

Proper recording of an interview is essential. Writing notes during the interview is no less a formidable challenge. Interviewer need to do a few things simultaneously without causing attention dilution. For example, interviewer has to ask questions, listen to answers, make observations and record the proceedings. Many a time, interviewee gets involved and presents huge data very fast that interviewer find difficult to record quickly without losing words and spirit. Therefore, enough precautions must be taken to avoid any situation that thwarts effective recording. For example, taping the interviewee proceedings can save the interviewer from writing on the spot, but can cause discomfort to the interviewee from sharing certain concerns and information treated as confidential. So, situational sensitive remedies must be adopted.

Similarly, for how much time, an employee should be interviewed is a question that interviewers often face without a definite answer. Generally, interviewing an employee for about 90 minutes is considered acceptable in interviewee method in competency mapping. However, the actual time spending can differ from person to person in relation to the position that person holds. Further, interviewer need to have a sense to gradually end the interview when interviewee is no longer adding any new, meaningful and valuable information.

Third issue is how many interviewers are required or what should be the ratio of interviewees and interviewers in competency mapping. Ideally speaking, there must be one interviewer for every five/six interviewees.

In order to ensure validation of interview, interviewee can be shown the recorded proceedings of interview, and comments can be invited. It provides an opportunity to sort out some ambiguous issues. However, this step is not a must but optional. Structuring means here, the pattern of commencing the interview, type of questions to be asked, method of questioning, and the format for recording the interview proceedings (A specimen format of semi-structured interview is given in Box 2.5).

BOX 2.5 Specimen Interview Format for Competency Identification

1. Name of the subject interviewee:
2. Title of the position (Job) the subject interviewee is holding:
3. Formal level in the hierarchy:
4. Department/Functional area:
5. Age:

6. Gender:
7. Location/Unit:
8. Years of experience in the organization:
9. Years of experience in the current job:
10. Academic background:

(Data for questions from 1 to 10 must be obtained prior to conduct of the interview)

Part I: General Information (to be answered/discussed by the interviewee)

11. Role and responsibilities
12. Nature of work/tasks/assignments performed on daily basis
13. Type of special work/tasks/assignments/performed by the employee
14. Other team members/colleagues with whom there is regular interaction
15. Details of other departments/functional areas with which co-ordination and collaboration is involved for effective functioning of the interviewee
16. Typical obstacles and problems involved in the incumbent's job for effective performance
17. Performance expectations of the position/interviewee in the future
18. Changes happening in the interviewee's job
19. Pattern of time allocation for various functions by the interviewee
20. Nature of work environment that is ideally suitable for effective performance

Part II: Specific Information (to be answered and discussed by the interviewee)

21. Share some of the incidents on the current job that excited you
22. Share the challenges and how you have managed them
23. Share the biggest problems you have dealt with and strategies adopted to resolve them
24. What upsets you in the job
25. Narrate some of the frustrating incidents and how you have overcome them
26. What according to you is most important for a person to perform well on the job
27. Share the concerns you have regarding the job
28. Narrate some of the problems/tasks you could not complete successfully and reasons
29. What technical knowledge and skills are essential, desirable and highly appreciable to perform on the job effectively

BOX 2.5 Specimen Interview Format for Competency Identification (Contd.)

30. What kind of attitude is necessary and how people demonstrate it for superior performance? Quote some examples
31. What kind of behavioural skills are required and how people on these jobs use them? Quote some examples.
32. What kind of organizational and industry knowledge is desirable for effective performance?
33. How the same or similar jobs are performed in other organizations. Are there any issues that other organizations are doing well?
34. How, why and when people in these jobs fail to deliver effectively?
35. What people in these jobs need to change in themselves and what they need to learn and acquire for effective performance?
36. What kind of behaviour demonstrated by the people on your job can make customers delighted?
37. What kind of changes people in your job seek and why?
38. What according to you are the competencies that are required for superior performance?
39. What should be the key responsibilities for this job for effective performance?
40. Share features and work behaviour of one or two of the most successful people on this job.
41. Share features and work behaviour of one or two averagely performing people on this job.
42. Some other additional questions.

Name of the interviewer:
Date:
Location:

Note: These questions are sample ones and framed for the purpose of illustration of competency related agenda points/questions/issues. Depending on the context of organization and type of jobs, the actual questions do vary.

Ten critical elements in competency interview

Interviewer has a critical role in interviewing the subject employees in order to collect the information on competencies. Interviews can produce counterproductive results if interviewer is ineffective, and over steps the role. Ten of the most important elements that an interviewer should be conscious of are described here:

- *Understanding and managing limitation with interview technique:* Interview itself is not self-sufficient in exploring knowledge, skills and attitudes of people. Even in its best form, i.e., when interview method is implemented under extreme professional conditions, it can obtain only partial information about an individual. Again, some amount of this partial information may prove to be imaginary and factually incorrect in due course. Being sensitive to this issue is very important while interviewing people. Sometimes, assessors behave in a fashion that everything about an individual can be elicited using interview method. Therefore, interview method must be associated with other information/knowledge/skills/attitude identification methods.
- *Understanding background of interviewee:* In considerable number of instances, candidates are interviewed without understanding primary information about them. Professionally speaking, interviewers must peruse the basic data about a candidate before interviewing. However, a common practice with interviewers is browsing through basic data of an employee while interviewing. There is a fertile chance of missing the vital clues and information in such a situation. Interviewees also tend to be internally unhappy with a feeling that the interviewer is not quite clear about him/her. Therefore, it is of utmost importance that interviewer must thoroughly read, understand basic data of the subject employee and write notes on issues of importance/relevance/irrelevance/clarification before commencing the interview process. Such a behaviour can enhance effectiveness of interview technique in competency mapping.
- *Understanding purpose/context:* Interviewers must be very clear why and what for is employees being interviewed. In other words, what the interview exercise is intended to serve, must be clearly defined. Interview process can be made meaningful when objectives are clear. In some cases, there can be a gap between the expectations of competency project sponsor/manager, and that of interviewers resulting in interview gathering/

yielding conflictive or low-value information. Therefore, implementing managers and interviewers must sit together and set the objectives of interview before getting on to the business.

- *Interviewer to be honest and straight forward:* Credibility for interview process largely comes from the attitude of the interviewer. A professional interviewer is one who is honest and straight with interviewees on one hand, and with competency project managers on the other hand. Honesty here does not necessarily mean only zero manipulation, but rightly evaluating the candidates. Suggestive and indirect questions only can contribute towards generating distrust rather than clever assessment of people. It is far better to converse with interviewees in a direct manner as much as possible rather than trying to find holes in interviewee's dialogue.
- *Interviewer keeping self in high pedestal:* Position of interviewer provides for a trap of superiority feeling. Therefore, interviewers who become victims of this trap tend to believe in themselves too much. This over confidence contributes towards manifestation of an authoritative behaviour. Authoritative behaviour constrains subjective employees from expressing themselves freely and comfortably. Unless, interviewer truly believes that people on the other side of the table are equivalent to him/her, it is difficult to ensure effectiveness of interview process.
- *Warming up is interviewer's responsibility:* It is primary responsibility of every interviewer to receive every interviewee warmly and help the candidate to overcome initial shock as quickly as possible. Hurrying up and not allowing candidate to settle down psychologically can only constrain rather than facilitate. Further, in such an incomplete scenario, subject employees perceive interview as biased and irrational. Hence, at least 3 minutes of time must be allocated for courtesies at the beginning of the interview process.
- *Advance briefing to interviewee:* It makes absolute sense to communicate in advance about the nature, purpose and process of interview along with details of interviewer.

There will be no benefit of worth to keep such information confidential, especially with distrust that candidates may pretend or manipulate their behaviour to suit the conditions of interview.

- *Trap of symbols and artifacts:* Interviewer and competency implementing managers must be conscious enough in not buying anything at face value. Substance is more important than style. Tendency of interviewers to see some kind of behaviour and extrapolating it to suit the decision can mar the effectiveness of an interview. Therefore, any information that is available on the surface must be cross-referred with an in-depth information. If such substantial information is not available, the same must be sought for cross-verification through the other data collection methods.
- *Making generalizations:* As a sequence to the above, there is a tendency to make generalizations and approaching the interview with such a mindset. There can be interviewers, who even without seeing candidates, draw conclusions about them internally. Such a behaviour can be proved to be dangerous in obtaining effectiveness on interview. For example, making up mind about candidate based on his/her age, gender, nativity, religion, function and other demographical data. Interviewers must be made sensitive to this issue; especially generalizations appear to be the common syndrome with many interviewers. The only difference can be the kind of generalizations they tend to make.
- *See-off subject employees with positive mind:* Effectiveness of an interview process depends upon how positive are the subject employees about interview. This is one occasion through which companies can send right signals and communicate about their company in right perspective.

Tips for effectively interviewing for competency identification

- *Establish rapport:* Interviewer must strike a rapport with subject employee for effective results. Employees tend to feel free to share the information when the environment is conducive. This establishing rapport must be a genuine process rather than doing it as a matter of routine.

- *Encourage interviewee to be expressive:* Subject employees must be encouraged to speak. Interviewer must resist themselves from interfering or disrupting the flow of interviewee. It is this uninterrupted flow that yield valuable information.
- *General yet specific questions/issues:* Interviewer must begin the interview process with general issues, but must facilitate the interviewee to progress to specific issues. Interviewee can be motivated to raise issues and problems that were encountered and how those were managed instead of interviewer asking specific questions at the first instance. Based on these incidents and narration of the interviewee, specific details of the case in the light of competencies can be sought.
- *Open-ended issues:* Interviewer must always raise issues open-ended instead of asking an objective pattern of questions. Objective type of questioning can lead to collecting information what interviewer wants rather than what interviewee possesses the information. Interview should be structured that does not mean the questions must be objective type. An open-ended discussion can help in gathering valuable information.
- *Collect the basic data about subject interviewee:* Interviewer can impress the subject interviewee as well as can save time if the basic information about the interviewee is collected in advance and behave accordingly. In this process, interviewee also can feel close to the interviewer and someone who has understanding about him/her.
- *Adhere to the format to a large extent:* Interviewer need to facilitate the interview in a meaningful manner. There must be clear agenda and follow that agenda as much as possible. The pre-designed format can guide the interview and assist the interviewee process to progress purposefully. However, such format should not become hurdle in eliciting additional information which may be more valuable in identifying the competencies.

The purpose of basic format is to guide the progress of interview as much as possible.

- *Facilitate and no directive:* Interviewer need to facilitate the interview and should not make attempts either to direct or to lead forcefully. In such an eventuality, interviewee may feel deprived of freedom to express and share certain vital incidents and how that person had manifested the competencies. Therefore, interviewer must be very conscious of this and respect the individuality and freedom of the interviewee.
- *Friendly language:* Interviewer must use the language in a manner that interviewee understand it fully. In some circumstances, language can put-off or discourage the interviewee to express freely. Unknowingly, language may make some expectations which interviewee would not comfortable with. Therefore, language must be used to the comfort of the interviewee.

Interviewing subjective employee's supervisor

The format given in Box 2.5 helps in interviewing the subject employees. The interview method however can be used for collecting the data regarding the subject interviewee from supervisors or seniors. However, interviewing the supervisors is not compulsory. This source can be used at the discretion and on need basis. The sample questions can be as indicated here:

- Who are your best employees on a particular job and why is it so?
- Which are the employees who need the help of supervisor the most and why?
- Share what kind and level of knowledge is required to deliver effective performance on this job.
- What are the skills required?
- What kind of attitude, interpersonal skills and values are required. Cite some examples.
- What are the competencies, the most successful employees on this particular job demonstrate?
- What are the barriers for effective performance of this job? What remedies are available, especially from the employee development point of view?

- Why and how employee on this job fail to perform effectively?
- Share some of the experiences you have with effectively performing employees.
- How employees on these jobs in other organizations perform and what is the difference comparing to your organization if at all differences exist?

Documenting interview proceedings

Building proper documentation based on the interview is an essential part of this data collection method. Interviews tend to produce huge volumes of data—both useful and superficial. The data as collected must be meaningfully classified. It is advisable that a pre-designed format must be developed for classifying the data as it also helps in codifying the data uniformly. For example, the data as collected must be organized into issues relating to technical competencies, inter-personal competencies, skills and conceptual related issues. There must be a separate section for recording the interviewer's observations.

These interviews along with observations of interviewers must be maintained employee-wise, discipline-wise, job-wise and high performing and averagely performing and poorly performing employees-wise. Based on all these data classification, a list of competencies required for effective performance in a particular job/job families must be developed. The limitations and reliability of the proceedings and extent such data can be utilized also must be dealt with in this document. For this purpose, all interviewers can have a group discussion before and after writing these reports. It must be noted that preferably an interviewer must be used for interviewing for the all same or similar jobs where the number permits. In other words, using the same interviewer for interviewing people on different jobs must be avoided as much as possible as it helps in developing document on a particular job comprehensively.

Data Collection Method 2: Behavioural Event Interview (BEI)

BEI is a key data collection method in competency mapping. The objective of this method is to collect behavioural data of a person at work. This method has been developed by McClelland

and his associates at McBer (McClelland, 1976) while working on a competency mapping project for US State Department. This method was developed to overcome the limitations of traditional interview method in collecting the most reliable data on competencies. According to McClelland (1993), BEI process gets a subject to describe three peak successes and three major failures in short story fashion. The interviewer acts as an investigative reporter asking the questions such as:

- What led up to the situation?
- Who was involved?
- What did you think about, feel and want to accomplish in dealing with the situation?
- What did you actually do?
- What happened?
- What was the outcome of the incident?

The advantages and disadvantages of using BEI method for competency mapping are:

Advantages

- BEI results possess high face validity due to its focus on collecting data on facts rather than beliefs.
- BEI process can gather the data which is underlying and pin point the real competencies due to its in-depth approach.
- BEI can reveal the competencies data which is not known to even an incumbent of a job.
- BEI is found to have high predictable value in predicting what competencies cause success on a job.
- BEI process is unbiased and can collect the data objectively.
- BEI yields the data that is useful not only to map competencies but also to help developmental plans for employees.
- BEI is a rigorous process that meets the research standards.

Disadvantages

- BEI can be used only when a job is well-established and in existence for a considerable time. This method would not be helpful in collecting data on emerging jobs and competencies.

- BEI involves use of well-trained assessors/interviewers. It can be difficult to train interviewers to a perfect level since such a proficiency comes only by repeated exposure and practice of using BEI technique.
- BEI is time-consuming. Developing BEI from inception to completion usually takes about six to eight months.
- Analysis of data obtained using BEI requires application of statistical methods for which finding software may not be easy.
- BEI is cost-intensive in comparison to other data collection methods in competency identification project.
- Analyzing and interpreting BEI data is very specialized job.
- BEI is a comprehensive process which some organization find it difficult to cope up with.

Despite some limitations, BEI is a powerful competency identification method as it brings out the feelings, thoughts and latent behaviour of subjects through its rigorous and systematically administered process. BEI especially is sensitive to the fact that even incumbents of a job may not be having a clear understanding of their own strengths, weaknesses and precisely their competencies. Also, employees may not always be willing to reveal their real attitudes, motives and behaviour. This sensitivity precisely helps in identifying the real competencies. Because of its short story approach, interviewee's tend to narrate their actual experiences at work and how they have approached various tasks and performed without making 'principled statements'. This narration style brings out the essence of an employee's behaviour. Based on this narration, BEI interviewer codifies and analyses data, describing the competencies involved.

How BEI is implemented?

BEI is generally conducted on the highly performing employees. However, BEI is evolved with the popular practice and now it is expanded to include the averagely and poorly performing employees. The following steps are involved in using BEI for competency identification:

Step 1: *Preparing for BEI:* Highly-skilled and efficient interviewers are required to conduct BEI. Interviewer must do a proper homework before getting down to the business. Details of the person to be interviewed should be known to the interviewer. However, interviewer should not be informed whether the person who is to be interviewed is highly or poorly performing employee. Person to be interviewed should not be known to the interviewer. BEI is generally spans for about 2 to 3 hours. The actual duration may vary by about 30 to 60 minutes. Interview need to be conducted in a closed place where possibility of disturbance is minimal. Recording the BEI is critical activity. Interviewee generally shares the experiences in a narration form. There would be many key issues in this narration, especially feelings, motives, thoughts, situational behaviours and the type of language and words used to describe the experiences. These aspects form the basis for identifying the competencies. Many times, the narration gets so intensified that it becomes difficult for the interviewer to observe, make notes and record the entire proceedings in its natural flow. Therefore, taping of the interview is recommended. It is useful if the taping is done with the consent of interviewee. Interviewer should be clear in his/her mind how to start the BEI, when to seek clarification and additional information and how to switch over from one experience to the other of interviewee. Interviewer essentially need to be an effective listener, possess empathy and demonstrate it in a subtle manner. Competency mapping project managers also should know the salient features of BEI so that it can be employed in a way that organization accrues maximum benefit out of it.

Step 2: *Implementing BEI:* BEI is conducted as described here:

(a) Subject employee is communicated in advance, at least three days before, that an interviewer would meet to conduct BEI. The purpose of BEI, venue, timing, and brief details of interviewer such as name and basic format of BEI along with a few issues likely to be addressed in such an interview are communicated. This can be done by issuing a formal letter or through an oral communication by the competency mapping project manager.

(b) Interviewer and interviewee meet as scheduled. Interviewer begins the conversation by introducing him/herself and commences the process explaining the basic purpose and format of BEI. Interviewer must make sure that interviewee is relaxed and clearly understood the purpose of BEI. Interviewer, must take lead to clarify if interviewee has any concerns on the BEI process and utilization of its outcomes. There must be trust and openness between both of them for effective conduct of BEI. Interviewer, if intended to use tape, must obtain permission of interviewee. Interviewer must start BEI only when it is clear that interviewee is relaxed, has developed confidence in the process and on the interviewer method and ready for the interview. Interviewer in order to gain confidence, encourage subject's participation and open talk and must conduct the whole process in an informal and friendly manner rather than in a typical interviewee process. About 10 to 15 minutes can be allocated for this phase of interview. The objective of this phase is to have mutual introduction, instill confidence in the process and motivate the interviewee to actively participate in the BEI.

(c) Once, the ice is broken and interviewee's concerns are addressed to his/her satisfaction, it is the time to get on to the core business of BEI. Interviewer can start this part of BEI asking the role and responsibilities of interviewee and tasks performed on daily basis. This issue should be approached in such a way that the interviewer just want to know the daily routine of interviewee. For this purpose, interviewer is advised to commence the process by briefing about self daily routine, professional activities, tasks and role and responsibilities so that interviewee gets the clue how and what to share. Interviewer must gather the basic information about interviewee's title of position, who reports to that person, to whom this person reports and the nature of their activities. Information to be collected must be very specific and if required, interviewer must seek clarification from the interviewee. For example, interviewee tells that about 6 sales executives report to him/her, interviewer must seek specific information what actually these sales executives do and what kind of reporting relationship exist and how the interviewee helps/motivates/facilitates/manages them. This phase takes about 15 to 20 minutes. The deliverables of this phase is to gather the specific information about the interviewee's role, tasks, responsibilities and other team members. Interviewer also must clearly understand the interviewee's job. If there are any doubts or issues that interviewer is unclear about, the interviewee's job must not hesitate to seek the additional information. Further, interviewer must also use this phase effectively to prepare the interviewee for the next phase, i.e., behavioural event interview.

(d) This phase is core to the BEI. In this phase, interviewee is encouraged to share about six to eight major incidents/ experiences in the job. However, the actual number of incidents may vary person to person, but a minimum of four and a maximum of ten needs to be ensured for a reliable BEI. Interviewer has to play a catalytic role by facilitating the interviewee to come out with the full details of the experiences. In other words, interviewee must be induced to experience emotionally the past incidents. Interviewer must observe the following guidelines:
- Interviewee must be encouraged to recall the details.
- At a time, the sharing of experience must be limited to one incident.
- Preferably begin the BEI with a positive incident.
- Interviewee must be helped to narrate the experience in a sequence such as (i) how the problem was detected; (ii) how serious the problem was; (iii) what were the existing remedies; (iv) how the existing remedies failed to resolve the issue; (v) how the interviewee thought a particular action was appropriate; (vi) how he/she gone about it applying the solution; (vi) what motivated to think in that way; (vii) who were the other persons involved in it and opinion of them; (viii) what was interviewee's feeling about the situation; (ix) what type of behaviour was demonstrated and (x) what was the end result.
- Interviewee must be motivated to dwell into in-depth aspects of the experience.

- Interviewer must present him/herself as a genuine and curious listener and at the same time be perform the role of scientific investigator/researcher.
- Interviewee should not be asked questions in such a way as it seems like critical probing, inquisitiveness and in a way that throws the person into defensive mode.
- Questions and additional information sought by the interviewer must be relevant, and must impose confidence in the mind of interviewee that interviewer is grasping the things in right direction.
- Interviewee must be facilitated to progress beyond the superficialities of experience and present the substantive aspects.
- Interviewee must be helped to examine the underlying aspects his/her actions in that particular incident. For example, interviewee can be asked what are the other alternatives considered while opting a particular course of action. What was the reason behind that action, but must be sought such information as additional details.
- Interviewer must gather the background information of the incident such as circumstances and other accompanying factors (contributory factors) for interviewee actions.
- Details must be collected what are the other minor actions/decisions/behaviours used by the interviewee in that particular incident.
- Find out how the interviewee feels about the situation.
- Some interviewees tend to be vague so that efforts should be made to bring specific points into the discussion.
- Interviewees also tend to make plain statements. For example, saying that I am a team player may not explain, what actually they do at work, and instead they speak what they desire to be in that role. Therefore, interviewer must look for specific incidents that demonstrate their behaviour.
- Interviewees also at time get very emotional. Interviewer need to use therapist skills.

- Rarely, interviewees also try to get out of the interviewee process as much as possible especially when they still feel uncomfortable despite interviewer's effort to relax that person. In such circumstances, it is better to take a break and meet after a gap of two or three hours.

Another important aspect is that interviewer in BEI should never jump into conclusions and generalizations. They would be smart managers and effective communicators, who can prolong the discussion describing how valuable their achievement is instead of presenting the real incidents with core details. Interviewer must exhibit curiosity and seek information into the specific details of that achievement. Interviewer also throughout the BEI must use friendly language. Interviewee should be respected in the entire proceedings as an expert presenting the views.

Interviewer towards end of the BEI can introspect at the whole proceedings quickly and seek additional information, if any, especially on what characteristics are needed to do the job that interviewee is currently performing. Interviewer can seek the opinion of the interviewee directly by raising the issue on what kind of competencies deliver superior performance on the job. At the end of this phase, interviewer must have accumulated valuable data such as responsibilities, role and job tasks of interviewee, and six major incidents in the job life of interviewee comprising success and failure, and interviewee's opinion of desirable competencies to perform exceedingly well on the job.

Step 3: *Concluding BEI:* The last phase in BEI is report writing. BEI report must deal with the following issues in detail:

(a) *Role and responsibilities of subject employee:* This must be the first part of the report. Daily routine, tasks and activities carried out by the subject employee, role in the organization/department and responsibilities, details of other team members, interaction of the job/person with other departments must be explained here.

(b) *Behavioural events:* The major successful and failure incidents occurred on the job of subject employee must be recorded in the second part. The report must be written here in the same way and style adopted by the subject employee. Each of the experiences must be written separately and with clear delineation. All small and big events, supplementary aspects and background of the incidents shared by the subject employee must be captured without any loss of data in the report. Interviewer must refer to the tapes, if used, and notes while writing the report.

(c) *Performance characteristics:* In this part of the report, the performance characteristics described and demonstrated by the subject employee must be dealt. These characteristics either the subject employee might have quoted while narrating an experience or indicated expressing the general opinion. These are the characteristics that contribute for effective performance on the job or reliable predictors of superior performance. These performance characteristics must be explained clearly and in operational terms. Performance characteristics as well could be drawn from the behavioural events discussed above.

(d) *Inferences and interpretations:* This is the last and final part of the report. This part is critical too for identification of competencies of high performance. Interviewer's analysis, observations, inferences and recommendations are dealt here. Such observations, inferences and conclusions must be based on substantive proof and logic rather than a simple feel or perceptual factors. The first three parts of the report are dealt here in combination, in order to identify and explain the competencies involved in that particular job. Further to these, interviewer must record self-observations on issues such as the general behaviour of the interviewee during the BEI such as the conversation style, expressions, language used, pattern in the explanation of major incidents (behavioural incidents), interviewee's seating arrangement, behaviour with other persons, arrangement of things on the table of interviewee and interactions with other persons if such things happen while the BEI was in progress, etc. All these observations essentially help to present physical and relationship settings of interviewee to some extent. This part of the report must give a clear picture on the following:

- Brief about role and responsibilities of the interviewee
- Behavioural events of interviewee
- Performance characteristics of interviewee
- Analysis, inferences and observations of interviewer

Copy of original proceedings such as notes and tape, if used, must be attached with this report. How this BEI report is used to actually identify the competencies and for competency modelling are discussed in Chapter 2 on Competency Modelling.

Data Collection Method 3: Focus Groups in Competency Mapping

Focus group is another key data collection method in competency mapping. Focus group method in the context of competency mapping is defined as a small group of high performers that meet at a predetermined venue and timing to have an intensive discussion facilitated by a moderator to identify and draft the most pertinent competencies those can produce high performance in a job/job families. Focus groups can be primarily classified into two:

- *Formal focus groups:* As the name suggests, formal focus groups are formed deliberately with a well-defined agenda to serve a particular purpose. There would be certain basic ground rules for functioning of this type of groups. Formal groups also made as structured by adhering to functional aspects such as representation to all sections of people, nomination of members through a rational procedure, defined agenda, code of conduct, duration, and defined outcome from such group. Mostly, formal and structured focus groups are used in competency mapping for the purpose of identification of competencies.
- *Informal groups:* These are the groups formed on their own and in a natural way. There may or may not be a logical end to the activities undertaken by such groups. People with common interest get together voluntarily in order to create opportunities or defend themselves in

some situations. Results of informal focus groups reported to be extreme. Rarely informal focus groups are highly effective and mostly they fail to serve any meaningful purpose and disappear automatically. Informal focus groups are seldom used in competency mapping as a data collection tool as its design does not suit to the purpose of identification of competencies in a systematic fashion.

Process of focus groups in identification of competencies

Focus groups for competency identification purpose are the functions which go through the following steps:

Step 1: *Forming focus group:* In the first step, focus group is formed with a membership of about six to twelve employees depending on the requirement. The chief criteria for inviting an employee to be member of the focus group is consistent outstanding performance in a particular job for which competency identification exercise is taken up.

Step 2: *Identifying moderator:* A neutral and well-trained moderator is to be identified either through internal or external source to facilitate the focus group discussion.

Step 3: *Briefing of participants:* Employees who are identified as participants of focus group must be communicated the purpose, methodology, and agenda of focus group meeting well in advance enabling them to seek any clarifications and also to do their own preparation.

Step 4: *Conducting focus group meeting for identification of competencies:* Focus group meeting should be conducted at stipulated venue, date and time. Moderator must start the discussion with a positive note and encourage members to participate actively. Generally, focus group members are handed over a chart of competencies primarily identified for job/job families and asked to select the competencies that contribute for exemplary performance on the job. Members are also invited to add any competencies that the list has not considered. Towards the end of this meeting, focus group is expected to come up with a draft list of competencies for a particular job.

Step 5: *Final version of competencies list:* After break of about a couple of hours from the meeting or during the next day, focus group meets again to have a fresh look at the first draft of competencies it has finalized. Focus groups generally improve upon the first draft and bring out final version of competencies list. The list as finalized by the group is passed on to the competency project manager. Moderator also submits a report with his observations on how the focus group has approached the issue and mentions the overall comment on the effectiveness of the focus group in terms of group processes.

Competency mapping project manager seeks comments of experts of that particular job within or outside the organization, and review in the light of such comments before accepting the same.

Similar to other methods, focus groups too have their own advantages and disadvantages when used as a data collection tool for competency mapping. These are as follows:

Advantages

- *Fast:* Since people involved are internal and readily available, the focus groups approach really helps to cut down the time in competency mapping.
- *Cost-effective:* Using focus groups is highly cost effective since no special resources are required for this purpose.
- *Simplicity:* Using focus groups as a tool for competency identification is comparatively a simple process. Competency project manager is just need to identify a group of internal employees on a defined criterion and convene the meeting with the help of a moderator. The result just comes out instantly.
- *Realistic:* Experienced and successful people on the jobs form as a focus group. Therefore, competencies identified by such group tend to be realistic and well defined in operational terms.

Disadvantages

- *Less comprehensive:* There is a possibility that focus groups can fail to bring real issues onto the surface. Often, focus group members attend focus group meeting without ample preparation. They also tend to not taking such assignment serious enough since it is not part of their jobs. As a result, they pay inadequate attention. Therefore, data obtained using focus group method can be less comprehensive.

- *Amateur moderator:* Quality of focus group discussions and output depends on the quality of moderators. Organizations either use internal moderator or external moderator. Both of them are likely to bring with them their own disadvantages. Often internal moderators lack sufficient experience in conducting focus groups and external moderators lag behind in the functional knowledge of the agenda issues.
- *Group dynamics:* Each focus group comprises six to twelve members drawn from the organization. They bring with them their historical differences, past differences and prejudices those adversely affect the discussion on the competency identification.
- *Superficiality:* There is a criticism against focus groups that they tend to be very superficial and benign in their approach, discussion and solutions. Focus groups are susceptible to behave in a manner that they just need to finish the job of finalizing some competencies for a job rather than committing themselves to bring out the best of results.
- *Too wide:* Another disadvantage is that focus groups tend to identify too many job competencies. Every member of the team wants to contribute by adding some competencies. Members see their role in quantitative terms rather than in qualitative terms. In such eventuality, it becomes too difficult to cover such a long list of competencies.
- *Influence of minority:* Regardless of actual strength of focus group, one or two members tend to dominate the whole proceedings affecting the quality of focus groups contribution negatively.
- *Imbalanced composition:* Effectiveness of focus groups is largely influenced by the nature of composition of focus group. In a few cases, the composition tends to be imbalanced with over load or less of representation to some. Such imbalanced composition can lead to identification of incorrect competencies.

The list of disadvantages may appear long, but all of them can easily be tackled with a professional approach. It is no denying the fact that quite a few focus groups fail to deliver expected results due to one or the other reason. However, often such reasons can be attributable to non-professional and casual approach adopted towards conceptualization and implementation of focus groups for identification of competencies. Moderator plays a key role in ensuring the effectiveness of focus groups in identifying the competencies successfully. Eight skills and characteristics of professional moderators are described in Box 2.6.

BOX 2.6 Focus Groups: Skills and Characteristics of Effective Moderators

1. *Effective communication skills:* Moderator must possess and demonstrate oral and written communication skills effectively. Apart from communicating across the participants, moderator also must exhibit good listening abilities.
2. *Sensitivity to others:* Moderator should have sensitivity to others logic, perspective, limitations, behaviour and need to show empathy. This enhances the acceptability of moderator among the participants.
3. *Professional image:* Moderator must carry credibility and professional image through demonstrating knowledge and abilities in facilitating focus groups to function effectively.
4. *Memory:* Moderator should have a good memory. Several things happen while focus group is in progress. Moderator need to intervene, facilitate and recapitulate certain facts happened in the beginning or middle of the discussions in order to bring them to the notice of the members. Further, moderator needs to write a report describing the focus group experience and analysis of group discussions after the discussions. Moderator, in order to do this, has to recollect even the minor details.
5. *Patience:* Moderator needs to have high degree of patience levels. Sometimes, it takes lot of concentrated effort to ignite the participants to come out with real good ideas. A few participants at time tend to be casual, some may not grasp quickly and others just behave in an unprofessional way. There would be conflicts and misunderstanding among the members. All these need to be tackled by moderator without losing patience.
6. *Ability to establish rapport:* Moderator should possess and demonstrate interpersonal skills for establishing rapport with participants of focus group. Most of the effectiveness of focus groups comes from the rapport building. Moderator also must ensure the rapport among the members of focus group.

BOX 2.6 Focus Groups: Skills and Characteristics of Effective Moderators (*Contd.*)

7. *Ability to motivate and encourage active participation:* Moderator should have adequate skills to break the ice as quickly as possible, and motivate the participants of focus group to share their views and contribute for the discussion actively.
8. *Ability to Obtain Consensus:* This is the most critical part of moderator's role. Eventually, every focus group is expected to make contribution by identifying the relevant competencies of job/job families. However, this needs to be achieved through consensus since consensual approach can ensure identification of right competencies. It is also natural that members of the focus group do differ in their perceptions and beliefs. Some of them may refuse to see other's points of views. Here, moderator needs to perform an effective role by bringing out commonalities in their opinions, though they may appear as differing on the surface.

Especially, by adopting a scientific focus group method, these disadvantages can be overcome easily. Six principles for effective focus groups are illustrated in Box 2.7.

BOX 2.7 Six Principles of Effective Focus Groups for Competency Identification

1. *Get the right people into group:* Quality of discussion and ultimately outcome depends upon the competency of group members. Therefore, competency project manager and other team members must ensure that right people are nominated as members of focus group representing all age, gender, experience and locations of the organization on that particular job/job family. Further, though focus group method in competency mapping suggests induction of highly performing people into focus group, sometimes some of these people may lack communication and inter personal abilities. Reason being, traditionally companies treat technically and functionally competent people as high performing people. In reality, it can only be partially true. Therefore, utmost care must be exercised to nominate only highly competency people in the focus group.
2. *Set the right ground rules:* There must be a clear procedure, guidelines, dos, and don'ts for conducting and concluding focus groups. If the ground rules are hazy or non-existent, it may contribute for ineffective focus group proceedings. Such ground rules must be adhered to right from identification of right members to finalization of group proceedings for identification of competencies.

3. *Create the right psychological atmosphere:* The psychological atmosphere surrounding the focus group event is extremely important. Members must feel absolute freedom, honest and commit to contribute their best. Focus group may fall short in delivering expected standard of performance if the atmosphere creates some kind of suspicion or skepticism. Such right psychological atmosphere can be ensured only through straight talk and commitment of top management and behaviour of competency project team apart from the way the focus group members are treated.
4. *Make advance briefing:* Focus group members must be clearly communicated how they have been identified, what is the problem, what they are expected to contribute, how they can progress in identifying the competencies in a systematic way and what are the ground rules for functioning of the focus group. Such briefing, in advance helps members to prepare themselves and frees them from any anxiety or apprehensions.
5. *Chose neutral and professional moderator:* Moderator has a key role in facilitating the focus group to perform effectively. Moderator has to establish rapport, motivate and encourage focus group members to participate and also is required to record and analyze the proceedings. Further, the image of moderator must be neutral in the eyes of participants. By choosing neutral and professional moderator, focus group event can be conducted successfully.

Further, any focus group meeting should be opened with a positive mode, all members must be asked whether they have received advance information regarding the agenda, seek views of the members on competencies one by one: must be ensured that every members gets an opportunity to express freely and fully, and record the proceedings in a professional manner without loss of any critical and supplementary information.

DACUM

There are many methods within the formal focus groups that organizations adopt for identification of competencies. A method called DACUM popularized by Robert Norton (1987, 1997) is immensely useful in implementing focus groups method. Dacum is the acronym for **D**evelopment of **a Cu**rriculu**m**—widely used as an occupational analysis tool. It is a one or two days story boarding process that provides a picture of what an employee does in terms of duties, tasks, knowledge, skills and traits.

Dacum process begins with the identification of job title, and builds in detail up to and a thorough job analysis. Dacum method is developed on a premise that expert employees can better describe the duties and responsibilities involved for superior performance than anyone else. Dacum process precisely starts with identifying the major duties involved in a job, tasks included in each of such duties, knowledge and skills needed to perform well in the job, personal attributes needed to be successful in the work and finally identifies the competencies based on all the steps discussed. Similar to any focus group method, Dacum engages a panel of expert employees for the discussion, a neutral facilitator and person to make observation and records the proceedings.

Data Collection Method 4: Critical Incident Technique in Competency Mapping

Critical Incident Technique has been developed by Flanagan during 1950s while studying the effective and ineffective performance among air force officers in administrative positions. According to Flanagan:

- The critical incident technique consist of a set of procedures for collecting direct observations of human behaviour in such a way as to facilitate their potential usefulness in solving practical problems, and developing broad psychological principles.
- The critical incident technique outlines procedures for collecting observed incidents having special significance and meeting systematically defined criteria.
- By an incident is meant any observable human activity that is sufficiently complete in itself to permit inferences and predictions to be made about the person performing the act.
- To be critical, an incident must occur in a situation where the purpose or intent of the act seems fairly clear to the observer and where its consequences are sufficiently definite to leave little doubt concerning its effects.

In competency mapping, critical incident technique is used to collect the data on exceptionally effective or exceptionally ineffective behaviour in particular conditions. Generally, critical incident technique in competency mapping is used as a part of BEI. Critical incident technique has its advantages and disadvantages while used as a data collection method in competency mapping.

Advantages

- Critical incident technique can yield valuable data on effective performance behaviour in exceptional situations/ circumstances in a job.
- Implementation of this technique is simpler comparing to other methods since either as part of BEI or in simple interviews, the job incumbents can be asked to explain the critical incidents happened and their behaviour in those situations.
- Implementation of critical incident technique for data collection on competencies is cost-effective since no extra or special facilities need to be created for this purpose.
- Data of critical incidents and exceptionally effective behaviour of incumbents in these incidents is critical since competency mapping is aimed at understanding the high performance-oriented competencies rather than simple daily tasks and duties.

Disadvantages

- Critical incident technique is more a job analysis technique than competency tool, because critical incident technique focus on knowledge and skills rather than on personal attributes.
- Difficult to implement critical incident technique in its existing form since high degree of discipline is required in the job incumbents. It is because job incumbents are expected to maintain a diary and record all the critical incidents systematically. Incumbents who are fully occupied with their responsibilities would find it difficult to create such documentation.
- Critical incident technique after all provides information that is rare and infrequently used behaviour. Therefore, such data would not have universal appeal in job.

Retrospective critical incident technique

Asking the incumbents of a job to maintain a diary and record the critical incidents, can be a major limitation. Further, when organization plan competency mapping such data will not be available since practice of maintaining diary by incumbents is generally not followed. For the want of critical incident data, competency mapping cannot be waited. Therefore, critical incident technique is used in competency mapping project in its retrospective form. Job incumbents will be asked to recollect the critical incident and narrate how they have dealt such incidents.

Process of retrospect critical incident technique

Major steps involved in conducting a critical incident technique in retrospect is described below. Course of critical incident technique is illustrated in Box 2.8.

BOX 2.8 Course of Progress in Critical Incident Technique

The course of critical incident technique focus on three critical issues:

1. *Cause:* This deals with details of the situation. What was the incident, circumstances, problem nature and whether new of its kind or that occurs seldom on this particular job and whether was there any precedence for resolving it?
2. *Response:* How the incumbent responded to the situation? What behaviour was demonstrated to resolve the problem? What was the expectation of incumbent while responding in that matter?
3. *Result:* What was the outcome of that behaviour in that situation? Whether the result was positive or negative? Was the result as anticipated by incumbents? What is the learning? What would have happened if such behaviour was not exhibited by incumbent?

- In the first step, jobs for which competencies are to be mapped are identified. In most of the cases, such a data is available ready since the same must have been done at the beginning stage of competency mapping project.
- In the second step, successful incumbents of such jobs are identified for retrospective critical incident reporting.
- As a part of third step, the successful incumbents are either asked to write down or to be spoken about while

someone else is recording some of the critical incidents took place in their jobs and how have they responded and what behaviour was exhibited to resolve them. Interviewer should possess reasonable knowledge of the job for effective capturing of the incident. Sub-questions must be asked and additional information should be sought wherever required by the interviewer.

- In the final step, the competencies demonstrated by the job incumbents in a particular situation are identified based on the recorded version and interview notes.

Critical incident despite its focus on job tasks and responsibilities does provide valuable data on behavioural attributes of exemplary performance. Much experimentation also can be done with critical incident technique for collecting holistic data. For example, instead of a single incumbent, a group of incumbents can be gathered together to brain storm on the issues of criticality and kinds of behaviour demonstrated to manage them for superior results.

Data Collection Method 5: Survey in Competency Mapping

Survey technique is another powerful data collection tool in competency mapping. Survey technique is implemented with the help of open/close-ended questionnaires administering on a group of identified employees with an objective to gather large scale information on competencies. Survey is immensely useful where the data is to be collected from large number of respondents. The pros and cons of this method are described here:

Advantages

- *Quick and efficient:* A carefully planned and executed survey method is quick and efficient in collecting valuable data. Data can be collected from even hundreds of respondents within 2/3 days. No other method can probably gather information from so many respondents within such a short time.
- *Cost-effective:* The method is also cost-effective since data can be collected without disturbing employees from their work setting. Further, there can be no special

expenses for creating any conditions for implementing survey in organization.

- *Consensus:* Survey method provides opportunity to all identified employees to express their views and contribute for competency identification. This helps in ensuring involvement of all employees and also to bring in consensus.
- *Breaks through geographical barriers:* Survey method has inherent advantage over other methods in reaching to all respondents regardless of geographical location. Survey can be administered wherever employees/respondents are available.
- *Frank feedback:* Employees tend to be frank in survey in comparison to other methods where they would not have the complete privacy. In other methods there would be some more employees participating with the respondents or a moderator. Presence of others has its own disadvantages especially from the point of view of collecting the frank feedback on competencies.
- *Study of large number of jobs:* Survey method also enables to study large number of jobs of same type or different types. Once the survey methodology is adopted, the same can be adopted for all jobs.

Disadvantages

- *Minimal flexibility:* The greatest disadvantage with survey method is it offers limited flexibility. Even in an open-ended questionnaire, there would be a menu of fixed competencies from which a respondent has to select a few and give ranking to them in order of preference/importance to that particular job. Respondent would be given freedom to add one or two new competencies. These restrictions which are in-built in any survey method works unfavourable to a competency identification study.
- *Quantity focused:* Survey method heavily relies on quantitative techniques for developing data collection questionnaires as well as in their analysis. Many of the competencies are soft in nature which is difficult to be measured using the hard measures. Real essence of competencies lies in quality and not in quantity.

- *Casual responses:* There is a possibility that some respondents, especially those who do not take this task seriously tend to give casual responses due to the very fact of absolute privacy. Such responses dilute the quality of data that adversely impact the competency mapping.
- *Not effective for small samples:* Survey method may not be effective where the data is to be collected from a small size of sample. It would be far more efficient if they are assembled and invited views directly instead of asking them to indicate their views in a pre-determined criteria.
- *Absence of emerging competencies:* Survey method would not provide opportunity for identifying the emerging competencies since the main menu of competencies is drawn from the existing lot of competencies. Respondents also would not have much of freedom to suggest or supplement any new competencies.

Process of survey method

Survey like other data collection methods, in competency mapping, must be dealt carefully and in a professional manner. The procedure for implementing survey in competency mapping is discussed here:

Step 1: *Collection of raw data of competencies:* Survey method begins with collecting raw data on competencies required for performing a job. This data can be collected by simply asking few experts of the job, successful incumbents of the job, job supervisors, senior managers, gleaning the job descriptions and key result areas.

Step 2: *Development of schedules/questionnaires:* Based on the raw data as collected at Step 1, schedules and questionnaire can be developed. A model questionnaire is given in Box 2.9. Such questionnaire, if required, must be pilot-tested, and reliability must be ensured.

Step 3: *Administration of schedule/questionnaire:* Schedule or questionnaire, as the case may be, must be administered on the identified sample either using paper-pencil test or electronic version. The sample must comprise respondents such as employees currently working on those jobs, reporting officers and peers of that job. The sample must represent the universe, and should be selected carefully. Further, care must be exercised while administering the questionnaire like briefing, and providing the clear guidelines to respondents for making right responses.

BOX 2.9 Model Competency Identification Questionnaire for an HR Professional

The purpose this survey is to identify critical competencies of superior performance for HR professionals in our organization. Respondents are requested to peruse the below described competencies, and assess them using a five-point scale based on their importance for performing exemplarily on the job of human resource professional.

The five-point scale mean:

- 5–Very essential for superior performance
- 4–Essential for superior performance
- 3–Desirable for superior performance
- 2–Seldom required for superior performance
- 1–Not required for superior performance

I. Technical Competencies

- Knowledge of HR-business alignment applications
- HR scorecard
- Performance management applications
- Crafting HR vision, mission and objectives for organiza-tional and employee growth
- Knowledge in competency based HR systems
- Human resource information system
- Understating of labour laws and regulations
- HR automation technologies

II. Behavioural Competencies

- Self understanding
- Skills in social processes
- Articulation
- Fairness

Step 4: *Statistical process of data:* Based on nature of data and its purpose, appropriate statistical tools like t-test, ANOVA must be used for data analysis. Reliability must be checked before accepting the data. Software such as Statistical Package for Social Sciences (SPSS) would be very useful for analysis of data.

Step 5: *Inferences and competencies identification:* This is the final step in survey method. With the help of statistically analyzed data available at Step 4 above, inferences on competencies must be drawn. The competencies can be identified and classified in their order of significance for superior performance for particular job/job families. The data can be presented job-wise and competency-wise with relevant details.

Data Collection Method 6: Competency Card Sort Activity

Competency card sort activity is an efficient and cost-effective method that is primarily used to identify the most critical competencies for success in a job from a long list of generic and specialized competencies. Participants who would be selected using clearly-defined criteria would select the competencies using several cards.

Process of competency card sort activity

The following steps are involved in implementation of the competency card sort activity:

Step 1: *Preparing competency cards:* This data collection method begins with identifying a long list of competencies and organizing them into (writing) cards. For example, each competency is written with operational definition using 150 cards if there are 150 competencies primarily identified for a job of operations manager. Each card must contain a number like 1, 2, 3, 4.... On the top of the card facilitating the users to identify them with numbers. The language used for writing competencies and explaining their definition must be crystal clear and understood by the users.

Step 2: *Developing competency card sort activity guidelines:* Competency project managers also must put in place adequate guidelines for conduct of competency card sort activity. These guidelines essentially must explain how the activity should be started, and how competencies need to be identified and certain ground rules for the participants.

Step 3: *Selecting the participants:* A few employees from the total population of employees of an organization must be selected for participating in the competency card sort activity. The sample would consist of best in class performers, job supervisors, human resource executives, senior managers and other employees possessing adequate knowledge about the jobs under study for competencies identification.

Step 4: *Briefing to participants:* Participants as identified, must be given briefing about competency card sort activity and the ground rules for identifying the competencies need to be explained. Participants particularly should be clearly communicated the objectives of competency card sort activity and expected outcomes of the activity. There should be no ambiguity or confusion in the minds of participants.

Sorting of competency cards: Participants, soon after the briefing session must be assembled to commence the activity. This can be done in two ways—either each participant must be asked to carry out the activity independently and come together for discussion in a group or they can start the group activity straight away. At this stage, precisely stating, participants are expected to categorize and prioritize the competencies keeping in view their importance for superior performance in a job/ job families. From a list of competencies written in several tens of cards, participant has to choose a few cards, categorize and arrange them in an order based on their significance to a job. In a group activity, each participant needs to defend for the categorization and priority that has been accorded by that person. At the end of the activity, participants need to choose ten most critical competencies that would predict success on a job (see Box 2.10).

BOX 2.10 Approach to Competency Card Sort Activity by Participants

Participants of competency card sort activity should approach the task of identifying the most critical competencies of a job with following five objectives:

1. Categorize the competencies into technical, functional and behavioural classes based on the nature of a competency.
2. Prioritize the competencies into essential, desirable and least useful based on their significance for producing exemplary performance in a job.

3. Identify as few competencies as possible from a comprehensive list of competencies.
4. Accept and include a competency after substantive reasoning, analysis and visualizing in practical setting with exemplary performance as key criteria.
5. Do not mind to alter your previous position if you see the rationality in what other participants are saying in sorting out the competency cards.

Further, competency prioritization can be done keeping in view the following conditions:

1. Perceived present importance of each competency for superior performance in a job.
2. Perceived future importance of each competency for superior performance in a job.
3. Perceived past importance of each competency for superior performance in a job.

Some of the advantages and disadvantages of this method are indicated here:

Advantages

- *Flexible system:* Competency card sort activity is basically a flexible system that allows freedom to participants to choose any competency and also to add and supplement new competencies through introducing new cards with the consent of fellow participants. This method also permits to commence the activity in a group situation or alone in the first stage followed by a group activity.
- *Time effectiveness:* Experience of organizations with competency card sort activity proves that it is one of the most effective methods from time investment point of view. The whole activity may not take more than half-a-day in the first instance. Further, refining can be done in due course of period as in the case with any data collection method in competency mapping.
- *Few critical competencies:* Competency card sort activity advantage lies in its objective, i.e., choosing few competencies from a comprehensive list of competencies. This allows building competency model for job/job families with clear focus and linking it sharply to superior performance.

Disadvantages

- *Cumbersome:* Preparation of competency cards and planning and scheduling the activity is complex. Carrying out all these activities involve considerable investment of time, energy and skills of higher order on the part of competency mapping project manager and associated people.
- *Collection of primary data:* Competency card sort activity is preceded by an exhaustive study in order to identify the wide range of competencies involved in a job/job families. The real effectiveness of this method depends on the richness of data on competencies. Unless the competency list is exhaustive, participants would not be able to choose the most critical competencies.
- *Language of competencies:* Language used and definition of competencies plays important role in competency card sort activity. Participants may get mislead if they do not understand the precise meaning of a competency. Using not only an appropriate language but also making it relevant is the biggest problem. Many a time, competency card sort activity fall short of fulfilling the expectations due to language related problems.

All these disadvantages however can be managed effectively when there is perseverance and competency mapping project managers possess clarity and clear objectives.

Data Collection Method 7: Observation of Job Incumbent/Job Task Analysis

This method primarily is used to supplement the other data tools of competency mapping in order to reconfirm the existing data and also to obtain the fresh data. In this method, an expert spends the time in observing an employee performing the typical job tasks. Expert would record the observations in a diary either while making observation or at the end of the day. Such diary would be used to identify the competencies involved for performing in particular job. The method may appear as simple but actual execution involves careful planning and deployment of professionally trained experts. This method is also known as Job Task Analysis (JTA).

Here also, job analysts make investigation while an employee performing various tasks and work backwards to identify the competencies used in performing those tasks. The process involved in observation of job incumbent method or job task analysis is explained as follows:

Process of job incumbent observation method

Observing job incumbents for identification of critical competencies comprises three major steps:

Step 1: *Identifying incumbents:* The first task is identifying the right employees working in particular job/job families for implementing job incumbent observation method. There are different approaches that organizations use in identifying these employees. Some organizations confine their observation process only to highly performing employees while others to both highly performing and poorly performing. This depends on the overall objectives of competency mapping project of organization. In either case, careful selection of employees must be done with the help of well-defined criteria. The second issue is number of employees to be chosen for each job. This is largely contingent upon the total number of actually employees working in such jobs. Fourteen employees can be chosen if the number of employees is more than 100 and proportionately less or more in reference to actually number subject to a minimum of ten employees.

Step 2: *Identifying experts:* The second challenging task is identifying the professional observers. Observers have a direct role in ensuring the systematic collection of data culminating in identifying the real competencies of exemplary performance in a job. Experts should possess two broad competencies. Firstly, they must be having adequate understanding of the job under observation. However, they should limit such understanding to comprehend the underlying premise of the incumbents' behaviour rather than to use the same for making performance expectations on the incumbents. Secondly, they should have keen observing (processes and feelings) skills, drafting and analytical abilities. Observers should not cause any discomfort or unnatural behaviour in the job incumbents while carrying out this exercise. They must be capable of taking all precautions and right measures in this context in tune with circumstances.

Step 3: Implementing incumbent observation: Job incumbents must be communicated well in advance that their on the job behaviour is being subjected to observation by an expert with an objective to identify the critical competencies involved. The observation must not be obstructive to the normal performance/working of the employee. Expert is expected to make observation for duration as deemed right to capture all the aspects. The recording must be done carefully. Such recording must cover all the aspects like tasks involved, the way these have been performed, interaction with other departments/people, behavioural responses of the job incumbent, decision-making, complex situations, relations with team members and general work behaviour. At the end of the activity, the report must be analyzed and competencies involved need to be described in a categorized fashion like technical, managerial, behavioural and administrative competencies apart from listing the routine tasks of the job incumbent. Efforts must be made to capture all these in a natural setting encouraging employee to behave in normal way as much as possible. Effectiveness of this method is dependent on the natural work behaviour of job incumbent while under observation of expert.

This method too has a few advantages and disadvantages while using as data collection method for competency mapping.

Advantages

- *Ideal for semi-skilled jobs:* Job incumbent observation method is suitable to semi-skilled jobs where content of the total job is explicit and demonsratable. When the job involves visibly carrying out the activities, it is easy to make observation.
- *Simple to implement:* This method is less cumbersome and easy to understand the recording also. Further, many of the recordings can be verified by making repeat observation. Therefore, the data collected using this method tends to be very reliable.
- *Supplementary method:* Observation of job incumbent method can be effectively used when combined with other

methods of data collection of competency mapping. This method helps in capturing all of physically measurable performances while other methods can be put into use for understanding the abstract activities.

Disadvantages

- *Long spell activity:* Observing job incumbents can take longer period; sometimes it take weeks to complete the recording. It is due to the reason that some of the activities are to be carried out occasionally by the incumbent and that occasion can be infrequent.
- *Incomplete data collection:* The data collected using this method tends to be incomplete. It is impossible for any expert to observe all the activities and tasks while being performed. Employee may not be required to perform certain activities while during observation which otherwise is carried out sometimes. Further, certain mental focused activities like decision-making, intellectual analysis, etc., cannot be observed as they are invisible for normal observation.
- *Unnatural:* Whatever may be the precautions experts do take; it is difficult to collect the data in a natural setting. Employees are likely to develop a behaviour that is not their routine. Further, certain situations, which happen once in a while, make it difficult for capturing through observation.
- *Expensive:* This method is also expensive and involves considerable investment of money due to engagement of experts for prolonged periods.
- *Experts as part of work system:* While engaged observations, expert becomes susceptible to be influenced by the existing work system itself. This disables that person from making objective observations and consequently objective reporting of task and decision-making behaviour.

Despite some disadvantages, this method is immensely useful for identifying competencies of technical and engineering related jobs. Also, the data collected using this method is original, provide rare insights and is reliable.

Data Collection Method 8: Delphi Technique

This is mostly used and drawn as a group communication technique. Competencies ideally required for a job or position can be identified by involving the current incumbents and through the Delphi technique. This technique prescribes a process where there are three phases involved. In the first phase, the participants are encouraged to discuss about the problem statement and suggestions in the second phase, and finalization of actions in the third phase. The discussion will also go in a round one by one where a person need to add only additional points and not expected to repeat what earlier participants are already stated. Through this way, a rich data will be collected in each phase. The data that has developed in the third phase of Delphi technique can be sharply relevant for identifying what competencies are related to a particular job or position.

Secondary data collection methods

Valuable data for identification of competencies can be collected using secondary data collection methods. These secondary data methods are of two types:

- *Secondary data sources (internal resource):* Every organization would possess enormous data within and in various forms regarding competencies. For example, job descriptions, training curriculum, key result areas, compensation system, performance appraisal system and career planning system (promotion policies) etc. All these systems contain some kind of description regarding competencies required at various levels and in various jobs. Such data may not be perfect enough, but still highly valuable from data collection point of view for identifying the competencies. These sources must be effectively tapped for mapping competencies.
- *Secondary data sources (external source):* There may be organizations in the same industry which have implemented competency mapping. For example, a petro-chemical organization must find out whether any other petrochemical organization had already adopted the

competency approach. If so, the data on the competencies so identified by that organization must be collected. Similarly, there are professional bodies which might have mapped the competencies for their professionals. For example, a professional body of chartered accountants might have mapped the competencies for a chartered accountant. Such data would be immensely useful to the competency mapping work. Similarly, there are many generic competency dictionaries available with other organizations and in academic books. These need to be referred and appropriately used.

These secondary data collection methods are discussed in detail in the next section.

Secondary Data Collection Methods

Data Collection Method 1: Job/Position Descriptions

Job or position descriptions can be rich source of information for identification of competencies. It is easy to identify the competencies if job descriptions are well-written. A good job description would provide information on what knowledge and skills one need to possess, what are the tasks, responsibilities, what precisely the role is, formal authority and powers vested with, administrative and managerial accountabilities, what outcomes/ results are expected from that position and the connection of that job to other functions in the organization. Analysis of these aspects would facilitate in identifying the relevant competencies required to perform the position/job effectively. The competencies as identified can be categorized into knowledge, skills and personal attributes. However, job descriptions cannot be relied upon in totality for the identifying the competencies. It is one of the potential sources of information.

Time logs also called work diaries maintained by shop floor men helps in understanding the tasks. Though, they do not provide any direct information on work behaviour and characteristics, still valid inferences can be drawn on work-role based on these logs. Studying time logs can be one of the best methods for identifying competencies for shop floor jobs.

Data Collection Method 2: Training Curriculum

Training curriculum and courseware of jobs are also useful in collecting information that contributes for identifying the competencies. Especially, training curriculum of induction programmes as well as advanced courses helps to understand the basic and specialized knowledge and skills required to perform a job effectively. Similarly, managerial and behavioural programme targeted at jobs would throw a light on the soft skills requirement. Knowledge and skills prescribed in the form of course contents can be drawn as basis and transferred them into competencies. However, this can be tapped as more a supplementary method than a standalone data collection instrument that facilitate identifying the competencies. Further, utility of this method depends on the quality of training system of organization. This method would present substandard data, if the training system of an organization is unprofessional and unsystematic.

Data Collection Method 3: Key Result Areas/Indicators Statements

A considerable number of organizations do follow the practice of setting Key Result Areas for the managerial staff if not for all the personnel. This KRA statement indicates the kind of tasks, assignments and responsibilities involved in the job. Study of these Key Result Areas can be proved to be a good source of information for identifying the competencies. Another advantage with this method is that, what construes exemplary performance in a particular job is also defined. Such standards of performance can be drawn as a basis for deriving competencies of exemplary performance. Competency mapping team must explore the source of performance appraisal system in organizations where there is no practice of setting Key Result Areas. In many organizations, setting Key Result Areas is a part of performance appraisal system. Often, performance appraisal does provide relevant information in the lines of Key Result Areas. Performance appraisal typically contains dimensions of performance against which employees get appraised at the end of the year or half/quarterly year as the case may be by the reporting supervisor. The said dimensions must be studied carefully in order to identify the competencies.

Data Collection Method 4: Compensation and Benefits System

Compensation and benefit administration largely draws its basis from job evaluation and other methods used for establishing value and role of a job. Such methods take into account tasks, performance factors, knowledge, skills and other motivational and interpersonal aspects. Therefore, studying compensation and benefits programme of organization yield valuable information that helps in identifying competencies for jobs. Similar to other secondary methods of data collection discussed here, the information of compensation and benefits would not be directly useful for identifying competencies. However, such information would offer significant assistance in supplementing exiting data of competency mapping study. Disadvantage is compensation and benefit system of an organization would not necessarily be having drawn based on worth of a job or competency profile. Therefore, drawing such information for the purpose of competency project can cause serious anomaly. In some cases, it can distort and nullify the objectives of competency mapping project.

Data Collection Method 5: Functional, Processes and Administrative Manuals

Work manuals such as production, maintenance, erection, quality, financial, human resource, service, sales and processes manuals explaining how an activity is to be managed and administrative manuals clarifying the formal authority of jobs etc., present an idea of the performance, role and responsibility involved in jobs. Studying daily logs, performance reports and perspective plans too provide large chunks of information. Competency mapping project team either on their own or with the assistance of experts must get perused these documents and relevant inferences can be drawn for identifying competencies. However, this method would help to identify competencies mainly at the organization and functional level rather than at the job level. There is also a view that manuals and policy documents cannot provide the data that can be real value for competency identification. At the best, these manuals may contain the data from which knowledge and skills required to perform a job may be identified, but not certainly the behavioural and personal attributes. Personal attributes constitutes the real competency in competency mapping rather than knowledge and skills. Further, drafting inferences those can be of value to competency identification from these manuals is an abstract and complex task. Even when executed, much value added information may not come forth from such exercise. Advantage with this method is that, data can be collected without disturbing the employees and in an academic manner. Like other secondary methods, this method too can be largely used as a supplementary tool rather than self-sufficient data collection method.

Data Collection Method 6: Customers Perceptions

Surveying customers' perceptions on what kind of performance they would expect from the staff generate precious data. For example, customers have their perceptions on what kind of product knowledge, service orientation, customer preferences, etc. the staff should possess. This survey of customers can be internal wherever the survey is to be conducted on internal customers and it would be external for external customers. For instance, internal survey involving all the employees is to be conducted in case of human resource staff. Similarly, external survey is to be conducted for sales staff. The gambit of survey can also include vendors, suppliers and distributors wherever required. However, conducting such surveys is an arduous task. In many cases, questionnaires/formats are to be developed at least with minimum of explanation while inviting the perceptions/opinions of subjects. If the size of respondents is too large it becomes unmanageable. Response rate also, especially in external surveys, tends to be poor. Further, once the data is collected which is mainly in the form of text/sentences form need to be classified and arranged in a meaningful shape before the same are transferred into competencies. Unless, carefully planned and executed, this data collection method can create confusion than adding value to the competency identification project. In exceptional cases in which perceptions of customers are ought to be obtained, this method must be adopted.

Data Collection Method 7: Academic and Professional Specifications

Curriculum of academic courses and professional specifications laid down by professional bodies can be used for identifying competencies for particular jobs. For example, referring to the professional conduct and technical expertise defined by Chartered Accounts Association would be useful in order to identify the competencies for Chartered Accountants. Similarly, browsing through the academic curriculums also can be a reliable source especially in identifying the knowledge and skills required in jobs. However, this method is fraught with one major limitation, i.e., academic curriculum and professional specifications can just would not be sufficient basis from which competency identification can be taken up. Also, such professional specification would not be available to all the jobs and academic curriculums in many a time take longer time to include the merging professional developments. Therefore, relying upon this method can deprive the competency mapping project from identifying the emerging competency fabric which is more important.

Data Collection Method 8: Generic Competencies

Competencies for different jobs of an organization can be identified based on the review of existing literature on competency mapping, conference proceedings, and journal and research articles in the area of competency management, best practices and study of competency lists of other organizations. In addition, many off-the-shelve commercial competency tools are available with consultancy firms. Competency mapping project team can refer to these sources, evaluate their relevance and adopt the competencies that suit to subject jobs. While adopting, prior consent and permission of patented organizations/authors/sources would be required to be obtained. Careful analysis must be carried out before opting for the competencies from such sources since they must have been developed in all together in a different context using different language and in a different cultural context. All or most of the competencies on surface may appear similar, and also would appear to be suitable to an organizational context. However, when one get into the depth of it, realization would struck that they are substantially different and may or may not suit for the jobs of an organization under competency mapping. This method has some inherent advantages as well as disadvantages.

Advantages

- *Fast and wide:* Data can be collected fast. Using this method, wide range of competencies, their descriptions and operational definitions can be gathered. It would consume several months of skilled man days to develop and operationally define such competencies. This method can save such long hours of hard work and also in some way it avoids reinventing the wheel. Instead of developing which already exist, it makes sense to adopt them and improve upon to suit to one's jobs and organizational context.
- *Insightful:* Gathering competencies based on review of existing literature and from other organizations and studying them can prove to be very insightful. It takes less time and still enables to learn what others might have taken years of effort and spending huge money to reach such learning level. Further, able analysis of existing information would present opportunity to gain immensely valuable insights. Such insights are imperative for identification of right competencies.
- *Credibility:* It gives significant credibility when competencies are developed after critically examining state of art competency practices, best competency methods and competencies of high performance. This approach also helps to avoid the common traps and pitfalls that other organizations might have encountered in their journey of identifying competencies.
- *Few resources:* Resources (specially, few people) are required for developing competencies using this method. There would be no disturbance to the work setting, and no air of tension while implementing the competency project. What it takes is, about three to four experts referring to others' practices and existing literature and choosing the most relevant to the jobs for which competencies identification is targeted.

Disadvantages

- *Imitation:* Adopting others practices based on literature review or on examination of industry best practices can never be an original work. Culture has pivotal role in competency mapping. Competencies are identified in any organization in tune with operating culture of those organizations. Therefore, adopting competencies of other organizations can lead to conflict as they may not be compatible with adopting organization. Best practices of other organization can not necessarily suit to all organizations. Literature on competency mapping and competencies described in literature also would not be a straight jacket material that they can be simply copied. After all, competencies described are more academic in nature rather than practical which are duly tested on the ground. Therefore, simply adopting them can cause problems than value addition.
- *Copyright permissions:* Competencies, best practices and off the shelve competency tool and generic competency lists are commercial commodities in today's era of knowledge business. An organization by law needs to procure advance permission from the sources and these many times cost money. Even when permission obtained, it may come up with many riders that ultimately dilute an organization's objective of competencies identification.
- *Weak institutionalization:* Competency mapping project apart from identifying the competencies for various jobs/ job families is also expected to institutionalize competency culture in organization. Such institutionalization would not occur when competencies are imported in a readymade fashion. This is due to the fact that employees' would get an opportunity to participate and involve in competency identification exercise when mapping is done internally. The same opportunity would not be there when generic competencies are adopted.
- *Weak integration:* Corollary to the above reason is poor integration of competency framework. It is difficult to understand the underlying premise and logic of competencies when adopted from outside. Many a time,

the inside logic plays an important role in driving the competencies and making rational expectations out of their implementation. Such appreciation would not come with copying others' competency frameworks beyond a limit. Another key aspect is, competency identification is not merely just to identify the competencies or for the sake of competency project. The ultimate objective is to use such identified competencies/framework for larger purpose in terms of human resource applications. A large number of practical problems would erupt while trying to extend the competency framework for human resource applications when internal logic, nature and process of competencies is not properly understood which can be acquired only when an organization develop such competencies internally and its own.

Data Collection Method 9: Competency Dictionary

Another secondary source for collecting data on competencies using external source is referring to the competency dictionary. The subject of competency dictionary is discussed in greater details Chapter 2, on Competency Modelling. Competency dictionaries are available with vendors and also with some organizations, who must have developed for their own purpose. Generally, management consulting firms with special focus on competency and assessment center technology, assimilate the competencies, subject them to content and reliability tests and compile them in a meaningful manner. An organization which has decided to develop competency framework/identification of competencies, but not inclined to initiate a full scale study can prefer this method.

Process of using competency dictionary

Step 1: An organization once has taken a decision to identify competencies for a particular job/job families or group of jobs must define the nature of jobs, broad tasks, responsibilities, role in the organization, brief history of organization and organizational context including technology, markets, customers and products.

Step 2: When step one as above is complied with, competency identification project team can short list two or three consultancy agencies known in the area of competency management for soliciting the competency dictionary. These agencies must be contacted with the data on jobs for which competencies identification is to be done with other specifications, chiefly detailing the quality standards and time limits.

Step 3: The agency must be asked to come up with competencies suitable to the identified jobs with operational definitions, measures and the evidence of their use in other organizations. Once an agency submits a report describing the competencies, the same must be examined thoroughly in terms of their value, expected contribution and relevance before adopting them.

Advantages

- *Benchmarking:* Competency dictionaries generally comprise competencies which are well-tested and implemented in world class organizations. Therefore, competencies adopted from competency dictionary tend to serve as benchmark practices. Precisely stating, this method enables organizations to follow the refined competencies, which in normal case, takes years of effort to reach to such a state of maturity.
- *Fast and rapid results:* Competency mapping project managers can save substantial time by following this method since many of the steps that normally an organization need to follow for mapping competencies like interviewing, surveys, job observations, etc., are done away with. Results also tend to be rapid since within few weeks of time the competencies for various jobs can be mapped without much effort and disturbance to the normal working.
- *Suitable for generic competencies:* This method is the most appropriate for mapping generic competencies at jobs as well as organizational level. Since these competencies are filtered from a wide range and long list of competencies and also based on study of competency framework of similar organizations they would more likely in the state of fineness.

Disadvantages

- *Superficial:* Competencies which are acquired using generic competency dictionaries run the danger of being low in quality and superficial. Competencies in dictionaries sometimes get included more for the purpose of having large number than with any utility. Competency dictionaries, are in some sense, more of encyclopaedias than actionable manuals which corporate organizations do require.
- *Irrelevant competencies:* Consultants when approached for identifying the competencies based on competency dictionaries can suggest list of competencies those may or may not relevant to the client organization. Some competencies when perused appear required, but in practice they may become irrelevant. Such irrelevant competencies can adversely impact the outcome of competency system.
- *Cost intensive:* Competencies identification which is based on competency dictionaries with the help of consultants can prove to be expensive. It would be quite possible to initiate a full scale competency identification project right from the scratch with the same amount of money.

As discussed, competency dictionary method is more appropriate in the context of identifying generic competencies than specialized competencies. Further, this method is more useful to large-sized organization where such competencies are required for many jobs in the organization in comparison to medium and small-sized organizations. This method is widely used to curtail the time schedules and also to complete the competency identification process within short time.

Data Collection Method 10: Repertory Grid

This is also known as theory of constructs. Repertory grid has been developed by Robert Kelly mainly for the purpose of identifying personal constructs. Methodology of repertory grid is used for identification of competencies. Repertory grid method is rigorous in nature and if followed correctly it can lead to identification of competencies of jobs in a systematic manner. However, the rigorousness to this method comes from its quantitative as well as qualitative approach to identification of competency constructs. The process of repertory grid in the context of competency mapping is:

Process of repertory grid

This method encompasses three major steps. These are:

Step 1: *Identifying top and poor performers:* In the first step, a group of employees chosen based on a well defined criteria would identify about 10 to 15 top and poor performers in a given job. The actual number of employees to be identified can differ in line with actual strength of total employees working in that particular job. The identification must be based on performance criteria. This does mean past 2 or 3 years of performance rankings/rating must be taken into consideration for identifying top and poor performers.

Step 2: *Identifying differentiating behaviour:* The group of experts would use appropriate methods to bring out the work behaviours and characteristics that distinguish the top performers and poor performers. These differences would be converted into competencies.

Step 3: *Developing constructs based on competencies:* Based on the competencies as defined at step 2 above, competency constructs are developed for testing the same whether they would contribute for high performance on those particular jobs.

Listing, Classifying and Arranging Identified Competencies

The last and final phase in competency mapping is three fold:

Listing Competencies

Organizations would use one or more data collection methods as discussed in data collection method, step 1 for collecting data on competencies of jobs/job families. Implementation of these data collection methods yield-mine of data on competencies.

Competency mapping project team must list these competencies with all definitions and supplementary details as arrived on. This may run into several hundreds of pages. Once data is listed, a final review and appraisal should be done to weed out unnecessary details.

Classifying Competencies

Successful implementation of first step, as described above, would contribute for listing several competencies. At this step, these competencies must be arranged in a classified manner. For example, competencies can be arranged into motivational related, customer service-oriented, communication related, decision-making-oriented and so on. This step must result in removing duplication of competencies and putting all related competencies at one place. Also, all related competencies must be arranged under one dimension. For example, all communication related sub competencies must be brought under one dimension. At the end of this step, competencies would be indexed into several types and each job/job families wise. For example, competencies of marketing jobs, competencies related to production jobs and likewise. There should also be a list of generic competencies classified into different classes. In many cases, such classifying of competencies does take place during identification of competencies themselves. However, this step at this phase emphasizes to take a fresh look at the classification, and make improvements wherever required. Competency mapping project team with the help of other team members can have a review of classification.

Arranging Competencies into Hierarchy

Once, competencies are structured into classes based on their nature, they must be arranged in an hierarchical order keeping in view the degree and intensity of their relevance to a job/job families in terms of exemplary performance. This means, competencies must be arranged in order of priority. Relevance and value of predictability of exemplary performance on a job must be the fundamental basis for it. Many a time, arranging them in a hierarchy becomes a complex task. In such a case, this activity must be taken up along with competency modelling process.

Once competencies are listed, classified and arranged in a hierarchical order for each job/job families, organization must move to the next major part of competency management, i.e., Competency Modelling.

Summary

In this part of the book, salient features of competency mapping are discussed in detail. Approaches to competency mapping such as top-down approach, bottom-up approach, beginning from the scratch approach and adopting generic competency model approach are discussed in the beginning of the chapter. Limitations of competency mapping that include issues like living in the past, irreconcilable differences, shoddy job, cloning and short-life cycles of competencies are discussed to caution the competency managers from making tall expectations.

Competency mapping process is presented in five parts. First part of competency mapping is devoted to preparing organization for launch of competency mapping process. This phase prescribes four major steps. These are:

- Appraising top management and key resource persons about competency mapping process.
- Planning competency mapping project on obtaining green signal from top management.
- Forming competency mapping project team and training them on conceptual and methodological issues of competency mapping.
- Defining objectives and targets of competency mapping project.

The second part of competency mapping deals with issues related to identifying jobs/job families for competency mapping as well as determining the method of competency mapping. Two broad methods of competency mapping are discussed. These are—adopting generic competency models with suitable modifications, and initiating the competency mapping project from the scratch. Each one of these has their own advantages and disadvantages. In addition to it, existing competency mapping methods such as job competence method, modified job competence assessment method, generic model overlay method, customized generic model method, systems method and accelerated competency system method are briefly described.

Setting performance effectiveness criteria for choosing the sample subjects for competency mapping is discussed in the third part of the chapter. Two methods for setting performance effectiveness criteria: defining performance effectiveness criteria based on secondary data and collecting primary data on performance effectiveness criteria, are presented.

Data collection methods for identification of competencies are discussed comprehensively in concluding section of competency mapping. Both person and job-based data collection methods are illustrated profusely with practical examples. These are: interview in competency mapping, behavioural event interview, focus groups/DACUM approach, critical incident technique/retrospective critical incident technique, repertory grid, survey, competency card sort activity, observation of job incumbents/job task analysis, position description, study of training curriculum, key performance indicators, data of compensation and benefits, study of functional, process and administrative manuals, customers perceptions, referring to academic and professional specifications, adopting generic competencies and seeking help through competency dictionaries.

In the fifth and final part of competency mapping, issues like listing, classifying and arranging competencies in hierarchy based on their degree of relevance to jobs are discussed.

Questions for Discussion

2.1 Discuss approaches to competency mapping. Which is right approach for competency mapping: top-down or bottom-up approach? Substantiate with reasons.

2.2 Launching competency mapping from the scratch, though pain staking and resource intensive effort is still worthy exercise from the benefits point of view. Is this statement valid?

2.3 Describe limitations of competency mapping and how these can be overcome?

2.4 In your opinion, what are the few preparatory actions those should be implemented before actual launch of competency mapping?

2.5 Discuss various person based data collection methods in competency identification?

2.6 What is competency dictionary? How is it useful to organizations in competency mapping?

2.7 Why defining performance effectiveness criteria are important for selecting the sample of subjects for competency identification? How performance criteria are defined?

2.8 Discuss job based data collection methods: Are internal sources are better than external sources for identifying real competencies of jobs?

2.9 What a competency mapping project team should do when competencies for various jobs are identified?

2.10 Compare and contrast the interview and behavioural event interview methods?

2.11 Critical incident technique cannot be used for competency identification since it is difficult to position observers when critical incidents happen since such incidents happen spontaneously. Do you agree with this statement? If you agree what should be done to use this method. Explain why is it so, if you disagree?

Case Studies for Discussion

1. Mr. Vijay Prasher is Chartered Accountant with Global Finance Company (GFC) at Mumbai. His job mainly involves investment banking and credit management, offering loans to new entrepreneurs. He is one of the top performers of the company exceeding set targets almost by 200%. He has been chosen as one of the subjects for identifying competencies of exemplary performance for the finance jobs, especially with the responsibilities of investment banking and credit

management. Preliminary data reveals that Mr. Prasher has a knack of taking right decisions at the right time. All those decisions appear as momentary for a casual onlooker, but the same decisions have benefitted the company with crores of rupees. All his decisions related to investment banking and loans proved to be logical, and right from all respects such as risk and profit to the company. Competency mapping project team has decided to conduct behavioural event interview on Prasher, in order to identify the competencies. Discuss (i) The steps involves in BEI, (ii) How BEI is to be conducted, (iii) How interview is to be recorded and (iv) Analyzed with inferences for identification of competencies. Make mock demonstration of BEI using this case if it is a classroom situation using students as BEI interviewer and Mr. Prasher.

2. Elix Automobiles Limited, is a joint venture promoted by Japanese automobile giant and an Indian Company based at Gurgaon. The company is engaged in manufacturing of radial tires for mid-sized vehicles. The company had identified following generic competencies based on survey, focus group discussion and survey applicable to a wide range of jobs such as sales and service staff, production managers, technical support positions, administrative and finance positions. As a next step, competency project team of Elix has decided to identify five of the most relevant competencies for marketing executives from the following generic list of competencies using competency card sort activity. Assuming you have been identified as one of the members for the said exercise, discuss how would go about implementing the competency card sort activity.

If it is a classroom situation:

- About 5 to 6 students must be distributed the competency cards (scripting each competency on each card with a card number).
- Asked to arrange the cards in a sequence according to the priority of competencies they accord for marketing jobs.
- Once students have done arrangements for the cards, they must get together to discuss and substantiate their priority of five competencies.

- And come up with a consensus arrangement of competency cards that explains five top competencies.

List of generic competencies identified by Elix:

- Organizational information: basic knowledge about the company, products, technology, vision, mission, objectives and organizational structure.
- Knowledge of competitors and their products and technology
- Leadership
- Communication
- Customer orientation and customer behaviour
- Planning
- Basic computer knowledge
- Personal computing and understanding basic financials
- Marketing research
- Quality orientation
- Ethics
- Team building
- Time management
- Conflict management
- Service knowledge
- Coaching
- Managing and developing others
- Creativity and innovation
- Flexibility

References

Flanagan, J.C. (1954): "The Critical Incident Technique," *Psychological Bulletin*, **52**, pp. 327–368.

Guion, R.M. (1991): "Personnel Assessment, Selection and Placement," *in* Dunnette, M.D. and Hough, L.M. (Eds), *Handbook of Industrial and Organizational Psychology*, Palo Alto, CA: Consulting Psychologists Press, p. 335.

Klemp, G.O. Jr. (Ed) (1980): *The Assessment of Occupational Competence*, Washington, D.C.: Report to the National Institute of Education.

McClelland, David (1976): *Guide to Behavioural Event Interviewing*, Boston: McBer Company.

McClelland, David (1993): "Introduction," *in* Spencer, L. and Spencer, M. (Eds.), *Competence at Work*, New York: John Wiley.

Norton, E. Robert (1987): "A Tool for Developing Curricula," *Vocational Educational Journal*, **62**:3, p. 15.

Center for DACUM, (1997): *DACUM Handbook*, Center for Education & Training for Employment, Ohio State University.

CHAPTER 3

Competency Modelling

This part of the book presents competency modelling as a sequel to competency mapping. Unless mapped competencies are modelled subsequent to analysis, testing and validation of competencies, not much benefit can be attained out of competency mapping initiative. Therefore, present chapter of the book is aimed at equipping the readers with salient concepts and techniques of competency modelling, apart from illustrating generic competency models and competency dictionaries built for various jobs/job families such as sales, finance, operations, research, human resource, administration, etc.

Discussion on Competency Modelling as the following text unfolds is organized into five parts as shown in Figure 3.1. The first part of the chapter is devoted to analysis of competencies, thus identified using a variety of data collection methods

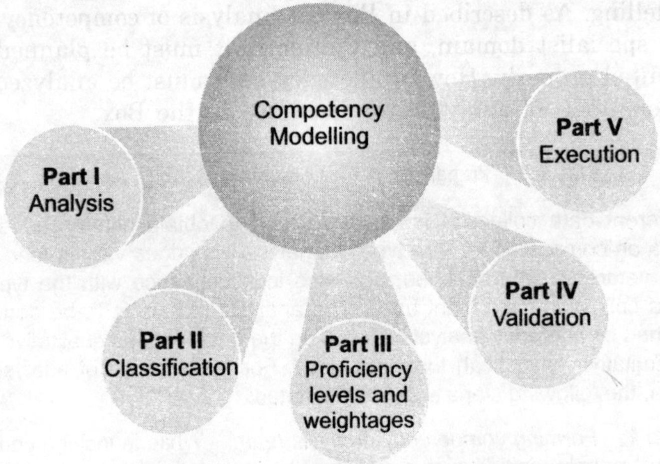

FIGURE 3.1 Competency modelling.

described in the second chapter of the book. Second part of the chapter deals with classifying competencies and in third part, how to accord weightage to each of the competencies assigned to a particular job-based on their predicative potential of success are illustrated. How to validate the competency model is discussed in the fourth part of the chapter. In fifth and final part of the chapter, a few generic competency models (iGATE) are presented to serve as examples and specimen models. Similar to the first part, here also few questions for discussion and exercises are included for facilitating readers to acquire practical familiarization with the techniques discussed here.

A competency model is nothing, but a set of competencies specifically and deliberately clustered together with varying importance that predict success on a job.

Part I: Analysis of Data of Competencies

In the first phase of competency modelling, competencies as identified using a variety of data collection methods should be analysed with the help of appropriate qualitative and quantitative analytical tools. The tools those should be used would be different for different types of data. This is very critical phase in competency management since quality of analysis determines the quality and effectiveness of competency modelling. As described in Box 3.1 analysis of competency data is a specialist domain, and therefore, it must be planned and executed properly. How competency data must be analyzed and various tools of analysis are discussed in the Box.

BOX 3.1 Preparations for Competencies Data Analysis

Different data collection instruments tend to obtain different kinds of data on competencies. The type of analysis also does vary in tune with the nature of data obtained, and also in consonance with the type of data collection instrument used. The analysis of data is to be done by trained competency analysts. Based on the data, various qualitative and quantitative (statistical) tools are used. For the purpose of analysis of data, the following steps should be initiated:

Step 1: *Forming competency analysis team:* While launching competency mapping initiative or soon after the completion of data collection, competency project manager must form competency analysis team.

The team members must have been trained on various analytical tools that include qualitative and quantitative (statistical) applications. It is advisable that people involved in data collection must be used as competency analysts as much as possible. For example, it is desirable that people who perform the role of an interviewer in BEI should be used in analysis too so that they can use their experience for better analysis of data apart from filling the gaps that come across during analysis stage.

Analysis is a complex and time-consuming activity. Therefore, sufficient number of analysts must be deployed since inadequate ratio of analysts can adversely affect the quality of analysis.

Step 2: *Training of analysts:* Competency analysis team must be exposed to a specific training on competency analysis methods especially in the light of data collection methods used in competency mapping study. Training also ensures uniformity in the approach of analysis. Uniformity is important in the analysis since it can ensure perception of equity and also quality of data interpretation.

Step 3: *Identifying tools of analysis:* With the help of competency management experts and with the active participation of competency analysis team, analysis tools must be identified and their application should be discussed thread bare. This can be done either as a separate exercise or as a part of step 3 above.

Step 4: *Analysis manual:* Wherever large data and a number of data collection instruments usage is involved, it is suggested that a manual of competency data analysis must be prepared by the competency analysis team. This manual must deal with all aspects of analysis such as the method of analysis, method of presentation, interpretation style, and preparation of competency modelling reports. The manual must be self explanatory with explanations and specimen formats.

Step 5: *Time frame:* Competency analysis must be taken up as soon as competency data is collected. Delay in analysis and report preparation can dilute the competency mapping effort. It is also possible that the memory experiences of persons involved in data collection can fade away. Therefore, time frame for data analysis must be defined.

Step 6: *Reconciliation meeting:* Wherever more than one competency analyst is involved in analysis of data covering a particular job, a reconciliation meeting must be held between them before competencies are finalized. Differences, if any, between their analyses must be sorted out beforehand.

Analytical Tools Used in BEI

Data on competencies collected using Behavioural Event Interview (BEI) tend to be in textual form (transcripts) with a few observations of the interviewer. Proper analysis of this is critical since the text on surface does not convey much about the competencies. Rather, the text presents incidences and events in the work-life of an interviewee. These incidents and events bear the key indicators of competencies. Competency analyst must understand the underlying meaning and essence of these events in order to identify the actual competencies. Two techniques which generally used in thematic analysis are employed in analyzing the BEI transcripts. These are:

Concept creation

BEI can generate valuable data that provide new insights and perspectives. This may be in the form of looking at a problem or resolving it in work-life entirely in a new way departing from the conventional mode. These problems would have been never thought or seen in this manner by many people working on them. A person may be demonstrating this new behaviour not only in a particular area/problem, but on many occasions. This means, there is a pattern in the way these events are looked at and resolved. For example, BEI of an operations manager who is immensely successful in a telecom company reveal that the person has shown the characteristic of fundamentally questioning any aspect and understanding it in an altogether a different manner than the others have understood. This person also has a characteristic of day-dreaming the success on an issue currently engaged on. This day-dreaming happens whenever a new challenging assignment is given. This does mean that there is a pattern in that person's work behaviour. The pattern is not accepting the truth that already exist (fundamentally questioning) and day-dreaming (rehearsing the success). Important aspect that should be noted here is that, these patterns would not be apparent from the BEI transcript. However, if the entire BEI script consisting many events and incidents are analyzed, these patterns would come out clearly. This is precisely what a competency analyst is expected to do while analyzing the BEI data, i.e., looking for patterns unknown so far. This is referred to as concept creation since such observed competencies are entirely new. The pattern analysis leads to identify the actual competencies. For example, in this case, the competencies are fundamental questioning and success rehearsing. Both these competencies form as a part of competency model for operations manager job in telecom organization. This type of analysis is called concept creation since the observed competencies are not known or not described in the mainstay competency dictionaries.

Relating concepts

Another way of analyzing BEI transcripts is using known concepts as a basis for identifying competencies, for example, communication skills. This is a well-known competency. How interviewee has made several observations and how the experiences are expressed, narrated and shared, the language used, etc., can help to analyze the communication ability. This coupled with interviewer's experience with interviewee would certainly throw a light on this aspect. Based on these, whether communication is a required competency or not can be identified. Similarly, looking in BEI transcripts against the well-known and generic competencies, and checking their application and use of these can lead to identify the existence of such competencies in a given job. In other words, competency analyst needs to check the existence of any known competencies in the BEI transcript carefully and analyze the competencies accordingly.

For the purpose of this twin analysis, i.e., concept creation and relating concepts, a competency analyst must follow eight steps as follow:

1. *Situation/experience:* Competency analyst must gather all BEI transcripts of a particular job (superior, average and poor performers) and look for similarity and dissimilarity in the experiences and situations put forward by them. Each of them may focus on particular aspects of job more than others. For example, BEI transcripts of human resource professionals show that someone talked more about training, other recruitment and the third all human resource functions and the need to align them with business strategy though all of them have same job description and role in the company. These differences in focus provide the clue about self-concept of interviewees. Someone want to play a developmental role more. Some a generalist, and some others more a regulatory job. These differences can account for differences in superior,

average and poor performance apart from presenting vital clues for identifying the competencies.

2. *Approach:* The next step that should be followed in analyzing BEI transcriptions is looking for points of emphasis. While performing on job, employees differ in their accentuation to different parts of the job. For example, an operations manager may give more importance for adhering to procedures and proper maintenance of equipment, while some others may accord more importance to people management and caring for people. These differences in their approach involve different competencies. It is possible that their approach may be the contributing factors for demonstrating different competencies, and in turn, these competencies influence who are superior and poor performers. Analysis following this aspect would result in identifying the different aspects of emphasis leading to demonstration of different competencies which hold the key for performance differences.

3. *Orientation:* Third step in analysis of BEI transcription is verifying the orientation of interviewees, i.e., understanding their thinking process. Employees differ in analyzing a problem, applying knowledge and seeking clarification, etc., for example, some employees seek greater details, data; past practices while some others on the same job would not like to peruse the data in depth and rather use their intuitive sense. Both these orientations involve different competencies, and a particular set of competencies may contribute for exemplary performance. It should be clarified here that each one of these orientations: intuitive vs. data-based decisions have their own advantages and disadvantages. It is the type of job and business environment that decides which of the orientations are suitable for superior performance. Therefore, BEI transcriptions must be analyzed looking for differences in orientations and also identifying orientations of superior and poor performers.

4. *Actions:* BEI transcriptions must also be analyzed in the light of actions of superior, average and poor performers. For example, superior performers may be

proactive, foresighted and approach an issue with a positive mind where poor performers can be reactive, do not foresee the things and just proceed to produce results without bothering the costs. These actions account for differing performance and their action orientation require demonstration of different competencies. However, on the surface of BEI transcription, it may be appear both these employees are equally committed and eager to give their best. But due to difference in their actions, some tend to perform better than others. Therefore, what a competency analyst must look for is not intentions, but for actions. Situations may be similar and intentions may be identical, but actions do differ that account for differences between exemplary performers and poor performers. BEI transcription analysis must find out the difference between actions and competencies used for producing those actions.

5. *Motivation:* How employees approach various tasks, and eventually, how they perform is contingent upon their motivation level. An employee who has motivation to excel, do approach with things differently, and another who just wants to finish the routine drudgery has a different approach. When motive is to excel, an employee would take various actions that lead to superior performance. That person tends to see end even at the beginning of an assignment and visualize various inter-connected things and synergy among them in integration, and act accordingly. Whereas, an employee whose motivation level is inadequate would refuse to see things in their integration and even would like to visualize an integrated thing in bits and pieces. Therefore, BEI transcriptions must be analysed in order to understand the level of motivation and their differences among employees.
6. *Feelings:* This refers to emotional aspects of employees. Jobs do create tensions to all people in some situations and some jobs by nature consistently throw people in high pressure zones. However, people on these jobs differ in their susceptibility to these tensions and pressures. Similarly, some people tend to get upset very easily

and others maintain calm and control even in adverse situations. These differences account for differences in performance level of employees. Therefore, a competency analyst must audit BEI transcriptions for understanding the feelings of employees working on a particular job, especially the difference between superior and poorly performing employees. Different feelings refer to different competencies, mainly emotional-related. Analysis of BEI transcriptions must lead to identifying feeling-related competencies wherever they do exist.

7. *Interviewer observations/comments:* Apart from behavioural event interview main text, the observations and comments appended to BEI transcription by interviewer is critical for pin-pointing certain competencies. For example, physical appearance of interviewee, physical setting, conversation style, articulation ability, inters-personal and intellectual skills displayed by the interviewee during BEI. For example, the way an interviewee narrates experience, understands a question and responds to it and processing some thoughts instantly, etc., demonstrate that person's analytical skills. Similarly, physical appearance has its own importance for certain jobs. These also must be analyzed for clearly defining and including them into competency list of job/job families.

8. *Results:* Finally, BEI transcriptions must be analyzed for finding out the results produced by different employees participated in BEI. This deal with both quantity and quality of outcomes. Specifically stating, the outcomes of all employees must be compared and analyzed with an objective to find out whether they differ in their outcomes. In some cases, quite understandably they may not differ in their outcomes when examined from quantity point of view. For example, all or most of them may be producing same amount of work/completing all the tasks/delivering the same level of results/meeting the targets as stipulated. However, they may differ when they compared on the measurement of quality standards. In some cases, it can be different. All of them may be comparable in quality standards while different in quantity outcomes.

Analysis of BEI transcriptions must clearly bring out the differences in outcomes. The outcomes must be referred against the initial classification of high, average and low performers.

Thc above discussed eight steps would greatly help in analysis of BEI data. Once, BEI data is verified in reference to these steps, the same would yield specific information of competencies. This information should be further subjected to the following questions:

1. What are the indicators of these competencies? Must be defined clearly citing examples. For example, rehearsing success can be cited as indicator of positive attitude.
2. Is there pattern in demonstration of competencies by job incumbents? For example, verifying whether all highly performing employees belonging to a particular job family demonstrate positive behaviour or only some of them or even poorly performing employees also have this behavioural quality, making it difficult to attribute the same as the cause to superior performance?
3. Which of the competencies are more important than others for exemplary performance in a job? This can be found based on frequency of usage of a competency in a job, its outcomes, the importance of outcomes in terms of contribution to the assigned tasks and analyzing what would be the consequence if such competency is absent.
4. Is there consistency and logic in the data collected using BEI? This can be verified comparing BEI transcriptions of the same job and comparing it again with physical reality and also holding discussions with the experts.
5. Which are the competencies accounts for major part of exemplary performance? In many cases, a quarter of competencies account for major part of performance. For example, it is possible that three competencies like self-motivation, communication and positive attitude out of about 15 competencies are responsible for 80% of high achievements in a sales job.
6. Whether any other data collection method is used for identifying competencies of a job apart from BEI? For example, in some cases, organizations would use two or

three data collection methods like competency card sort activity, job incumbent observation in addition to BEI in order to map competencies, for the same job. In such an eventuality, BEI data analysis must be compared to find out the agreement in outcomes of these data collection methods.

Answering to the above questions in the light of BEI data would lead to identifying and meaningfully analyzing the competencies of a job. At the end of all these analyses, a competency analyst must come up with a list of competencies application, which can result in exemplary performance in a job. There can be a BEI report detailing with the identified competencies along with their operational definitions, manner of interpretation, how the analysis has been done, answers to few self-expressed questions in the line of above discussion culminating into attributing the particular set of competencies for superior performance of a job/job families. Box 3.2 shows us the steps to prepare competency analysis report.

BOX 3.2 Competency Analysis Report

It is suggested that format for reporting competency analysis (competency analysis report) must be standardized. This helps in ensuring the quality of reporting apart from enabling its wide usage and acceptance. A typical competency analysis report must consist of the following:

1. *Analysis report must be specific:* Competency analysis report must have a well defined scope. In other words, competencies defined in the report must be specific to a job/job families or function or to an organization. This aspect should be dealt in the first part of the report explaining the job or function or organization.
2. *Objectives:* Second part of the report must deal with objectives of competency mapping and modelling. This part must focus on why competency initiative is taken up and what it intended to deliver on complete implementation to employees and organization. Objectives must be measurable as much as possible rather than simple descriptive version.
3. *Methodological issues:* Method used for selecting particular persons performing particular jobs, various data collection methods used for identifying competencies, tools used for analysis and limitations of the competency mapping study

must be discussed in the third part of the report. Factors such as dependability (reliability) of the data and why the selected data collection methods are used must be spelt out clearly. Rather than simple explanation, issues need to be substantiated deliberating why a particular method and persons are chosen for the study instead of other methods and persons.

4. *Competencies cluster:* Cluster of competencies so identified and analyzed must be presented in a group form in this part of the report. This means that all related competencies are grouped and presented in a logical manner. For example, competencies involved in managing self as one group and competencies required to manage other effectively as one group and competencies involved in managing superiors as one group. Similarly, competencies also can be clustered into topic/subject/class-wise. For example, competencies pertaining to managing people into one group, competencies related to customer orientation into one group, competencies related to motivation as one group and competencies related to influencing others into a group, likewise.
5. *Individual competencies:* In the fifth part of the report, competencies in their individual status must be dealt. For example, self motivation as a competency need to be defined operationally and behavioural indicators for that must be described apart from presenting sub competencies wherever feasible. This is critical part of the competency analysis report. Therefore, clear explanation and discussion must be conducted in a comprehensive manner. This is operational part of the report which would be used for different applications that include for the purpose of assessment center and human resource decisions.
6. *Relation to job tasks:* The nature of relationship and interaction between the identified individual competencies and competency clusters to job tasks and performance must be dealt in the sixth part of the report. Importance of each of competencies in terms of producing performance and frequency of appearance/presence of competencies can be dealt here.
7. *Application:* Seventh and final part of the report can present the possible application of competency report in the area of human resource management such as recruitment, training and performance management.

Analytical Tools Used in Survey Method

Type of analytical tools to be used in survey method is dependent on the nature of data and nature of tools used for data collection.

Questionnaires used in survey method are chiefly of two types as discussed here:

Unstructured and open-ended questionnaire analysis

There are no definite statements here. Lead items are given based on which respondents write their views and also add their observations/competencies not found in the lead items list. For example, seeking views and observations of respondents on the competencies involved in a sales job of electronic consumer goods. Competencies indicated in the lead list are like planning, managing sales representatives, motivation, customer-orientation, accounting, billing and realization of revenues, marketing research, networking ability, communication and leadership. Respondents would be expected to offer their views on relevance and significance of these competencies to the sales job and also asked to add competencies not covered here. Data obtained using unstructured questionnaires would be analyzed using content analysis. Views and observations of respondents would be tabulated, classified and grouped into related categories. For example, all views in favour of customer-orientation as one group and all views expressed against customer-orientation as one group are illustrated. Similarly, all views should be grouped and illustrated.

Based on these and in consonance with the expressions used by respondents, the data would be analyzed by competency analysts. Analysts also accord weightage to these competencies based on the strength of respondents' views on competencies that result in superior performance. A standard format that can be used for the analysis of unstructured questionnaire data is given at Tables 3.1 and 3.2.

Keeping in view the respondents positive and negative strokes to competencies and reckoning into added competencies, a competency analyst must list the competencies that cause exemplary performance in a job/job families.

Structured questionnaire analysis: The use of structured questionnaire based survey for competencies identification is growing in organizations. Reason for this is its reliability and possibility for objective analysis of data. Nature of questionnaire and data influences the choice of analytical tools. Tools frequently used for analysis of data obtained using structured questionnaires are as following:

TABLE 3.1 Analysis of Unstructured/Open Ended Questionnaire*

S.No.	*Competency*	*Positive rating*	*Negative rating*
1		√√√√√√√	√√
2			
3			
4			
5			
6			
7			
8			
9			
10			

* Total no. of Respondents: 10

TABLE 3.2 Competencies Added by Respondents to above List*

S.No.	*Competency*	*Positive rating*	*Negative rating*
1			
2			
3			
4			
5			

* Total no. of Respondents: 5

Comments of competency analyst
1. ______________________
2. ______________________
3. ______________________
4. ______________________
5. ______________________

(a) *Means and standard deviation:* Structured questionnaires use scales for measurement. Therefore, it would be easy to analyze and illustrate the data in means and standard deviations. Mean is the simplest measurement of central tendency, and is widely used measure. Mean convey the average weightage accorded by the respondents for each of the competencies. Additional advantage with using mean is that it helps in identifying the competencies cluster. Standard deviation would project the variation among respondents in their preference for a particular competency over others.

(b) *t-test:* This tool is used in the context of competency data analysis for two purposes. Firstly, it is used for judging the significance of sample mean. This essentially presents the importance of survey respondents' preference for a set of competencies apart from enabling to understand how significant such preference in overall condition. Secondly, this test is also used to compare and judge the significance of difference between the means of two samples. For example, some respondents have given a positive rating to particular competency and some other a negative rating. Using this test, the difference and significance of difference between the two groups of respondents can be analyzed.

(c) *Analysis of variance (ANOVA):* This test is also widely used in survey data analysis. This is similar to t-test, but more a robust test and widely used when more than two sets of samples are involved. This test is relevant when competency data is obtained from various units of an organization. This tool is also immensely helpful for analyzing the data obtained for building generic competency models. ANOVA test is used to understand what is the variation between two sets of data and significance of such variation. For example, this test enables to understand how significant is the difference between high and low performers due to a set of competencies. Further, this test is also useful to judge the predictability of a particular competency for effective performance.

In addition to above discussed commonly used tests, chi-square, co-relation analysis, factor analysis, regression and multi-variate analysis are also used to analyze the survey data of competencies. It is important that prior to subjecting the data for statistical analysis using above tests, the reliability of data must be verified using appropriate reliability tests such as test-retest reliability, parallel forms of reliability, split half reliability or inter-rater reliability.

Analytical Tools Used in Competency Card Sort Activity

Competency card sort activity itself is designed to end up with identifying and listing the most relevant competencies of a job those result in effective performance. Therefore, strictly stating there should not be a need for special effort in analyzing the competency data obtained using this method. However, analysis of supplementary data and the approach adopted by participants of competency card sort activity can present useful insights. For example, the analysis can provide which are the competencies have been given high importance, which are the competencies selected for inclusion by some participants but dropped at a later stage and what are the factors that influenced the choice/ judgment of participants in selecting competencies: whether they are influenced by future demands of job or present demands or to reach consensus, etc. The analysis also provides valuable information on gauzing the relative strength of competencies in producing the high performance. There is no one standard method for analyzing the competency card sort activity principal and supplementary information. The following procedure can be adopted:

1. Competencies identified by participants based on sorting must be clearly recorded with their operational definitions. The listing of competencies must be done in the same way that participants of competency card sort activity followed. The preferences and weightage must be taken into consideration while arranging the competencies in an order. Analysis can be limited to describing the order, operational definitions and comments of participants.
2. Supplementary information as discussed above must be provided in the second part of the report. This part can deal with issues like how participants have reached to consensus, degree of variation between individual preference and group preference for a particular competency and competencies that are least preferred.

Basis for choosing particular competencies over others also must be described here. This interpretation need to be done by at least two observers/moderators who facilitate the competency card sort activity. The second part of the report should not be used for individual comments of moderators. If there are any comments by the observers, the same should be discussed in the third part of the report.

The language used in describing the identified competencies must be the same that is given in competency cards. At the end of the analysis, there must be a self-explanatory report detailing the competencies identified for a job using competency card sort activity.

Analytical Tools Used in Interview Method

There is no specific tool recommended for analysis of interview scripts. This is due to the reason that the data collected using interview method tends to differ widely from one study to another. Both qualitative and quantitative techniques are used to analyze the data if such techniques in the context of the obtained data are appropriate. Thematic analysis is also used to identify behavioural attributes. Broadly, the data collected using interview method must be analyzed on three parameters:

1. Firstly, information collected must be analyzed in the light of knowledge aspects. Issues like what functional expertise and information is involved in performing job exemplarily must be dealt.
2. Secondly, skills related information must be analyzed in order to describe their importance and outcomes for the job.
3. Finally and most importantly, personal attributes such as communication, articulation, attitude, motivational level, inter-personal competency, etc., need to be identified from the interview text and based on interviewers report.

Interpreting and analyzing interview scripts are critical and sensitive task since interviewer's observation and personal perceptions play an influential role. Therefore, utmost care must be exercised to avoid personal biases and personal opinions. In order to ensure objectivity, it is advisable that apart from the interviewer, a neutral person not involved in the interview process, but has reasonable understanding of the job, must be put on to the task of analysis. Wherever more than one interviewer is used for study of the same job, interview scripts must be compared, reconciled and consolidated. Further, interviewee scripts tend to generate two types of data on competencies. One is the specific data on competencies wherever structured interview schedules are used, and the other is descriptive text in an essay form wherever the technique of open-ended questions is used. Therefore, analysis must be done separately and later these must be assimilated for identifying competencies. The analysis report must describe competencies involved with clear definition and frequency of usage of such competencies for superior performance on a job. Further, report must deal with factors that differentiate superior performance from average performers. There must be substantive explanation for every observation made in the report. Importantly, interviewee responses on surface may appear different from its inner meaning. Therefore, efforts must be made to understand the essence of content rather than mere verbal meaning of interview scripts.

There can be an exclusive section in which interviewer can make her/his observations that include psychological as well as physical aspects such as articulation ability, physical features and mind set of the interviewee, etc. Interview scripts when analyzed in professional manner can provide valuable insights that other method find difficult to garner such information due to inherent limitations.

Analytical Tools Used in Observation of Job Incumbents

In this method also, there is no one specific tool recommended for analysis of observation data. Based on the recorded observation and type of formats/schedules used in collection of data, analytical tools are used. Data need to be classified at three levels as described in the interview method. At each of these levels, knowledge, skills and personal attributes observed while job incumbent performing various duties must be identified from the general data so collected. In selective cases, organizations do use video recording of the job performance by incumbent. Analysis of these proceedings involves writing the observation by watching the video picture. Identified competencies and notes of observers must be reconciled wherever more than one observer is involved in study of same job. Differences, if any, need to be dealt separately analyzing the reasons for it. Observation reports of highly performing and poorly performing employees must be compared and inferences shall be drawn, especially knowledge, skills and behavioural attributes those contribute for the difference between these two categories of employees. Focus of the report must be on the factors that contribute for superior performance rather than simple observation diaries that present information of routine tasks of a job or job incumbent. The report must adequately deal with how incumbent approaches the problems, how resolves it and what unusual efforts are made by the incumbent to achieve higher levels of performance on the job. Report must be organized in such a way that competency description, frequency of use, relation between a particular competency and results of performance are dealt in a structured manner. Mere descriptive or narrative reporting must be avoided since language than the facts tend to overtake the reporting.

Competency Dictionary

The credit for pioneering competency dictionary goes to Richard Boyatzis (1982) who while analyzing BEI transcripts found that the competencies that distinguish superior performers from poor performers are mostly common across many functions in organizations. These commonly seen competencies that distinguish superior performers from poor or average performers in different functions are referred to as generic competencies. These generic competencies are defined in operational terms and illustrated in a competency dictionary. For example, Spencer and Spencer (1993) had identified 760 separate behavioural indicators from about 260 competency models that include sales, marketing, trading, human service, healthcare, education, managerial and administrative jobs etc., Out of these 760, about 360 behavioural indicators defining 21 competencies accounted for 90% of behaviours reported in each model. Each competency would generally consist of 6 to 8 behavioural indicators demonstrated on the job. These behavioural indicators belong to the same competency. Therefore, they are brought under a single competency.

Generic competencies are again grouped together based on their inter-relationship called competency clusters. For example, all competencies related to achievement motivation are grouped together. Each competency model can comprise about 3 to 6 competency clusters. A competency dictionary therefore is developed consisting of:

1. Competency consisting of behavioural indicators that result in effective performance in a job
2. Competency cluster consisting 3 to 6 competencies
3. Each competency is illustrated with its operational definition
4. Competencies illustrated are generic in nature implying they are equally valid for a wide range of jobs in an organization.

Competency mapping and modelling project team of an organization must undertake the task of developing a competency dictionary for organization. Such a task must be dealt after it is through with building competency models based on analysis of competency data. A competency dictionary is immensely useful to an organization. Competencies illustrated in the dictionary can be used to develop competency scales and metrics. These scales and metrics can be used for competency assessment of employees. In other words, competency dictionary becomes a primary basis for building competency-based human resource systems and application in an organization.

Competency dictionary, though immensely useful, is fraught with many limitations in real-life business world. It is possible that none of the generic competencies described in an organization's competency dictionary may precisely suit to any of the jobs. There are many unique competencies that high performing employee's possess and use which might not have been captured effectively. These unique competencies may contribute significantly for high performance. Therefore, while dealing with competency dictionary, this reality must be reckoned. Further, competency dictionary is dynamic rather than static. The dictionary is required to be revised and updated as often as desirable in tune with changing performance profiles and behaviours. Competency dictionary should also be improved upon in order to include unique competencies. Therefore, a competency dictionary must be developed in two phases. In the first phase, generic competencies must be identified and illustrated and unique competencies must be studied, defined and described in the second phase of competency dictionary. Box 3.3 shows the salient features of competency dictionary, and Table 3.3 shows model competency dictionary.

BOX 3.3 Salient Features of Competency Dictionary

The following aspects must be taken into consideration while developing competency dictionary:

1. *Competencies can be generic as well as specific:* Though, competency dictionaries are generally used to illustrate generic competencies, the same can also be used to include job-specific competencies. In such a context, the competency dictionary must be dealt in two parts. Typically, the first part can deal with generic competencies (primary competencies) those are common across many jobs in the organization. Competencies unique to a job can be dealt in the second part of the dictionary.
2. *Behavioural indicators:* Competencies must be defined in operational terms illustrating behavioural indicators. Each behavioural indicator must be sufficiently defined. Care must be taken to avoid bringing too many behavioural indicators under one competency. Similarly, every behavioural indicator should not be treated as a separate competency. All behavioural indicators related significantly to each other must be brought under a competency.
3. *Language/Expressions:* Competencies must be defined clearly in an unambiguous language. Language must be clear, simple and easy to understand. In order to accord professional status, some people tend to use technical jargon, thereby, making it difficult for wider understanding. Intention must be to communicate clearly rather than to achieve an academic goal. Further, definition must suit to practitioner's world.
4. *Content analysis:* Each and every competency in order to being qualified for inclusion in the competency dictionary must

have withstood to content analysis standards. It is also preferable that competencies listed in the dictionary must be subjected to face validation. For this purpose, help of competency experts and superior performers within the organization can be solicited.

5. *Tedious and long drawn:* Developing competency dictionary at times frustrating, and require enormous patience. Further, competency dictionary needs to be revised at regular intervals, failing which such dictionaries contribute problems than adding any value. Therefore, competency management team must evaluate all the pros and cons and its real necessity in the organization before undertaking the exercise.
6. *Not the end:* It must be remembered that despite many benefits of competency dictionary, this is not the ultimate. There would be always behavioural characteristics and competencies that contribute superior performance which existing dictionary might have not captured. Therefore, competency efforts always must look beyond competency dictionary. In such a context, competency dictionary works as a basic tool.
7. *Competency dictionary as a developmental tool:* Competency dictionary development effort generates developmental environment. Therefore, this instrument must be effectively used to build competencies and enable employees to overcome the weaknesses.
8. *Notify limitations:* Limitations of competency dictionary must be explicitly stated in the dictionary itself. In which circumstances, the limitation can have impact also must be described in order to avoid mal-implementation of competency dictionary.
9. *Availability of dictionary:* The competency dictionary on its notification/publication must be made available to all employees in the organization. Making it as a limited edition can cause apprehensions in the minds of employees.
10. *Relationship between competency and performance:* Conventionally, competency dictionary gets limited itself to illustration of competencies, their behavioural indicators description and definitions. The latest developments have widened this scope by including the description of outcome of each competency. It is preferred that the outcome of each competency in terms of performance (how each competency results in high level of performance on the job) must be dealt with.

TABLE 3.3 Model Competency Dictionary

Label of competency cluster	*Competency*	*Operational definition*	*Behavioural indicators of competency*
Problem solving	Conceptual thinking	Understanding a situation by connecting events/parts of information	• Sees basic relationships (understanding patterns/themes/ trends from a given information) • Sees multiple relationship (synergetic ability: understanding relationships among several components) • Clarifies complex data or situations • Applies complex concepts • Creates new concepts
	Innovative thinking	Thinking out the box. Innovating and encouraging innovation	• Open to new ideas • Questions conventional methodology • Thinks laterally (generates unconventional and radical solutions) • Agile in response to change (adaptability to changes and ability to anticipate and effectively deal with changes in external environment) • Champions innovative thinking (encouraging new ideas from employees)

	Strategic orientation	Understanding strategic direction and capabilities and weaknesses of the department	• Understanding strategies • Aligns current actions with strategic goals • Understand how the relationship of department with outside world and community • Contributes to strategic direction • Forges strategy with internal and external alliances
Leadership	Change leadership	Championing the change effort and motivating/ stimulating the group members to introduce changes	• Describes general need for change • Defines and articulates change strategy and disseminates vision • Building support and commitment • Challenges status quo • Executes change by addressing the challenges and managing barriers effectively
	Sharing responsibility	Fostering long term learning, development and sharing responsibility with individuals and groups	• Expresses positive expectations • Delegates routine tasks • Demonstrates trust
	Holding people accountable	Ensures that others perform as per set standards and procedures in order to achieve targets	• Sets clear, consistent expectations and goals • Manages for high performance • Takes corrective action

TABLE 3.3 Model Competency Dictionary (Contd.)

Label of competency cluster	*Competency*	*Operational definition*	*Behavioural indicators of competency*
	Team leadership	Teams up people, teaches, develops and motivates to work towards a well-defined outcome and demonstrates concern for people	• Manages expectations and informs others • Build team-effectiveness • Fosters team success • Cross-team collaboration • Defines a vision
Inter personal influence	Impact and influence	Persuades, convinces and influences others to gain an impact	• Takes action to persuade others through oral and written presentations. • Uses multiple actions to persuade and anticipates reactions to manage them effectively. • Uses indirect influence like exerts or third party initiatives • Uses complex influence strategies like forging coalitions and drafting broad based support and generating new/radical/unconventional ideas and initiatives
	Listening, understanding and responding	Responding to concerns of others appropriately	• Demonstrates openness and receptivity to new information • Listens actively • Listens and responds with sensitivity • Willingness to see others point-of-view

			• Capable of accurate assessment and sensitivity to the underlying complex root causes for individual or group behaviour patterns.
	Networking	Establishes, maintains and utilizes a broad network of contacts and also understands whom and when to involve in order to accomplish objectives and minimize obstacles	• Maintains a network of contacts • Utilizes established network of relationships • Broadens network of relationships • Creates opportunities
	Teamwork	Working together as opposed to working individually or in competition with others	• Carries positive expectation of the team • Communicates information • Solicits ideas and opinions and values others viewpoint and input • Encourages others and acknowledges others credit instead of taking personal credit • Build team spirit
Personal and corporate effectiveness	Results orientation	Setting goals, monitoring its achievement, maximizing resource utilization and progressing as per plans	• Works to meet performance standards • Strives to exceed expectations • Improves operations • Enhances programme outcomes

TABLE 3.3 Model Competency Dictionary (Contd.)

Label of competency cluster	*Competency*	*Operational definition*	*Behavioural indicators of competency*
	Commitment to learning	Pursuing learning and development	• Possesses interest in own filed, updates continuously, discusses with other experts about new ideas, technologies and methods • Actively uses all sources to be contemporary • Keep updated about contemporary with trends • Links newly acquired knowledge with departmental needs and clients requirements • Maintains broad learning perspective
	Client service orientation	Meets clients requirements and serves clients interest through a focused effort	• Responds to enquiries, complains and requests in a timely manner • Maintains clear communication • Aligns activities with clients needs • Anticipates and takes proactive action to ensure customer delight
	Flexibility	Adopts and works effectively within a variety of situations and with varied requirements and perspectives of individuals and groups	• Willing to change ideas and perceptions based on new information and evidence • Modifies procedures and processes to fit a specific requirement • Changes the overall, if required, in order to achieve goals and keeping in view overall situation

	Organizational awareness	Understand clearly organizational vision, mission, objectives, long, medium and short-term plans, various policies and decision-making process and budgetary issues	• Understands formal organizational structure, departments, functions and their role • Understands informal organizational structure • Understands organizational interaction and interface with outside world • Gauzes areas of improvement • Positions organization and resources for alignment
	Planning and initiative	Proactively not only planning, but also acting with right actions	• Shows persistence • Addresses current opportunities • Grasps opportunities and identifies potential problems and take timely action • Plans ahead and manages contingencies effectively • Plans for the future and creates solutions to problems that are likely to occur in future • Executes plans in short, medium and long-terms with precision

Note: The above indicated competency dictionary is illustrative and not comprehensive. Presented to serve as an example.

Source: The above competency dictionary is adapted with modifications from Management Competency Dictionary of Saskatchewan Public Service.

Competency Modelling

Based on the competency data analysis of jobs/functions, competency modelling must be initiated. Competency modelling chiefly involves the following steps:

Consolidation of competency data

Organizations do vary in their approach for competency data collection. Some use a single data collection method to obtain data, whereas others use a combination of methods in order to enhance the possibility of gaining rich data. Use of multiple methods is common when data being collected is for leadership/managerial jobs of the organization. In such context, data obtained using all these methods must be collected job wise. Similarly, some organizations collect competency data for a focused area, for example, competency data of senior level mangers of an organization. In both the cases, it is prerequisite that data of multiple sources must be reconciled. Data is to be reconciled in the manner illustrated in Box 3.4. However, assigning proper and equitable weightage to each of the data collection methods is a tricky issue. If required, resource persons involved in data collection and analysis must be utilized for deciding the rate of credit for each of the technique. The limitations, strengths and the most importantly suitability of data collection methods to a particular job must be taken into consideration while determining the credit.

BOX 3.4 Competency Model: Practitioner's Doubts

While actually building the competency models, a practitioner encounter many doubts for which there are no standard answers. Answers and solutions lie in the modelling process itself. Though, there are certain standard patterns for building competency model, the same are quite flexible and situational sensitive. Most of the competency building efforts need a functional deviation/introduction of new way at some stage due to dynamics associated with that particular organization and persons and jobs under study.

Validation of competency data

This is highly critical activity in the competency modelling. The consolidated competency data of jobs must be subjected to validation process in order to develop a competency model for a job/job family. As a part of validation process, a series of steps are followed. These are:

1. *Establishing inter-rater agreement between competencies:* The consolidated data would project four or more competency clusters for each of the job/job families that distinguish superior performers from average. There must be a statistically significant co-relationship between each of the competency with other competencies in the cluster. For example, four competencies such as accurate self-assessment, positive regard, managing group processes and power of socialization comprise the human resource management competency cluster. Each of these competencies should have a strong positive co-relationship with rest of the three competencies. Secondly, each competency comprises a set of behavioural indicators/demonstrable characteristics. There should be a positive co-relationship among all these behavioural indicators at one level, and all these behavioural indicators must have positive and direct relationship with the competency they represent at the second level. For this purpose, statistical tests like co-relation coefficients, factor analysis can be applied.

2. *Reliability test:* Competencies identified can be subjected to reliability test. For example, identified competencies are expected to result in effective performance and these are the competencies demonstrated by examplary performance in an organization. Using these competencies, questionnaires can be developed. Such a questionnaire can be administered on highly performing employees and averagely performing employees of that particular job seeking their responses. The data obtained can be analyzed to check the validity with the help of t-test and conventional reliability tests.

3. *Focus group discussion:* Using identified competencies; a schedule must be developed enumerating competencies and their behavioural indicators and definitions. Secondly, separate focus groups of exemplars and averagely performing employees to whom the identified competencies are relevant must be formed. Thirdly, they must be invited to discuss, analyze and offer their comments on the identified competencies. In tune with these discussions, competencies must be finalized.
4. *Refining competencies:* Based on the results of focus group discussions, survey ratings and reliability tests, competencies must be refined in terms of their definitions and descriptions. Only those competencies which stand to the standards of reliability must be included as competencies of a particular job/job families.
5. *Building competency model:* Subsequent to the refining of competency statement, competency modelling should be done. Competency model is a comprehensive statement consisting competencies, their behavioural indicators and definitions. Competency models are generally built in the context of a job or job families. Generic competency models are also built which are applicable to a large workforce in the organization. Individual competencies are clustered together based on the inter-relationship of individual competencies. For example, all customer-oriented competencies are grouped together as a single competency cluster. The cluster approach helps to bring the number of competencies in manageable size.

Competency clusters

Understanding competency clusters is essential for building robust competency models. Further, competency cluster approach is also helpful in implementation of competency models for various human resource related issues. Competency clusters can be of many types. For example, there can be function-wise competency cluster like human resource management competency cluster, sales competency cluster, finance cluster, telecom operation cluster and so on. Similarly, there can be discipline-wise clusters like leadership competency cluster, inter-personal competency cluster, communication competency cluster, etc. There can also be level-wise competency clusters like junior management competency cluster, middle management cluster and senior management cluster. Richard Boyatzis based on his extensive research into competencies has identified 21 generic competencies known as Boyatzis's 21 competencies.

Sample competency models

A few common models are discussed in the following subsections in order to illustrate how competency models look like, developed and used.

Leadership competency model

In accordance with Boyatzis, leadership competency model encompasses four competencies as described here. However, his studies have found that these four competencies are related to effective performance at middle and executive levels only, and not at the entry level. Further, these four competencies are significantly correlated thereby becoming a single cluster.

1. *Self-confidence:* This competency is demonstrated through behavioural characteristics such as self-awareness, decisiveness, self-esteem, self-belief, self-regulation. People with this competency tend to exhibit clarity of thought, and they know what they are doing. They come across as confident people who can defend their actions, reason out and convince others. They can be good team players and would forge collaboration with others easily. Studies have shown that all effective and successful middle and senior level managers demonstrate this competency. There is a positive co-relationship between self-confidence and leadership effectiveness.

2. *Use of oral presentation:* This is a competency of communication. Behavioural indicators are ability to communicate effectively using verbal, symbolic and non-verbal signs/ language. This competency helps in making clear presentations and effectively communicating in a way that others understand easily. Use of oral presentation doesnot merely mean talking to others, but talking with quality,

sense and complete meaning. People with this competency would be at ease to use various methods such as audio-visual techniques and also employ interactive techniques to ensure that audience understand what they want to communicate. Studies have shown that all senior level managers, who are successful in their roles, demonstrate use of presentation skills abundantly implying there is a significant positive relationship between leadership and use of oral presentation. All effective managers across the functions such as finance, operations, marketing, human resource, etc., have demonstrated the use of this competency.

3. *Logical thought:* This is a competency demonstrated by behavioural indicators such as insightfulness, establishing cause and effect relationship in the events, thinking in a logical sequence and analyzing the events in an orderly manner. Studies have found that though this competency may or may not result in effective performance directly, but all successful leaders possess this competency, whereas poor performers do not.
4. *Conceptualization:* This is referred to as cognitive skill. People with this competency have the ability to see the pattern in a given information however disorganized such information may be. They tend to explain the issues with the support of an analogy. They can connect even the disconnected information, and bring out a meaningful interpretation. Themes are identified out of information, and label is given. This competency reflects creativity too in terms of concepts and ideas. Studies have found that conceptualization is strongly related to effective performance of managers and all high performers demonstrate and use this competency frequently, and this competency is not found with poorly performing managers.

Leadership competency dictionary

Leadership plays a pivotal role in organizational effectiveness and growth. In realization of this fact, many organizations like GE, Motorola, Citi Bank, IBM and Microsoft have identified and developed a comprehensive leadership dictionary. The dictionary can offer multiple benefits to organizations since its applications are value added. Dictionary can be used in career and succession planning in order to groom future leadership, leadership training, and to design a leadership specific performance management system, and also to build leadership at many levels of an organization. In the absence of leadership competency dictionary, leadership training and career planning tend to be unsystematic especially from the point of view of competencies. Leadership dictionary similar to other competency dictionaries need to be specific and clear in their description. A model leadership competency dictionary is shown in Table 3.4.

TABLE 3.4 Model Leadership Competency Dictionary

Competency	*Behavioural indicators*
Accountability	• Accepts responsibility for own behaviour and job-related tasks • Takes steps to perform work at a higher level in order to achieve goals • Takes steps to perform work at a high level in order to achieve goals • Makes a contribution to the goals of others and to the team • Assumes responsibility for the performance and results of the entire team
Coaching	• Provides support and help to colleagues • Creates an environment that is conducive to high performance and growth and attracts talented people • Accepts accountability for helping people to develop beyond current role and in the interest of the organization
Communicating	• Listens in order to clarify information: sends both written and verbal messages in a clear manner • Provides timely, appropriate and useful information to others • Increases the value of information by providing sound interpretation
Composure	• Adjusts comfortably to demanding situations • Deals with issues forthrightly and with sensitivity • Achieves mutually agreeable results when faced with conflict or crisis

TABLE 3.4 Model Leadership Competency Dictionary (Contd.)

Competency	*Behavioural indicators*
Decision-making	• Makes timely and accurate decisions with readily available information and within clearly defined parameters • Makes good decisions by defining the parameters and acting on what is important • Makes good decisions by clarifying ambiguous situations and accurately assessing the risk • Makes decisions which are based on the values and principles of the organization when there is information which is incomplete or conflicting
Flexibility and adaptability	• Respects that there is more than one point of view or way of accomplishing results • Adjusts to multiple demands and shifting priorities • Responds openly and confidently when faced with ambiguity and uncertainty
Goal-setting	• Is motivated by achieving or surpassing challenging goals • Maintains focus by linking goals to the goals of the team and the organization
Influencing	• Involves others in setting and achieving common goals • Uses clear and reliable processes to build relationships and to gain commitment from others • Is highly regarded and sought out by the others, because of a sustained track record of collaboration
Innovating	• Uses the ideas of others to improve the quality of own work • Generates ideas that improve the quality of own work and that of others • Forecasts the impact ideas might have on the organization if implemented
Integrity	• Respects others • Communicates high personal standards which reflect socially accepted norms • Adhere to the organization's values and guidelines of conduct • Is open and honest • Actions are consistent with words • Represents self truthfully • Does not exploit people

Planning	• Organizes own work in order to complete routine tasks • Prepares plans which guide the activities of a team, project or multi-function team • Leads/sponsors complex projects which impact multiple stakeholders and the long-term success of the organization
Problem-solving	• Recognizes problems as they arise and uses good judgment and common sense to resolve issues • Uses all available resources to assess the problem and to identify the best solution • Takes initiative to identify conflicts within a team and fosters an environment which supports resolution
Self development	• Responds positively to feedback regarding performance and strives to develop in current role • Seeks opportunities for development • Takes advantage of opportunities to grow beyond current role
Service orientation	• Clarifies the client's expectations and respond promptly and courteously to requests • Demonstrates empathy, offers alternatives and describes likely consequences of each possible course of action • Views the relationships with the clients as ongoing. Displays an understanding of the client's circumstances
Strategic perspective	• Thinks several steps ahead in order to complete tasks and projects • Considers the implications of information, decisions and actions beyond the team/department • Develops and communicates a compelling yet credible vision of the future for all members of the organization
Sustaining functional, technical and organizational proficiency	• Applies new knowledge, procedures and skills to own job and assists others within the team and to do so • Helps others to make connections between own area of expertise and others functions within the organization

TABLE 3.4 Model Leadership Competency Dictionary (Contd.)

Competency	*Behavioural indicators*
	• Remains informed on the broader economic, political and social factors which could impact the organization and helps others understand these factors
Teamwork	• Participates in developing the goals and using the processes by which the team accomplishes its work • Uses a participative approach to leading and directing the work of the team
Understanding the organizational culture	• Accomplishes results through formal channels • Works through the complex informal networks of stakeholders and interest groups • Has an appreciation for and knowledge of the organization culture and can convey its strengths and complexities to others
Valuing diversity	• Interacts effectively with all people regardless of age, culture, gender, interests, nationality, orientation, perspective or race • Seeks out the ideas and perspectives of others, because they are different • Takes action which may be the mainstream, in order to provide opportunity to people on the basis of age, culture, gender, interests, nationality, orientation, perceptive or race • Holds people accountable for their behaviour with respect to others • Initiates change in systems and policies in order to eliminate inequities.

Source: Based on Wilfrid Laurier University's Leadership Competency Dictionary.

Compass competency model of leadership

Compass based on their extensive study developed and tested a competency model consisting of 7 competencies such as:

1. *Risk taking:* Undertaking calculated and prudent risks and taking responsibility for making difficult decisions.

2. *Credibility:* Behaving consistently and keeping promises and honouring commitments.
3. *Strategic thinking:* Knowing and identifying market demands, customer needs and taking a long term perspective.
4. *Customer focus:* Taking customers needs as basis for initiating decisions and demonstrating concern for customers.
5. *Consulting:* Encouraging participative and democratic work environment and seeking views and concerns of others prior to effecting changes.
6. *Influencing:* Reasoning, valuing and emphasizing.
7. *Recognizing:* Acknowledging and praising and appreciating the effective performance and significant achievement through appropriate means/behaviour.

Competency model for accounts/finance professionals

CGA association based on it's competency-based programme of professional application and competence evaluation (PACE) has identified a set of three types of competencies for accounting and finance professionals which include:

1. *Leadership competencies:* The sub and micro competencies here encompass strategic and organizational leadership, organizational effectiveness and individual and team leadership and development.
2. *Professionalism:* In order to ensure upholding the highest standards of ethical and professional conduct, CGA competency framework identifies a distinct set of competencies labelled as professionalism. The sub competencies here include: ethics and trust, stakeholder focus, communication, integrative approach, problem-solving, professional development and professional self-evaluation.
3. *Professional knowledge:* These set of competencies deal with technical competency requirements of accounting and finance professionals, these competencies prescribe

knowledge and experience proficiency levels required to perform the said job effectively. The prescribed competencies here are: financial accounting and reporting, management accounting, assurances and other related services, finance and financial planning, business environment, information technology, and taxation.

Competency model for first level supervisors

California government as a part of modernization of human resources project identified the following set of competencies for front level managers:

1. *Fostering a team environment cluster:* Sub competencies of this cluster are—communication, conflict management, inter-personal skills and team leadership. Communication is operationally defined as the ability to listen to others and communicate in an effective manner, the ability to communicate ideas, thoughts and facts. Conflict management is defined as ability to prevent, manage and resolve conflicts. The ability to get along and interact positively with co-workers and degree and style of understating and relating to others are the attributes related to inter personal skills. Team leadership is defined as the ability to effectively manage and guide group efforts. This includes providing the appropriate level of feedback concerning group progress.
2. *Creating organizational transformational cluster:* Change leadership is defined as the ability to manage, lead and enable the process of change and transition while helping others to deal with their efforts and vision. Strategic thinking is defined as the ability to support, promote and ensure alignment with the organization's vision and values and the ability to understand how an organization must change in light of internal and external trends and influences. These two are the part of this cluster and planning and organizing defined as the ability to define tasks and milestones to achieve objectives while ensuring the optimal use of resources to meet those objectives.
3. *Maximizing performance results cluster:* Sub competencies such as analytical thinking defined as the ability to

approach a problem by using a logical, systematic, sequential approach and customer focus defined as the ability to identify and respond to current and future customer's needs and the ability to provide excellent services to internal and external customers. Decision-making is defined as the ability to make decisions and solve problems involving varied levels of complexity, ambiguity and risk and thoughtfulness defined as the ability to ensure that one's own and other's work and information are complete and accurate. The ability to follow up with others to ensure that agreements and compliments have been fulfilled.

4. *Building trust and accountability cluster:* Ethics and integrity defined as the degree of trust worthiness and ethical behaviour of an individual with consideration for the knowledge one has of the impact and consequences while making a decision or taking action and personal credibility defined as demonstrating concern that one be perceived as responsible, reliable and trustworthy are the operational competencies under this cluster

5. *Promoting a high performance culture cluster:* Competencies such as developing others defined as the ability and willingness to delegate responsibility, work and others and coach them to develop their capabilities, Fostering diversity defined as the ability to promote equal and far treatment and opportunity for all and work force management defined as the ability to effectively recruit, select, develop and retain competency staff, includes making appropriate assignments and managing staff performance.

Human resource management competency model

Boyatzis identified human resource management competency model comprising four competencies as follows:

1. *Use of socialized power:* This competency is demonstrated by the tendency to form alliances, to become an active member of team/organization, seek people around, and influence them. This competency is found to be positively

related to human resource management role. People with this competency use socialized power to accomplish their tasks. They seek others views and act in a desirable manner instead of prescribing something unilaterally and expecting people to adhere to them. Though, this competency is demonstrated by all effective managers in organization, its usage is higher by human resource managers due to demand of the role and also on account of loose structure and less formal authority of the function.

2. *Positive regard:* Believing others, respecting their views and valuing their opinions are the behavioural indicators of this competency. People with this competency tend to exhibit an optimistic behaviour and use verbal and non-verbal language to convey their regard to people in what they say and believe. The relationship between performance effectiveness and positive regard, though positive, is found to be weak. This is attributed to the factor some organizational cultures may not be supportive of valuing and believing in people. Therefore, managers use this competency not so frequently.

3. *Managing group process:* This is termed as a collaborator role. People with this competency would stimulate others to work in a group setting. People with this competency believe in cooperation and forge alliances. Collaboration between and among groups. They use group identity, group pride and a group specific language to bond the members together. They use personal contact and friendly gestures more often. This competency is positively related to performance effectiveness of all managers. However, this competency is more strongly related to effective performance of human resource managers. Therefore, human resource managers tend to demonstrate this competency more often than line managers.

4. *Accurate self assessment:* This competency encompasses the behavioural indicators such as realistic view of self, knowing strengths and weaknesses and ability to evaluate objectively the performance levels of self in a given situation. This competency has positive relationship to effective performance of managers.

The above four competencies have a reasonable positive relationship among them, thus qualifying it as human resource management cluster. Some of these competencies are common and applicable to other line managers too since they hold human resource related responsibilities.

Competency model for technical professionals

Spencer and Spencer (1993) based on their study of technical personnel, identified 12 distinguishing competencies of superior technical professionals. These are described here. Technical professionals are basically knowledge workers working in software development, finance, research and development and other specialized services. These competencies vary in their degree of importance for effective performance in the technical roles. Competencies are listed here as per the said importance/priority for effective performance. This importance is established through measuring the frequency of use of these competencies in technical jobs. For example, achievement orientation is a competency widely and frequently used competency among others.

Therefore, it is listed here as the first competency of technical exemplars. In similar manner, the order of describing competencies is as follows:

1. *Achievement orientation:* This is demonstrated by innovativeness, seeking challenging goals and making continuous efforts to improve from the existing status.

2. *Impact and influence:* Behavioural indicators of this competency are—persuasion, showing concern and valuing others view-point and perspective, and communicating to others using suitable aids/means.

3. *Conceptual thinking:* Identifying underlying assumptions, patterns and themes from a given information and seeing the synergetic relationship between two or multiple indirectly connected events/information.

4. *Analytical thinking:* Visualizing future and anticipating problems. Challenges/obstacles and drawing rational inferences for action.

5. *Initiative:* This is demonstrated by proactive action/ behaviour; acting on problems before hand.

6. *Self-confidence:* Self-belief, knowing what one is doing, understanding self-strengths and weaknesses and demonstrating confidence in self-actions and judgment.

7. *Inter-personal understanding:* This competency is demonstrated by behavioural characteristics such as understanding values, attitudes and interest of others.

8. *Concern for order:* This is related to systems approach; seeks clarity, quality and logical order of arranging information.

9. *Information seeking:* Collects information, reads and attends meetings/conferences and uses all sources to have information.

10. *Teamwork and cooperation:* As the title suggests, this competency is demonstrated by a behaviour seeking contributions from others and involving all and encouraging group ownership for performance.

11. *Expertise:* Possessing and using technical knowledge and updating technical expertise and sharing with others developments in one's own field.

12. *Customer service orientation:* Continuously analyzes and identifies customer needs and takes action to meet customer needs timely.

Competency model for software professionals

1. *Competency* #1: *Management ability:* This competency is demonstrated by behavioural indicators such as providing direction and accountability, team facilitation, leadership/vision, coach and develop others, participate and lead productive meetings, influence and persuasion, organizational awareness, manage conflict and build consensus, oral presentation, ability to challenge current thinking and change management and follow up monitoring.

2. *Competency* #2: *Conscientiousness:* Behavioural indicators for this competency include: flexibility in terms of taking into account new information and changed circumstances, strategic/tactical perspective, creativity, adaptability/multi-tasking, persistence, application of knowledge and initiative.
3. *Competency* #3: *General cognitive ability:* Behavioural indicators are: reasoning—the ability to analyze information and to make correct inference, analytical thinking, problem-solving, communication, decision-making and attention to detail.
4. *Competency* #4: *Service orientation:* This competency is represented by behavioural indicators such as: teamwork, customer service focus and interacting with people and building relationships.

In addition to these four competencies, generic competencies such as self management, stress management and self development are identified as supplementary competencies for software professionals.

Part II: Classification of Competency Models

Part I as discussed above helps in analyzing the competency data, templating it and validating. The purpose of phase II in competency modelling is to arrive clusterization of competencies and establish co-relations among individual competencies. The competencies can be classified into meaningful clusters. The classification can be organization wide, function/job/department-wise, role/position-wise and based on nature of competency. Sample classification of competencies is provided as follows:

Organization Wide Classification of Competencies

There are number of ways that organizations can follow to classify the competencies. They are technical, functional, behavioural, leadership, specialist, and so on. The purpose is to create a meaningful cluster so that they can create a desired impact and also developing and nurturing them become easy apart from assessing them. Let us look at some of the classifications at organization level in a more detailed fashion.

Technical competencies

Every organization whether service or manufacturing or process will have core technical competencies to deal with in order to deliver goods and services to the end customer. For example erection, testing and commissioning, coal handling, water treatment, field survey, land acquisition are the technical competencies for an electricity generation organization, whereas programming, coding, requirement analysis, testing etcetera are core technical competencies for a software services organization. One important distinction is same competency can be technical competency for one organization and the same can be functional or enabling competency for other. For example, public communication is a technical competency for a media company, whereas the same can be either a functional or just an enabling competency for a non-media company. These competencies can fall within threshold as well as differentiating competencies. The easy part with these competencies is they can be imparted with a good training and course module, relatively easy to measure and assess the proficiency level of employees on these competencies and competencies can be used as reliable predictors of performance at organizational level. Often an organization identifies itself with the set of technical competencies it has. In that sense technical competencies are basic blocs. However, technical competencies also can assume the value proposition of differentiating competencies when an organization becomes leader in those by continually redefining the technical competencies from the state of status quo. This set of competencies is vital and imperative for survival of an organization though often they are not the change vehicles for revolutionary growth.

Functional competencies

These sets of competencies are similar to technical competencies in terms of the nature, knowledge base and trainability and assessibility. However, they differ in their business outcomes. Technical competencies are used for basic functioning and identity of an organization and functional competencies are used for enablement and growth of the organization. Functional competencies include, finance, human resource, marketing, sales, project management, innovation, corporate communications, technology management, administration, legal and shared services. There is as systematic body of knowledge within each of these functions. Proficiency in these functions can create value to an organization. No organization can function without presence of functional competencies. Sometimes functional competencies can assume the status of technical competencies. For example, finance which is a functional competency for non-finance organizations can be a technical competency for finance-centric organizations like banking, insurance and financial institutions. Similarly, information technology which is a macro technical competency for IT organizations can be just a functional competency for non-IT organizations. Therefore, the definition of technical and functional is contingent upon the prime nature and functioning of the organization.

Behavioural competencies

These set of competencies are known as soft competencies or broadly as inter-personal competencies. Competencies such as self awareness, self control, social skills, communication, team work, negotiation, conflict resolution, relationships, and empathy are considered as behavioural competencies. These are also called attitude-related competencies. These are vital for effective functioning of organizations. Latest research establishes that behavioural competencies are twice in their importance comparing to technical and functional competencies for success and growth of organizations. Unlike technical and functional competencies here trainability and assessment is a big challenge. Often organizations devote resources and efforts to impart technical training since the way it hurts organization is quite clear and direct. Training efforts that are centred around technical competencies also tend to yield results which are visible and quantifiable in linear fashion. However, the results in regard to training of behavioural competencies could produce often unclear results and may not easily susceptible to quantitative assessment. Therefore, some organizations tend to exhibit inhibition in their resource commitment to building behavioural competencies. Often than not organizations fail to grow not because of lack of technical competencies, but because of low level of behavioural competencies. This reality is spread in more organizations so as a result there is a growing effort to build behavioural competencies and especially to hire employees for their attitude rather than aptitude (technical competencies). In fact, credit for most of the competency movement goes to the upsurge in interest in behavioural competencies. Often it is also thought that competency mapping means nothing, but understanding and defining operational measures for behavioural attributes.

Leadership competencies

This is crucial and strategic set of competencies from organizational point of view. Decision-making, managing uncertainties, ability to see the big picture, inspiring, leading, visioning, managing paradoxes, empowering, risk taking, intuition, etc., are considered to be typical leadership competencies. These are also known as differentiating competencies. Leadership effectiveness is largely derived from proficiency of these competencies prevalent in an organization. In the past, it was widely believed that someone mere possessing large depth in technical and functional competencies can qualify someone as a leader. However, the recent experience and research clearly point-out that it is differentiating leadership competencies that contribute for success of an organization rather than technical competencies per se. this realization has given a fillip in renewing the interest in building leadership competencies as well as identifying and catapulting people with these kind of competencies into leadership roles. There are distinct tools developed to assess the said competencies, and customized courses are created to impart these to people holding leadership positions. Undoubtedly this set of competencies are king pin in the competency model of any organization.

Process-related competencies

These are more a catalytic competencies than bearing a direct impact on themselves in organizational context. These are more like compliance related, for example protocols, quality measures, discipline in execution or follow up, audits, reporting, documenting and sharing fall into the category of process-based competencies. These are more like intermediate competencies. They help maintain and preserve history and movements of organization in an orderly fashion. They help to reap benefits of implanting other competencies, and they help in preventing the reinventing the wheel in any given filed or activity. These competencies are more like functional competencies. Not difficult to measure, assess and impart training. It is also relatively easy to measure their application and success in organizations. These competencies are not essential for growth, but important from a method and order perspective and also from the angle of efficiency.

Department/Function-wise Classification of Competency Models

The next level that competencies can be described in any organization is at department and functional level. At this level, a competency is sliced into more at micro level. For example, finance, which is either technical or functional competency at organization level, can be further portioned into accounting, taxation, treasury, audit, compliances, business law, risk management, costing. Similarly, a human resource function which is a functional competency can be further broken into sub competencies like recruitment, performance, development, compensation, employee relations, and leadership development and employee engagement programmes. Each of these competencies can be defined into operational elements for a clear comprehension. It is helpful for any organization to have clearly-defined competencies at department level too. Unlike competency identification at functional level, it can be quite a complex exercise at the department level. This is due to the reason that at department level it is not one competency, but a set of competencies comprising functional, behavioural and process-related competencies that define a competency set of a department. For example, in finance department it is not only direct finance functional competencies but also a few behavioural competencies like communication, team work, integrity and process-related competencies like adherence to the system play a definite role in successful functioning of such a department. It is desirable that every organization must make efforts to clearly establish the competency set required at a department level as well as at the functional level. Such definition and standards can help hugely in hiring, assessing and developing employees apart from using such an application for enhancing departmental and functional performance. The nature and number of competencies, the functions and department of an organization has, are drawn from the nature of business and their operations. In summary, it is very important for an organization to define and classify the competencies associated with each function and department.

Role/Job-wise Classification of Competencies

Another way of classifying competencies is identifying and defining set of competencies required at each position and job level. In the same function as described above, the number of competencies and their proficiency level can differ depending on the role level. For example, the number of competencies required at a level of Accounts Supervisor can be lesser comparing to the level of Accounts Director. Similarly even for the competencies which are common across these both levels, they would differ in their proficiency requirements. Practices like job analysis, job description and job specification can be of relevance here. The performance expectations and KRAs of a role and job will determine the kind of competencies and proficiency level desirable for a role. Based on the criteria of success factors of a position/job, the competencies are drawn. Once the competencies are drawn, they should be classified into meaningful clusters like technical, functional and behavioural and leadership competencies. Proficiency levels and operational measures of each competency must be provided for greater clarity and understating. The classification of competencies at position level helps in variety of human resource interventions like hiring, rewarding, training and measuring performance. Often there are efforts to define the competencies at organization and department level and such a practice is seldom experienced at role level in organizations. Unless competency initiatives reach at the level of a position and role, it is difficult to obtain the benefits of competency management in organizations.

A job level competency classification is another way of approaching competency management. Primarily this can be done at various levels like:

1. *Individual contributor level:* There will be positions in the company which are by nature individual contributor level implying no people and management functions/tasks/ expectations involved in this job. Therefore, competency classification here may limit itself to technical or functional competencies.

2. *Leadership/manager level:* Competency classification especially at managerial and leadership level is a critical necessity. This is on account of a number and variety of competencies involved in a leadership role, which span into technical, functional, process and behavioural roles. Such identification and definition along with proficiency level will give a good comprehension and plan for management of these jobs in an effective manner.

3. *Specialist level:* One more perspective for classifying the competencies is specialist level. There can be a number of positions in an organization which are highly specialized in nature like java architects, functional consultants, taxation experts, head hunters, chefs, and so on. Here the competency classification may give more focus and emphasis to proficiency levels and less in terms of variety of competencies.

4. *Generalist:* This is akin to leadership and managerial set of competency classification exercise. Here the complexity and variety involve. A generalist is supposed to have comprehension not only in more competencies but also in more varieties like behavioural, process, technical and functional at an organizational level. The classification of competency sets at this level is of utmost importance. The typical roles in this category are CXOs, and business leaders whose job requirements span across the broader functioning and leading of an organization.

Part III: Proficiency Levels and Weightages of Competencies

The sequential phase, after classifying competencies, is determining and defining proficiency levels and giving weightage to both proficiency level and significance of a particular competency to a job and position/role. One of the most effective ways to communicate the relative importance of competencies and goals to employees is by assigning them weights on your employee evaluation forms. Knowing the relative weights helps employees to prioritize their work and efforts on a day-to-day basis, as well as make decisions when faced with competing demands. It is often used when compensation is tied to performance ratings, and in mature organizations that have established their core values and objectives.

The proficiency levels can be 2 or more depending on the clarity and depth, a competency would require. There are organizations which have two levels of proficiency and some three and many organizations also follow four levels of proficiency. For example, CGA has defined three proficiency levels which are described as follows:

1. *Level A: Mastery:* This level represents a thoroughly analyzed given information, synthesize information to form a sound evaluation of a situation, make recommendations that are well-supported and add value for the decision maker and apply and implement knowledge as a competent professional would be in normal circumstances within a reasonable time frame and without supervision.

2. *Level B: Comprehension:* This level solicits that a candidate should be prepared to apply concepts and techniques to a new situation, analyze given information and develop preliminary conclusions and break down information into its component parts, discriminate between relevant and irrelevant information and differentiate facts from assumptions or inferences.

3. *Level C: Awareness:* Here a candidate should be prepared to recognize why information is relevant, understand it well enough to be able to describe or explain it in their own words and summarize the information or provide examples.

iGATE follows four levels of proficiency as follows:

1. *Level 1: Knowledgeable:* This is primary level applicable to entry level employees. At this level, an employee is

expected to possess a thorough conceptual and theoretical understanding of a given competency and should be able to understand the models and literature on the subject.

2. *Level 2: Practitioner:* Here an employee is expected to have the abilities to apply a formal body of knowledge into work situations to solve problems and improve processes. This is more an application and practical perspective of any competency. This is also understood as a level of proficient execution level.
3. *Level 3: Proficient:* At this level, an employee not only know how to apply the knowledge and skill at work situations but also can find new ways fitting the situation and alter the way a problem to be approached and resolved. This proficiency recognizes a fact that every situation is unique and every time one would be required to make modifications in a set method. Hence, this proficient mandates dynamism into an employee.
4. *Level 4: Champion:* This is the most advanced and highest level of proficiency of any suggested competency for a role or job. An employee, at this level, should have the ability to innovate/create a solution which is high value and which cause disruption to the status quo. This is a mastery and innovator level competency. Also, at this level an employee gets identified as role model for that particular competency.

As discussed above, proficiency levels and their definitions and indicators do provide greater understanding and clarity on the breadth and depth of a competency. This is significantly helpful for assessments and developments. Also from an individual employee perspective, it is helpful to plan the learning and acquire the proficient in an evolutionary and logical manner since it provides a clear road map of progression in acquiring the competency. Proficiency levels also help to prescribe same competency to a job, but different proficiency levels can be made applicable to different levels like higher proficient for senior employees and beginner levels to junior employees.

Weightages ought to be accorded to competencies in relation to jobs and positions depending upon importance of such a competency for effective performance of a job/position. For example, communication is the most important competency for someone in media and the same can be of moderate importance for someone in accounting. So it is important that success factors of a job/position need to be identified and competencies those are sure predictors of such success factors shall be given higher weightage. Proficiency levels also can be used to assign the weightages like 25% weightage for beginner level, 50% for intermediate and 75% for proficient and 100% for champion. Proficiency-based weightage can automatically address the computation of weightages. The key purpose of weightage assignment is to ensure a job is associated or assigned competencies those are the most pertinent and vehicles of superior performance in a job/position.

Part IV: Validation of Competency Models

Reliability and validity of competency models at multiple levels like at organizational, function/department and job/position level is very important for success of competency-based human resource management. Unless the validation is done, it is neither desirable nor feasible to apply competency modes for predicting performance as well as using it for variety of human resource decisions like hiring, developing, monitoring and rewarding. It is also unethical and illegal to take human resource decisions-based on competency modes those are not validated. Broadly, there are three methods which can be used to validate competency models as described below:

Content Related Validity

Here the test is establishing that competency model has covered all the behavioural, knowledge and skills characteristics. This can be done based on performance criteria of a role/position or function. This also can be done based on literature reviews and job description and specifications of a role. There shall be a correlation between the elements of competency model and performance criteria. For example, a key performance criterion for a sales role is the ability to influence customers through good communication and the competency framework/ model of a sales role do not capture that reality, then the same may collapse in the content validation test. Therefore, testing the performance criteria of a role against the content of competencies of a role/job/department/function is essential. More importantly, it is often seen with organizations that a set of additional and supplementary competencies or generic competencies are added to a role those are not impactful for a good performance on the job. For example adhering to the company policies and discipline (compliance) as a competency for sales role do not espouse the theory of competency model which is designed to cut the flesh and retain only muscle in the form of high impact competencies. Each of the competencies listed and captured in a competency model shall be directly related to a performance criterion with a possible weightage implying the said competency can predict performance on a given scale with a good reliability. An assessment needed to be carried out in regular intervals on the content validity by following the steps as follows:

1. *Build a questionnaire/instrument:* A set of statements shall be created based on competencies citing that demonstration of the said competencies or possessing and applying the competencies would result in performance at a defined level. In other words, a particular proficiency in a given competency would likely to lead a particular level of performance.

   A good user language and sequence of questions/ statements covering all the competencies shall be ensured as a part of instrument building. It is advisable to do a pilot testing of the questionnaire for refinement.

2. *Administer on relevant sample:* Once the instrument is built the same can be administered on relevant sample consisting of employees who are the role holders, customers of that particular role, reportees and managers of that role. The prime purpose is to establish that a competency model is capturing the competencies those have direct impact or sure predictor of success of a role. Based on the responses and analysis the competency model can be validated.

3. *Expert face validation:* It is also advisable to just get verified and checked by subject matters expects whether the competency model captures all the relevant competencies required in a role to obtain superior performance. Based on responses and views of such a study the validation of the content can be done.

4. *Criterion-related validity:* This is an important method of competency model validation. These are also known as construct-related validation. Here the relationship strength between a competency and performance measure is tested and validated. Higher the direct and positive co-relationship between a competency of a role and performance produced, better the model in terms of validation. For example, the criterion validity goes into greater examination that a competency test scores is able to produce performance in proportionate manner. For example, whether a competency which has a recorded a test score 4 out of 5 in a given competency and is it 4 out of 5 when compared to performance scale?

There are two types of criteria validation—one is called as predictive criteria validation and second is called as concurrent criteria validation method. In predictive criterion method, all test scores of competencies of a group of role holders is obtained, and over a period of time their performance on the role is observed to find out the type and strength of correlation. In the concurrent method, scores both on competency tests and performance output measures are collected simultaneously and the data is analyzed to establish the correlation.

In such criterion validation studies, it is of utmost importance to eliminate all intermediate and moderating factors/variables those contaminate the validation studies. There can be circumstantial factors those contribute or inhibit the performance regardless of competency scores and similarly vice versa. Such factors shall be identified and eliminated for robust validation study.

Whether it is predictive or concurrent validation, establishing both the performance criteria and competency testing criteria are very critical. Each of it is also dependent on the other, competencies shall be defined based on the expected performance level and nature of performance in a role and similarly the performance criteria shall be defined exactly what a role is expected to produce the outcomes in an organization. Any over look or ambiguity in definition of these criteria can create barriers in competency model validation.

The test of reliability also must be given due importance while implementing validation of competency models. The reliability scores provide the consistency and durability of competency models. The standard tools of reliability can be used for competency model reliability exercises.

Unless a competency model is tested for its reliability and importantly for its validation, the same cannot be implemented in organizations for any purpose, whether it is for development/ assessment or reward management. A good validated competency model is just apt for a competency-based human resource management practice in organizations.

Part V: Execution of Competency Model: iGATE Experience

Competency management system was created at iGATE to adopt a focused approach in building a workforce that is agile, and is capable of achieving even the most challenging of business objectives of an organization.

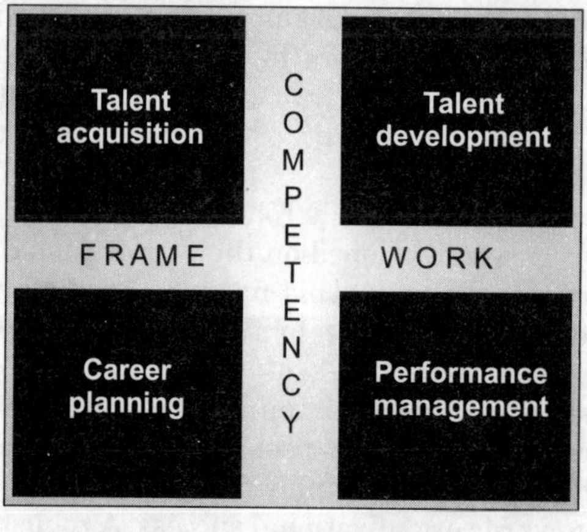

FIGURE 3.2 Design of the competency-based HR system at iGATE.

The competency framework of iGATE (as shown in Figure 3.2) is created based on the roles and the career ladders existing in the organization. The framework caters to all employees across business functions in the organization.

The behavioural and leadership competency framework covers all grades starting from Alpha A to Eta vertically, and all the business units (including BPO & CC) and business enabling functions of iGATE horizontally.

The technical competency framework covers IT delivery business units of iGATE. The grades covered by the technical competency framework include roles from the entry level up to the middle management layer.

The following are the benefits that iGATE has reaped in implementing a competency-based HR system:

1. Enhancing organizational capability and strengthening iGATE's core competency.
2. Bringing in a common understanding of critical aspects of a role. The system will provide the role holder with more information about the success factors of a role, thus minimizing ambiguity. The system minimized any differences in the understanding/expectation of a role across its various internal units that existed due to different business conditions, leadership styles, and other human factors.
3. Enabled the organization to channelize investment in the right development programmes critical for the role/organization and that caters to an individual's development needs. A competency framework will essentially result in the identification of the organization's core competency/cies.
4. Enabled iGATE build a robust system that will ensure employees are developed on their professional capabilities in a systematic way. This means a systems was built to ensure that the people in the organization will develop themselves as a part of being in the organization irrespective of their position, role, reporting structure, etc.
5. Ensure that the right people are put in the right job, thereby capitalizing on individual capabilities and directing them towards organizational success. A robust competency framework will support alignment of individual career

objectives with that of the organization thereby engaging its people fully with the organizational activities.

6. The competency framework will provide an employee with clarity on the critical success factors of a role.
7. The competency assessment exercise and the scores enabled individuals to understand one's capabilities better.
8. The CMS supports a role holder in understanding the nuances that lead to performance excellence in a given role.
9. The CMS ensures that the professional capabilities of an individual are developed systematically.
10. Creates a platform that can support systematic career planning with more information on the competencies to be built to take on more challenging roles and move up the career ladder.
11. The individual is better informed about one's opportunities for improvement, thereby working towards building specific competencies to excel in a role.

Phase 1: Creation of the Competency Framework

The first phase of the exercise involved setting up of a Cross Functional Task force based on the business verticals and domains. The competency definition exercise was carried out using this task force to ensure it is aligned with the vision, mission and values of the organization. This process aimed at providing the role holders with key information such as competencies required for the role, the expected proficiencies to be displayed at every role, this exercise became extremely critical in ensuring the initiative meets the objectives defined. As an outcome of this exercise the competencies that are required for successful performance of these roles were identified and defined.

Phase 2: Validation through Benchmarking

It was important for the competency management system not just to cater to the needs of the organization and its internal customer, but also to be able to attract and retain the top talent from the talent pool external to the market. Hence the benchmarking exercise was carried out to ensure that it is competitive enough and incorporates the best practices of other organizations. The benchmarking helped iGATE to understand that the competency-based career management system requires immense commitment from the organization in the form of systemic support, managerial time, etc., to be able to yield continued benefits for the people and the organization (see Figure 3.2).

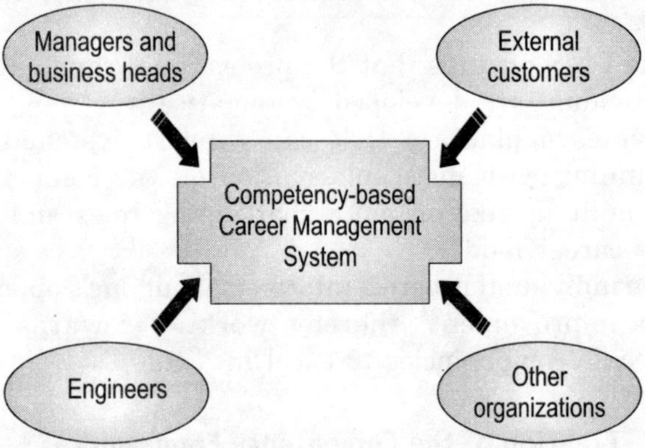

FIGURE 3.3 Pictorial representation of the design adopted.

Phase 3: Validation with the Customers

The third and the critical phase of this journey were to take it to our customer organizations to ensure that the career paths and the competencies defined for the roles in totality are meeting the expectations of the customers. Thus, the external and more importantly the customers' view brought in a new dimension that helped us refine the frameworks further and move ahead with confidence that the approach will positively impact the key stakeholders.

Phase 4: Internal Piloting of the Competency Management System

Since the new system will result in a significant change in the way people development and recognition of capability was carried out in the organization, we took a systematic approach required for a change intervention. The result of this decision is the piloting exercise. As a part of the piloting exercise, we implemented the new process to 10% of the organization. The objective of the piloting exercise was:

1. To ensure that the competency framework can be successful given the business realities
2. To ensure that the competency framework is adequate and easy to interpret aiding in the ease of use
3. To ensure that the competencies and the proficiency level definitions are not far away from the actual capabilities. This is because, if it's not setting a high standard it may result in not enhancing individual effectiveness and may fail to meet the larger objectives. On the other hand, if it's way too above, it might demoralize the people resulting in a loss of faith in the system.

Phase 5: Defining Development Interventions for Competency and Proficiency Level

This objective of this phase is to provide road maps for individuals to develop competencies and move to higher proficiencies. This exercise enabled the organization to understand and capitalize on different learning interventions such as formal training, on-the-job training, mentoring, and knowledge sharing through KM portals that can be used for developing specific competencies.

The exercise resulted in creation of 22 new learning modules for building leadership and behavioural competencies, and 53 learning modules for the technical competencies (Figure 3.4 shows architecture of iGATE competency framework). The key differences between the development initiatives of the organization that existed earlier and the ones created as a part of this initiative are as follows:

1. Formal training was the only development engine that was used earlier and in the new competency-based learning maps, newer methodologies such as mentoring and e-learning have been studied and incorporated.
2. The process helped in tapping the tacit knowledge that existed in the organization. iGATE could identify around a minimum of 25 people for every competency across various proficiency level defined who were capable of playing the role of mentors and SMEs.

3. The knowledge management portal was revived to align it with the competency framework.

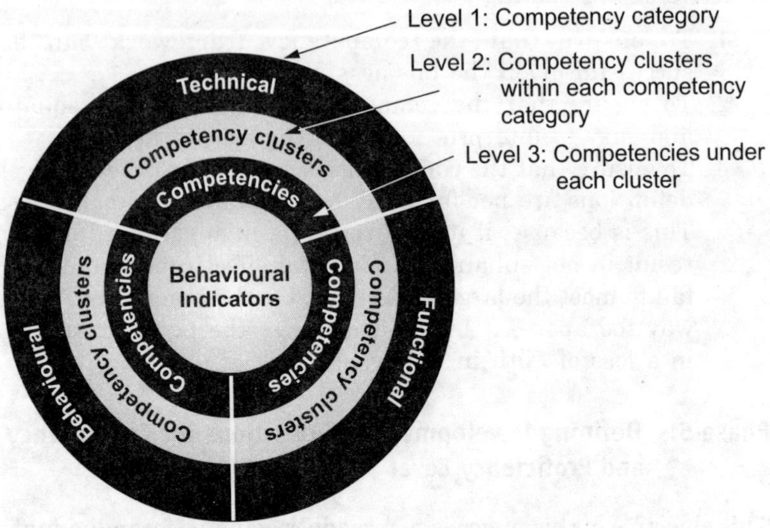

FIGURE 3.4 Architecture of the iGATE competency framework.

List of Competencies

The list of competencies were reviewed to ensure adequate coverage of roles and required capabilities across the grades (see Figures 3.6 and 3.7), and to maintain reasonable level of detailing while terming them as a competency with the following features:

1. Each competency has four proficiency levels.
2. These four proficiency levels are knowledgeable, practitioner, proficient and champion (Fig. 3.5).
3. For each competency, in each proficiency level, multiple behavioural indicators have been provided for ease of usage.
4. These behavioural indicators are written progressively, i.e., any latter mentioned behavioural indicator is expected to subsume any formerly-mentioned behavioural indicator.

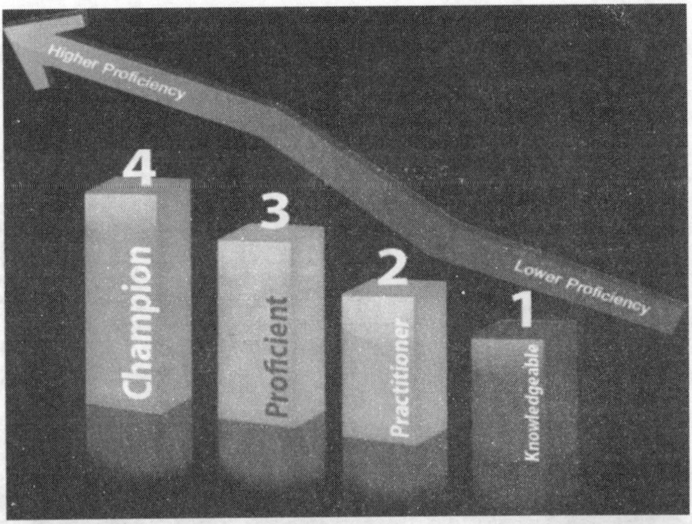

FIGURE 3.5 Four proficiency levels of competency.

The competencies were identified and defined using a set of approaches as detailed below.

The study of the organization structure and the business model gave insights on the following:

1. The IT delivery function works on application development and maintenance projects on various functional/business domains. These projects are based on technology domains such as JAVA, .NET, etc.
2. The business units are organized based on the following:
   (a) Global customer accounts (For example: GE, ING)
   (b) Geographies of customer concentration (For example: ROW, NAM)
   (c) Service offerings (For example: IVV, ERP, IMS, DW/BI)
3. The business deliverables of these business units were similar in nature following the project life cycle of a typical IT project. Thus, the business critical competencies were common across the units though the environments in which they are applied are different.

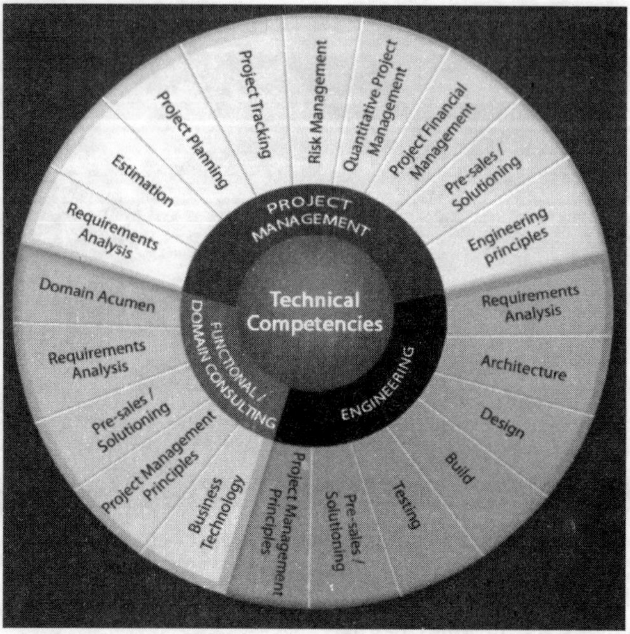

FIGURE 3.6 iGATE technical competency framework.

Thus, this helped in arriving at the following set of competencies which were applicable across all the business units which is based on a project life cycle.

Leadership and Behavioural Competencies

This leadership and behavioural competency framework consists of 17 competencies in 6 clusters. The framework provides definitions, key features, 4 well-defined proficiency levels [knowledgeable, practitioner, proficient, and champion], and multiple behavioural indicators for each of these 17 competencies. These competencies and categories are:

1. *Foundational:* Citizenship, and customer leadership
2. *Enabler:* Psycap [broaden and build]
3. *Connector:* Communication, team-effectiveness, and persuasive negotiation
4. *Expander:* Coaching and mentoring
5. *Business leadership:* People leadership, Financial and commercial acumen, Appreciation of business reality,

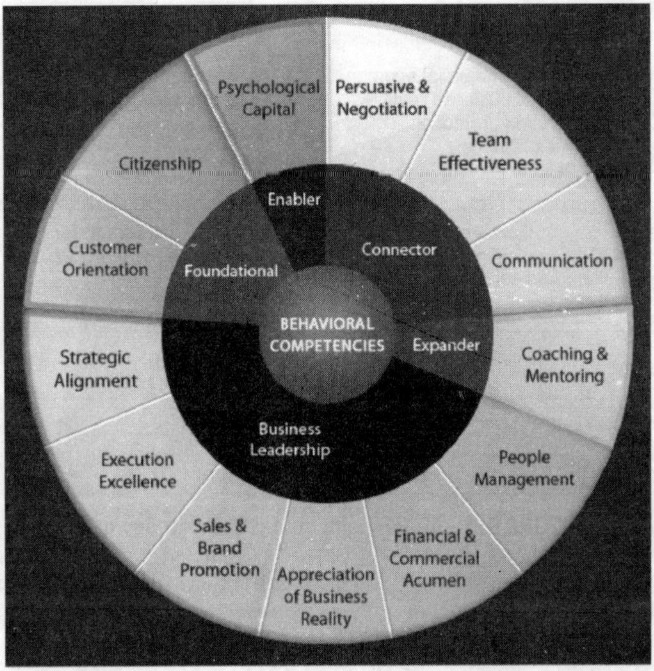

Figure 3.7 iGATE behavioural competency framework.

Sales and brand promotion, Execution excellence, and Strategic alignment.

6. *Distinguishing:* Outcome orientation, Aspiration, optimism, and Cultural agility. These are depicted in Figure 3.8.

Foundational

The foundational competency is that which guides the employee in all his/her endeavours, and therefore, it has got an all encompassing nature. The iGATE foundational competency category consists of two competencies, citizenship, and customer leadership. These are the threshold competencies.

Enabler

The enabler competency is that competency which enables an employee to effectively use all the other competencies that he/she may possess. The enabler in this framework is Psycap. Psycap is a unique competency in this framework. By definition,

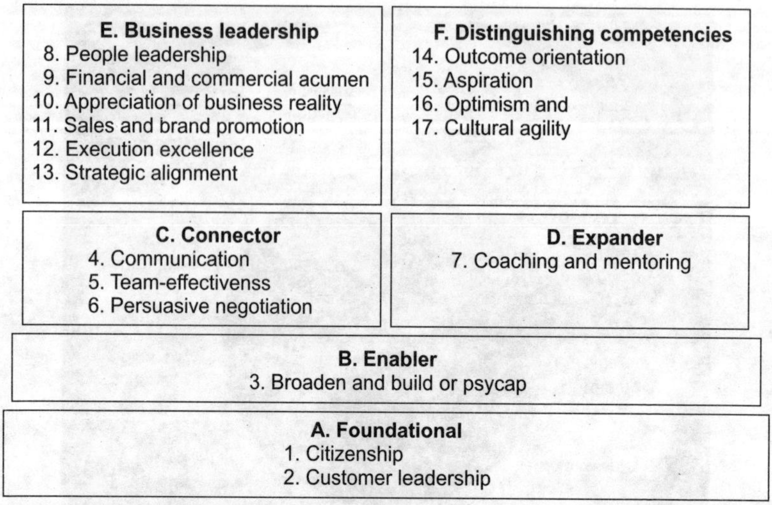
E. Business leadership
8. People leadership
9. Financial and commercial acumen
10. Appreciation of business reality
11. Sales and brand promotion
12. Execution excellence
13. Strategic alignment
F. Distinguishing competencies
14. Outcome orientation
15. Aspiration
16. Optimism and
17. Cultural agility
C. Connector
4. Communication
5. Team-effectivenss
6. Persuasive negotiation
D. Expander
7. Coaching and mentoring
B. Enabler
3. Broaden and build or psycap
A. Foundational
1. Citizenship
2. Customer leadership

FIGURE 3.8 iGATE behavioural competency grid.

psycap is that competency without which all other competencies are rendered useless.

Connector

The connector competencies are those that enable the employees to work as a cohesive whole, toward a common goal. These competencies create synergies. This category includes such competencies as communication, team effectiveness, and persuasive negotiation.

Expander

The expander competency is that which enables an employee to build capabilities of others. This category includes the competency of coaching and mentoring.

Business leadership

Leadership is all about bringing the future to the present. It is about envisioning the future together and then reaching there first. The competencies in this category are meant for nurturing credible leaders for organizational transformation, and continuous renewal. These competencies are, people leadership, financial and commercial acumen, appreciation of business reality, sales and brand promotion, execution excellence, and strategic alignment. It is through these competencies that leaders realize sustainably the goals of the organization.

Distinguishing

The five categories that have been discussed so far are all permeating, and often functional in nature. The sixth category is the category of distinguishing competencies which seeks to trace its origin to the philosophical quotation of William James, "A difference that makes no difference is no difference at all." It is this search for meaningful differences that necessitated the inclusion of this sixth category with four competencies—outcome orientation, aspiration, optimism, and cultural agility.

Proficiency Levels and Behavioural Indicators

The iGATE LBCF–V.1 depicts each competency with four proficiency levels, namely, knowledgeable, practitioner, proficient, and champion. However, it may be noted that the citizenship competency in the foundational category consists of only one proficiency level, i.e., champion, because each employee of the organization is expected to be in the level of champion in this competency. The typical meaning of the four proficiency levels is furnished in Table 3.5.

TABLE 3.5 iGATE Four Proficiency Levels

Proficiency levels	*Descriptor*
Knowledgeable	Adequate awareness level
Practitioner	This competency has been adequately imbibed by the incumbent, and the incumbent is practicing it with great deal of confidence.
Proficient	The incumbent has developed expertise in this competency and is now practising it avidly in a spontaneous manner.
Champion	Personifies the competency. This person is not only an embodiment or example of the competency, but is also naturally imparting that to others such that whosoever gets in contact with that person, naturally starts learning that competency.

Distinguishing Competencies

As we have already seen in Section 2, the iGATE LBCF–V.1 an all encompassing framework consists of 17 competencies which have been divided in to 6 categories. The sixth category amongst these is the category of distinguishing competencies consisting of four competencies which are expected to propel the competency development of the employees to still greater heights. This category includes four pro-competencies and four con-competencies. The pro-competencies are the ones that must be present for superior leadership performance, while the con-competencies are the ones that must be absent for superior leadership performance. In other words, for each of the pro-competency there is a mirror image that has been called con-competency. For example, for the pro-competency outcome orientation, the mirror opposite is the con-competency transaction orientation. Each competency in this framework is a top level competency which subsumes within it some other competencies as well. Those other competencies are also detailed in the Accompanying Ready Reckoner.

Structure of Distinguishing Competencies

The structure of the distinguishing competencies is slightly different from the remaining five categories as would be apparent from the ready reckoner. The distinguishing competencies are applicable to grade/s epsilon and above only. Each pro-competency has four proficiency levels, knowledgeable for grade epsilon, practitioner for grade zeta, proficient for grade eta, and champion for the ex-com members.

Like the other five categories, the ready reckoner presents this category also in the most user friendly manner. Albeit a bit different, the presentation format is quite similar to the other five categories. In case of the pro-competencies, the competencies have first been defined, and after that the key features are listed. Thereafter, the sub-competencies have been defined along with the key features. Subsequently, an illustrative list of the behavioural indicators for these competencies has been furnished. In the behavioural indicators section there are two extra boxes here as compared to the other categories. These two boxes are, lacks competency, and misunderstands competency. This has been provided for the sake of greater clarity, and for facilitating the resolution of any dilemma. It is believed that these additions will further enhance the usability of this framework. In each category of behavioural indicators around 12 to 20 behavioural indicators have been listed. The first three indicators in bold in each category indicate the behaviours directly related to the main pro-competency, and the other indicators are directly related with the other sub-competencies that are included in that meta competency.

Subsequently, details about its mirror image, i.e., the details about the corresponding con-competency have been provided.

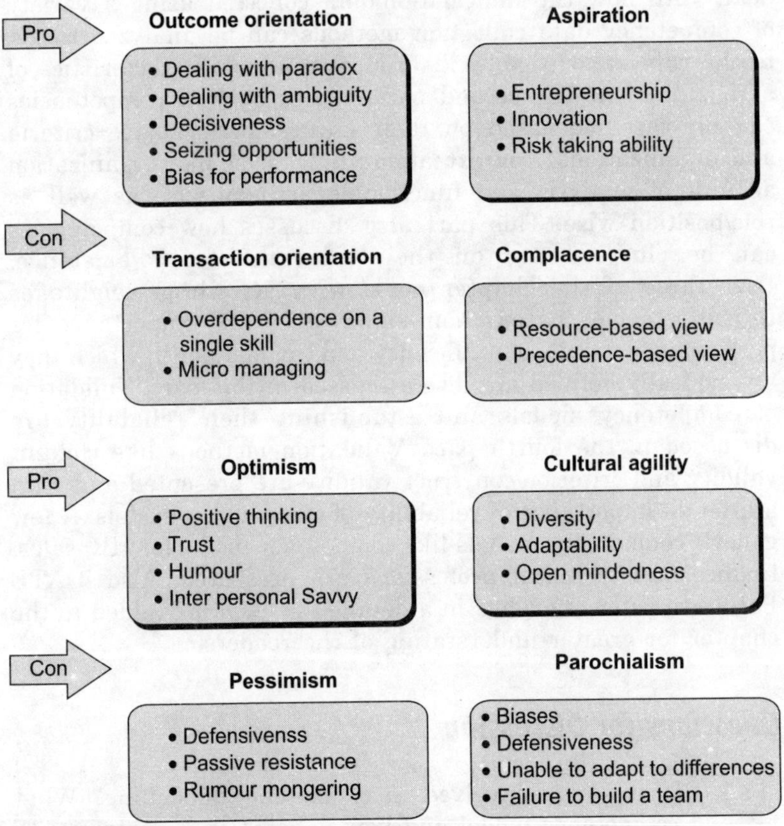

FIGURE 3.9 Structure of distinguishing competencies.

These again have been defined, keywords have been provided, and a list of pointers is furnished thereafter that suggests when these are real big problems, and when they are not. This segment closes with a short list of some of the causes for the same. Figure 3.9 elaborates the pro- and the con-competencies of this category.

Summary

In this chapter, competency modelling process is discussed which is key for extension of competency practice to human resource management in organizations. The first part of the chapter has dealt with how the information/data collected using a variety of competency data collection methods can be analyzed to get to the core knowledge, skills and attitudinal characteristics of a role/function. The second part focuses on how competencies can be classified based on their nature, performance criteria and organizational context at multiple level like organization as unit of analysis and function/department-wise as well as role/position wise. This part also discusses how competencies can be cluster-based on their relevance for co-existence. Part three of the chapter deals with according weightages to competencies based their significance and importance for performance. Levels of proficiency and the manner in which they are typically defined are also discussed in this part. Validation of competency models and establishing their reliability are discussed in the fourth part. Validation methods like content validity and criterion/construct validity are presented and with a brief on importance of reliability of competency models. A few generic competency models like competency model for HR, sales, finance and technical professions are presented. Also iGATE Patni competency models in a detailed fashion are added to the chapter for greater understating of the readers.

Questions for Discussion

3.1 Discuss steps involved in competency modelling? What a competency model and how it helps an organization?

3.2 Discuss analytical tools used in analysis of competency data? Why different tools need to be deployed for different data collection methods? What preparatory work is involved in analysis of data?

3.3 What is a competency dictionary and how the dictionary is developed? What a standard competency dictionary shall encompass? What is the core purpose of a competency dictionary?

3.4 What a competency cluster means and discuss methods how competency clusters can be created?

3.5 How do you model the competencies related to a function/department and how they are classified and operational measures are defined? Is the model can be different for each function/department? If yes, on what basis such distinction can be made?

3.6 What is classification exercise of competency model? How different it is to classify competency at different levels like organization-wide, department and role-wise?

3.7 Why competency proficiency levels need to be defined and how the weightage for each competency arrived on? What purpose the proficiency level definition intended to serve?

3.8 What is the difference between content validity and construct validity? Which is more important for establishing correlation between performance outcome of a role and competency scores?

3.9 Why validation of competency model is important for competency based human resource management? Whether competency model and competency approach can be applied in an organization without validation?

3.10 What is reliability test of a competency model?

Case Studies for Discussion

1. SalesOne is a company engaged in marketing and sales of consumer products. The company neither manufactures nor have any products produced on their own. The company essentially helps consumer product organizations in marketing and sales of the products through their expertise in sales. About 145 employees work in this organization out of which about 130 of them are direct sales people. Their job involves direct sales of products: door-to-door sales of consumer products. SalesOne in its earlier efforts have identified the following sales competencies: accountability, always learning, ambitious, analytical, builds trust, change agent, communication skills, competitor awareness, composure, customer focus, customer strategy development, deals with ambiguity, decision quality, deliver results, delivery value, detail orientation, determined, financial discipline, initiative, integrity, inter personal skills, manages priorities, networking, persuasive, planning, problem-solving, professionalism, profit management, prospecting, resourceful and work ethics. The competencies now need to be classified into meaningful clusters. If you are given this task, how do you approach in order to cluster the competencies for SalesOne. Explain in detail.

2. AB Limited, is a company engaged in manufacturing of consumer electronic goods. The company has over 45 frontline supervisors whose role include planning, directing and monitoring of workers performance on daily basis. The company's HR department in a detailed study has identified competencies like: communication, teamwork, conflict resolution, empathy. Process knowledge, mentoring and coordination as the critical competencies for effective performance on the role. How these competencies can be validated and their reliability can be established? Discuss how AB Limited, can approach and establish validation of the said competencies.

References

Boyatzis, Richard (1982): *The Competent Manager: A Model for Effective Performance*, New York: John Wiley.

Spencer, Lyle M. and Spencer Signe (1993): *Competence at Work*, New York: John Wiley & Sons.

CHAPTER 4

Competency Assessment

Competency Assessment (CA) is a critical and comprehensive activity in competency management. Unless, competency models are transformed into assessment tools, it is difficult to obtain significant advantages from competency mapping and modelling processes (see Figure 4.1). The key objective of competency assessment is to assess job incumbents on a set of competencies (based on competency model of a job) that are critical to job and organizational success. As this chapter unfolds, the competency models are converted into various assessment tools and exercises. These tools and exercises would be applied to assess and identify the competency profile of a job incumbent/successor/aspirant of a job apart from using for development, career and selection processes.

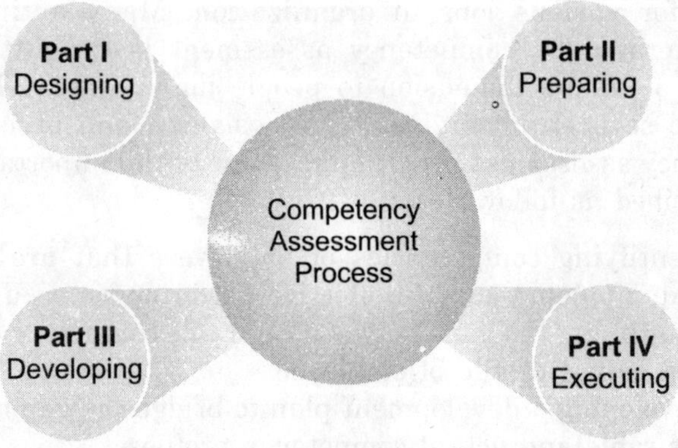

FIGURE 4.1 Process of competency assessment.

Competency assessment programme should not be launched unless a full-fledged competency mapping and modelling exercises are successfully conducted. It is not unusual with organizations seeking to implement assessment interventions based on generic competency models. Experience of many a corporate across the world shows that such assessments have not yielded real value to organizations. This is due to the reasons that generic competency models have many limitations and their suitability with organizations is far from being perfect. Organization-specific competency models not only enhances the reliability but also helps in developing valid assessment tools and exercises melding with organization's environment and culture.

Why Competancy Assessment is Required?

Competency assessment programme is a logical sequel to competency mapping and modelling. Without CA, the efforts made to map and model competencies would render less useful. The value-addition to employees and organizations comes from competency assessment rather than from mapping and modelling. They are prerequisites for a CA and not sufficient themselves to accrue employee and organizational advantage. A well-designed competency assessment programme provides rich data on competency profile of organization. This data can be effectively used to create internal benchmarks of competency profiles for various jobs in organization. Many a time, the data generated by competency assessment is insightful, and presents a unique dimension to people management. Though, there are several advantages with designing and executing a competency assessment programme, some of the important ones are described as follows:

1. Identifying competencies of employees that are critical and supplementary to effective performance on a job
2. Identifying the gaps between desirable competency profile and actual profile of employees
3. Developing a development plan to bridge the gap between desirable and actual competency profiles
4. Providing valuable data of existing competencies of employees that can be used for multiple purposes
5. Contributing as reliable tool in understanding strengths and weaknesses of employees

6. Helping in effective management of employees performance
7. Contributing to ensure person-job fitness
8. Creating competency benchmarks
9. Helping career and succession planning
10. Assisting in recruitment and selection processes since many of CA tools and exercises can be adopted straightaway
11. Enabling supervisors and managers to form compatible teams
12. Providing data on other perceptions about employee behaviour
13. Providing sensitive information to employees about their personal behaviour and the way it affecting others
14. Enabling individual employees to compare their personal and professional strengths and weaknesses and compare with standards of organization to achieve particular goals and objectives.
15. Establishing performance accountability through defining the competency specifications for various jobs.

Prerequisites for Launching a Competency Assessment Programme

As discussed above, competency assessment must be a sequel to competency mapping and modelling rather than a standalone and independent activity. A successful competency assessment assumes fulfilment of various prerequisites as discussed in the sections to follow:

Is top management approval obtained?

First and the foremost in competency assessment is obtaining the explicit approval of top management for conducting the assessment. Top management not only must be willing but also must manifest its commitment towards a systematic assessment initiative. Competency assessment can cause moderate to severe discomfiture at times, while the assessment intervention is in progress. Patience and positive attitude can remove the practical obstacle that arises in the way when top management embraces such a programme willingly.

Do the competency models exist?

In order to take up competency assessment programme, there must be well-established competency models which are validated. For example, there must be a reliable and tested competency model (comprising well-defined competencies for effective performance as finance executives) for the purpose of assessing the competencies of finance executives. In the absence of competency models, no assessment could be possible. Generally, a successful competency modelling programme would provide an organization with job-specific and organization-specific competency dictionary. These dictionaries would offer immensely valuable outputs and can be converted into assessment instruments.

Is cost-benefit analysis performed?

Instead of directly embarking upon competency assessment programme, it is preferable that a realistic cost-benefit analysis of competency assessment programme to organization and employees is carried out. This would help in two ways. Firstly, it helps in budgeting the resources requirement for conducting a competency assessment programme. This would also help when approval of top management is to be obtained for launching the programme. Secondly, it becomes easy to gain the approval of top management once the likely benefits to organization and employees are clearly analyzed. Competency assessment administrators also can develop a clear perspective of several critical aspects involved in conducting the programme. There is a possibility of derailing of assessment programme when organizations proceeds without understanding of cost-benefit analysis.

Are resources available?

Merely having competency models would not be adequate for preparing for competency assessment programme. Many resources other than finance budgetary allocation such as the following are prerequisite for launching a competency assessment programme:

1. Expertise to develop assessment exercises, tools, tests based on relevant competency model

2. Guidelines and manual for conducting Competency Assessment programme
3. Facilities for conducting assessment programme
4. Availability of sufficiently trained competency assessment assessors
5. Data of employees who are targeted for undergoing assessment
6. Expertise to generate valid competency assessment reports based on assessment exercise
7. Analysis of assessment reports and
8. Expertise for testing the reliability of the assessment reports.

Competency assessment administrators must audit the resource availability based on the above parameters and must ensure the fulfillment of above before initiation of assessment programme.

Are organization and employees ready?

It is quite possible that the internal environment of organization and its employees may not be ready for an assessment programme. This can be due to a variety of reasons. In some organizations, the level of trust between employees and organization may not be satisfactory. In some other cases, an organization may be currently undergoing a restructuring programme indicating uncertainty and in still others, the basic requirements such as organizational communication and preparation of employees for participating in assessment programme may be falling short of requirements. These issues must be addressed prior to conducting the assessment. Many a time, training employees before participating in the assessment activity would be desirable so that all their concerns are addressed. It is prudent to wait rather than rushing through the competency assessment programme when there is organizational uncertainty. The timing, circumstances and preparedness both physically and mentally is of paramount importance for a successful execution of competency assessment programme.

Are protocols defined?

Who will be interpreting the assessment reports? What precautions are put in place to ensure absolute confidentiality of the assessment reports? What are the various procedures involved in identifying and inviting the participants from a list of employees? How the assessment reports will be made available to concerned employees? These issues must be given due importance. Unless they are clarified in the most professional manner, they can create potential problems in actual implementation of assessment programme.

Are endorsement of key resource persons obtained?

The first step in competency assessment programme is: (i) designing competency assessment tools/instruments/ exercises, (ii) developing the right survey methodologies and (iii) identifying the appropriate statistical and non-statistical methods for analysis of data. Competency assessment tools as discussed in the forthcoming text are to be developed based on competency models and competency dictionaries. Once, these tools are developed, the methods for applying them over employees must be identified. For example, certain tools can be applied using survey, whereas others through interview methods, and still others by employing interview method. The methods to be followed for analysis of data also would depend on nature of the data obtained and methods used for collecting such data. It is suggested that endorsement of key resource persons in the organization such as members of top management, assessors, and employees (to be subjected to these tests) must be obtained. In the absence of such an endorsement, the acceptance for competency assessment tends to be low.

Process of Competency Assessment

A systematic competency assessment programme consists of three principal activities. Accordingly, the following contents are organized into three parts. First part deals with designing a competency assessment programme, second part dwells on executing a competency assessment programme and third part discusses the elements of evaluating a competency assessment programme (cost benefit analysis). These are discussed in detail.

Part I: Designing a Competency Assessment Programme

Once, all the prerequisites as described above are met, an organization can initiate a full fledged competency assessment programme. Such an assessment must start with designing an assessment programme. Designing a competency assessment activity typically comprises the following major steps:

Step 1: Deciding on implementing competency assessment programme

The first step is consciously deciding and obtaining approval of top management for implementing a competency assessment programme. More specifically a competency manager must question himself/herself and motivation behind proposing a competency assessment programme. Merely, other organizations are implementing such a programme or this is the latest technique in the area of human resource management that ought to be practised in organization should not be the factors of significance. Competency manager/human resource manager responsible for competency management must follow the following sub-steps for obtaining support of top management for successful competency assessment programme.

1. The objectives of competency assessment should be defined clearly. While doing so, issues such as why assessment must be implemented, what business needs it can address, and what benefits it would offer to organization and its employees, what will be the disadvantages if competency assessment is not in place etc., must be considered. It would be effective if the statement of objective flows from business needs citing two or three current ones and how a competency assessment imitative can address them.
2. The scope of competency assessment must be defined clearly. This includes the details of positions and persons to be brought under the purview of competency assessment. Each of the issues must be substantiated and no issue must be assumed without subjecting it to thorough analysis. Wherever the competency assessment programme is being proposed only for a section of

employees instead of total population, the reasons for identifying that specific group need to be elaborated.

3. Methodological aspects must be given due emphasis. At this stage, it may not be possible to identify and discuss all the methodological issues of competency assessment, but attempt must be made to outline the broad methodological strategy to be followed with reasons. Many a time, methodological aspects, especially the manner the assessment needs to be conducted, is of great importance from administrative and human relations perspective. This opportunity can be availed to describe some of the important and commonly used terms in a competency assessment programme.
4. Resources required for designing, executing and evaluating a competency assessment programme need to be worked out. This must include financial cost, infrastructure requirement, technical requirements like preparing the in-house competency assessors and logistics and other arrangements. Suitable time schedule, normally the slack period of the year for the organization can ideally be proposed for implementing competency assessment programme.
5. Wherever possible, the details of organizations that have implemented/implementing competency programme must be gathered, especially organizations in the same industry to serve as a reference point. Benchmarking practices together with benefits gained by the corporate organizations if studied would prove highly beneficial. The benefits of competency assessment programme accrued to people and organization must be studied and illustrated in financial, motivational, intellectual and innovation terms.
6. The possible applications of competency assessment results in the area of human resource management must be dealt. As much as possible, the use of results should be limited to developmental purpose, especially for creating and reinforcing the competencies rather than for any promotional and reward purposes. The extension of results to career and reward related issues can be taken up in subsequent running up of competency assessment and after obtaining the acceptance of wide section of employees and management to the competency assessment as a reliable tool.

7. A briefing/presentation must be made to senior executives and key resource persons of organization in order to gain their approval for competency assessment programme. Unless, all the above issues are clarified/homework is done adequately, the briefing session must not be taken up. Competency manager should have answers to all possible questions before such a session is planned. It is preferred that a brief document containing all the relevant details of proposed competency assessment progarmme must be circulated among senior executives for their advance reading. The observations made during the presentation must be recorded. If answers were not available during the presentation phase, the same must be addressed immediately after the formal presentation. The presentation need to specifically focus on concept of competency assessment, uses of competency assessment, benefits to organization and employees, objectives of current programme, scope of the programme, resources required and methodological issues and time frame. It would also have strategic advantage if competency manager discuss and gain confidence of a few key managers before the formal briefing session is held. The changes and suggestions advanced by the executives present in the briefing session need to be incorporated into the assessment programme as much as possible.
8. Most importantly, the presentation need to focus on limitations and challenges involved in pursuing a competency assessment programme. This part of the presentation unequivocally must state the sacrifices involved and initial disturbance it may create in management of people. The benefits it would accrue when all these challenges are effectively managed can be juxtaposed while putting the progress barriers in perspective. This can ease the emotional burden and provide great strength to competency managers in systematically implementing competency assessment. It need to be abundantly clear that a competency assessment programme will not produce dramatic results over night, but do so when pursued through a reasonable period with perseverance.

The option of presenting the case of competency assessment can be planned in two parts. The first part can be devoted to introduce the plan and proposal of competency assessment programme for obtaining the approval of top management. The second part of presentation can be considered for receiving the budget sanction for estimated cost. At the end of this step, competency manager must have gained the formal approval and budget sanction for implementation of competency assessment programme. Also, senior executives of organization are well-informed about the competency assessment programme, its salient features together with challenges and advantages to organization and employees. All the proceedings of briefing session together with views of senior executives, if documented systematically, can be valuable during the course of implementation.

Step 2: Preparing for competency assessment programme

Once the approval of top management is obtained and financial budget is created to meet the cost of project, the work on designing the competency assessment programme must be taken up. A few important sub steps are discussed here which can support designing a competency assessment initiative. These sub steps are only illustrative and not conclusive since the series of steps to be taken up differs from organization to organization. However, the objective of second major step would be making preparations for designing a competency assessment programme.

1. *Defining responsibility center:* Though, all the managers involved in competency assessment programme, especially the beneficiaries, are responsible for implementation of competency assessment programme, a few employees need to be categorically identified who would perform the role of competency assessment team members. The actual volume of team depends on the scope of competency assessment programme. Ideally, there must be a project leader and a few members. The project manager can either be competency manager himself or a senior level line manager with competency manager acting as deputy project manager. Members need to be drawn from all the departments/units which would be eventually covered under competency assessment programme. The role

of project manager and members need to be defined to the understanding of all concerned. The record of briefing proceedings held at the Step 1 above should be circulated among the team members to provide them an understanding and objective of competency assessment programme in the context of their organization. Efforts are also required to delegate requisite powers to project manager and other members that enable them to function effectively and take decisions timely. The composition of competency assessment team and the functions of team must be notified for information of all employees of organization.

2. *Adopting competency model:* The project team manager in consultation with other members must identify the valid competency models of the jobs. The identified competency models would be related to those job incumbents who are to be covered under competency assessment programme. The competency models are discussed in Chapter 1 of this book in detail. It is not possible to design a competency assessment programme without valid and reliable competency models. Therefore, an organization first must develop competency models for jobs before the competency assessment is carried out on the job incumbents. Wherever valid competency models are not developed within the organization but still keen to proceed ahead with competency assessment programme can adopt the competency models of other organizations having similar business operations. However, caution must be taken to ensure the validity and relevance of such competency models to your organization. If required, discussion must be conducted with job incumbents and other key managers to determine the validity of adopted competency models. It is highly desirable that an organization must build its own competency models before assessment of incumbents is initiated. Despite the best efforts, the adopted competency may fail to deliver the expected results since the competencies required tend to differ from organization to organization though the job is similar. The competency models form as core basis for competency assessment of job incumbents.

3. *Communication to employees:* All employees of organization must be well-communicated about the salient features of proposed competency assessment programme, the purpose and benefits along with answers for frequently asked questions. This would help to avoid confusion and also disseminate the information in a proper fashion. In the absence of authentic and comprehensive communication, possibility of spreading rumours would exist. In large size organizations, this communication assumes significance. The possibility of assembling and holding discussion with employees who are likely to be covered under competency assessment programme can be explored. Objective of all these attempts is to avoid any misconception and misgivings about a competency assessment programme. In some cases, the assessment programme tends to encounter constraints in implementation not due to lack of well designed competency assessment programme but because of doubts and misconception in the minds of people. Therefore, effectively communicating employees about the proposed programme should not be taken as a peripheral activity. Communication ensures mental preparation of employees for impending change.
4. *Mobilizing resources:* As a part of preparation, the required resources must be mobilized in a planned manner. This mobilization may include procuring the necessary aids like off the shelf commercial business games, computer hardware and software and hiring of a competency assessment expert for advising the successful implementation. Wherever required, a day-long orientation course on competency assessment can be conducted. Such a programme may not be required where already competency mapping and modelling as discussed in Chapters 1 and 2 are already implemented.
5. *Training resource persons:* Apart from orientation programme, resource persons identified as assessors and members of project team need to be given intensive training on competency assessment technology and conceptual inputs. Expert lectures by practising managers having experience with assessment programmes must

be invited to share their experience. They also need to be trained on various assessment exercises, the method of developing assessment exercises, their administration and interpretation of results. This is generally known as assessors training programme. At this stage such full fledged assessors programme would not be required unless the assessment tools and exercises to be used in the organization as a part of present competency assessment are completely ready.

6. *Developing time schedules:* Time schedules for completion of various activities must be prepared. This time planner can serve as targets for monitoring the progress of competency assessment programme. In the absence of time schedules it is quite possible that the implementation may get derailed. A specimen schedule is given in Table 4.1. The time schedules should be developed keeping in view all the practical aspects and in consultation with all implementation partners. This opportunity must be used to obtain commitment from all the concerned for implementing the programme as planned.

TABLE 4.1 Schedule for Implementation of Competency Assessment Programme

S.No.	*Activity*	*Responsibility center*	*Time schedule*
1			

Step 3: Developing assessment exercises

Quality, reliability and validity of assessment exercises are of paramount importance to the management of competencies. Unless, assessment exercises constitute the value of predictability, there would be no use with such exercises. Exercises that are devoid of the value of predictability instead of benefiting can cause enormous damage to the organization and to the whole process of competency management. The following principles must be reckoned while developing assessment tools, exercises and tests:

1. *Dimensions:* Assessment tests and exercises must be developed in order to assess the employees' potential on relevant and well-defined dimensions those believed to

cause superior performance. These dimensions must be drawn from the competency models of a particular job or cluster of jobs. For example, in Chapter 2, we have illustrated many competency models. Competency models like these must form a basis for developing the assessment tools, tests and exercises. Each of the competency models consist a set of competency dimensions. There can be one or more assessment tools to measure each of the competencies. Therefore, identifying the most relevant dimensions for building robust assessment exercises is the most fundamental step.

2. *Assessment based on dimensions:* The assessment must be carried out based on identified dimensions and not using the principle of superior and poor performers discussed in competency mapping (Chapter 2). Not the individuals, but dimensions of superior performance ought to be taken as the basis for assessment. This element can be fulfilled if the assessment test are developed strictly, keeping in view the identified dimensions of competency.

3. *Use of multiple assessment techniques:* Competency assessment must not rely on a single test or technique or exercise. Rather, there must be a combination of all these. Despite taking utmost care in order to ensure reliability, still there exists a possibility of error. Multiple assessment tools help in avoiding such error. In other words, there must be more than one assessment test to measure the same dimension of performance. Cross verifying and reconciling the results of both of these, significantly avoids the possibility of error in competency assessment. For example, using critical incident technique and the in-basket exercise to measure the decision-making capability, enhances the reliability of the assessment instead of only one such tests.

4. *Tests must be developed by well-qualified assessors:* Various assessment tests, tools, techniques and exercises must be developed by well-qualified, trained and experienced assessors. Developing assessment tests is a highly specialized job. Assessors should possess the

knowledge not only about the dimensions of competency for which the assessment tests are to be developed but also about the organizational culture and the nature of job for which the assessment test are to be developed. Assessment tests tend to yield desired results only when they do fit into the organizational culture, and when they are not away from the reality of job. Assessors also must be well-informed about the population on whom the assessment tests are to be applied.

5. *Interpretation guide:* Each of the assessment tests should have a well-explained interpretation guide. The interpretation guide must consist of details like: operational definition of competency, explanation about the scale such as what constitutes high potential, average potential and low potential. Alternatively, there can be a scale classification like more than acceptable level, acceptable level, less than acceptable level and much less than acceptable level behaviour. The limitation of the test, guidelines for its administration and a specimen interpretation copy must be included. In the absence of interpretation guide, there is a high probability for multiple ways of administering and evaluating the outcomes of the test. Such deviations can be avoided and a scientific interpretation of the results can be ensured with the inclusion of interpretation guide.

6. *User friendliness:* The assessment test must be designed in such a way that they are user-friendly. Easy to administer and interpret tests provide fillip for their wide use and also helps in their proper application. However, the quality of tests should not be diluted merely for the sake of ensuring user friendliness of the tests. The test should possess all the qualities of a robust research tool and at the same time it should not have the abstractedness. Continuous improvement of assessment tests make it possible to achieve both these virtues. Assesses also feel comfortable with user friendly tests especially with interpretation since they are easily understandable. Ultimately, it is the assesses acceptance of the tests that make the assessment exercise fruitful.

7. *Unbiased:* The assessment exercises must be free from biases. If proper care is not taken, sometimes assessment tools, tests and exercises by their very nature may end up favourable to some section of employees and disfavourable to others. Tests must be customized to ensure absolute compatibility with organization and its employees. For example, the language used must be equally understandable and the subject/dimension/competency items used must be relevant to the job universally. Any complacency and lack of critical evaluation on this issue can create constraints in the way of reliability of the tests.
8. *Uses of assessment test:* The purpose of application and uses of assessment tests must be clearly spelt out. The objective of the test at the stage of its design itself must be very clear. A test developed for example to measure communication ability should not be used to assess decision-making capability.
9. *Appropriateness of tests:* The type of assessment exercise to be used to assess the competency dimensions must be appropriate to the type of job and to the incumbents of such job. Otherwise, the assessment exercise may not be successful in objectively assessing the competency potential of subjects how objectively the test might have been designed.

Types of Assessment Exercises

There are several exercises used as a part of competency assessment in order to assess the competency profile of job incumbents. There are singular tests like paper and pencil intellect assessment test, knowledge assessment tests, personality profiling inventories and integrated assessment techniques like assessment center and multi-rater assessments. Both these type of test if required can be used in combination or independently depends on the requirement. These exercises are briefly discussed Box 4.1.

BOX 4.1 Signs and Samples

The assessment exercises can be fragmented into two types. The first type is called as signs and the second is popularly known as work samples. Signs as the term suggest constitute tests that provide us general proficiency of individuals on competency dimensions rather than proficiency in the competency itself directly. For example, test like paper pencil, personality tests and aptitude tests provide us with results that help us as indicators of possessing competency. This means, sign tests are helpful to measure the knowledge level of a person in a given competency rather than the proficiency in using that competency.

In contrast, work samples measure the competency proficiency directly by using simulation and replicating the processes of a job. In basket exercises, assessment centres, business games, focus group discussions, leaderless group discussions and other problem solving exercises fall in this category. Simulating does not mean the conditions of job need to be created exactly the original job. Only the processes such as communication, decision-making process, problem solving method etc., are to be created as exercises using similar circumstances.

Both these tests have their own advantages. In combination, they can provide rich data and measure accurately a person's proficiency on a given competency.

Paper and Pencil Tests

Paper and pencil tests are age-old method of testing the aptitude, knowledge level and intelligence of a person. Intellectual abilities such as intelligence, arithmetic, spatial and mechanical abilities, reasoning, perceptual consistency, etc., can be measured using these tests. In this method, subjects are asked to provide verbal or written responses/answers to a set of questions. Most of the government recruitment written test fall in this category. Paper and pencil tests can reliably test the knowledge level of a person in a given area rather than competency/performance potential. This is the biggest limitation with using this method in corporate organizations. Knowledge not necessarily can result in possessing the competency. Knowledge is mere a conceptual and theoretical ability, whereas competency is integrated that include hands-on and practical level skill. The gap between knowledge and actual application of skill can be wide due to several intermediate factors. Therefore, the reliability of paper and pencil tests as predictors of competency proficiency is highly moderate. Due to these reasons, paper and pencil tests have lost their popularity in contemporary organizations. Despite their limitation, paper and pencil tests are widely used, especially when large number of people are to be assessed for various human resource applications like recruitment, promotions, postings and training. Further, their simplicity in administration have made them omnipresent in assessment tests. Paper and pencil can be effective when used in combination with other assessment tests. When used in combination, the overall weightage for paper and pencil tests can be kept at reasonable level. Though there is limitation with paper and pencil tests, we should not overlook the fact that, this is the most reliable method in eliciting the knowledge of a person.

Written assignments

Written assignments though fall within the category of paper and pencil tests, they do vary in their content and outcome. Written assignments are generally used to assess the verbal comprehension, drafting skills, and ability to organize disconnected information to draw inferences for managerial action. There are two types in written assignments. In the first type, there would be a kind of open written activity in which assesses are asked to write essay on a given problem. In the second type, background of a problem with pros and cons would be presented to analyze and opt for a solution that ensures advantage. This kind of assessment is generally employed for managerial positions in which drafting and analysis is involved. This is similar to many recruitment examinations conducted by government and banking agencies. The reliability and content validity of written assignments as a technique of competency assessment is moderate. However, this must be used only for managerial positions and positions where document preparation and analysis is an important responsibility.

Case Study Method

This is comparatively old method, but has greater usefulness in analyzing decision-making and analytical capabilities, apart from comprehension and organizing of content-related competencies. Here participants are given description of an event or problem with few facts and descriptions which a participant on perusing must prescribe a path for progress. Though case study often is used as a learning technique, it also can be a potential technique for competency assessment. Observers based on method of organizing the facts and way of solving problems and generating choices by participants can interpret how participant is likely to perform in analytical and decision-making capability apart from ability to chose a scenario over the other. However, this technique is tedious and can be subjective when used as a competency assessment tool though some amount of standardization can help to reduce the variability in assessment.

Critical Incident Technique

This is also a well-established learning and appraisal method. Its usage as competency assessment technique is relatively lesser in vogue given that it tends to be cumbersome in interpretation and objectivity of findings. Here the participant is given either a crisis situation or loss of opportunity or probability of gain and sought to analyze and provide the best solution. Participant is expected to read through the content and consider facts and data in order to analyze and suggest way forward in that scenario. Based on analytical style and appropriateness of decision and attention to detail and questions raised seeking additional info helps to analyze analytical and decision-making capability of participants in addition to their pressure profile.

Intelligence Tests

Intellectual ability is an important component of managerial competency. Intelligence tests are often used for the purpose of recruitment and promotional decisions in corporate organizations. Intelligence tests can measure several cognitive and mental abilities. Verbal abilities such as meaning of words, synonyms and antonyms, precise writing, filling the blanks, grammar, vocabulary and numerical abilities like solving mathematical problems, identifying symbols, reasoning, etc., are tested in intelligence tests. Intelligence tests which were used to test the intellectual ability as a part of competency assessment have lost their significance in contemporary times. This is due to the fact that intelligence tests suffer limitations, as they can test only a part of intellectuality and not the wide spectrum. Further, research evidence highlights that the correlation between results of intelligence tests with actual performance on the job is significantly weak. Therefore, many organizations do not use intelligence tests as a part of competency assessment. This does not mean that intellectual ability is not a determinant of job success or important part in the competency. In fact, intellectual ability is a strong determinant of managerial success, but measuring it through intelligence tests found to be not very reliable. However, the method can be used wherever the reliability and content validity of the test is established to be a good predictor of job success.

Emotional Intelligence Tests

Daniel Goleman (1987) found that emotional intelligence is a reliable indicator of job success. Ever since, the evidence of correlation between emotional intelligence quotient and job performance is established, it has become a significant component of competency assessment. The continued research has contributed for development of a number of emotional intelligence testing and assessment methods. The number of organizations using emotional intelligence tests as a part of competency assessment is progressively growing. Emotional intelligence tests are used to measure the interpersonal competency, social skills, self-awareness and motivational level of employees in competency assessment.

Projective Tests

Projective tests are a type of personality assessment tests used in competency assessment in order to identify the motives and underlying assumptions of subjects' behaviour. Projective tests are unstructured. Ambiguous material is used as a part of projective tests. Rorschach inkblot test (Box 4.2), Thematic Apperception Test (Box 4.3), Worthington personal history, Horn picture arrangement, etc., are examples of projective tests.

BOX 4.2 Rorschach Inkblot Test

Rorschach Inkblot test is one of the oldest projective tests developed to identify and interpret the drives, motives and underlying assumptions of behaviour. The test is useful in analyzing the sub-conscious mind. The test was developed by Herman Rorschach in late eighteenth century. Unstructured and ambiguous inkblots are used in this test to interpret the subconscious mind. A participant is shown a white paper on which the inkblots are spread. Looking at those inkblots, participant is expected to imagine and come up with an explanation. Based on the participant's explanation of inkblots, the interpreter interprets the subconscious mind of the participant. In competency assessment exercises, this interpretation is used to identify the drive and motives those possibly have implication for managerial success.

The reliability and content validity of inkblot test as a technique of competency assessment is significantly low. This chief reason for this lack of validity is subjectivity of interpretation and absence of evidence that the process, i.e., inkblots, explanation of participants and its interpretation have any correlation with managerial performance/potential.

The author of this test had never used it as a test of personality analysis. The varying interpretation of the explanation given by the participants based on Inkblots also found to be inconsistent. Though, efforts have been made by several psychologists to standardize the interpretation, nothing much had happened making it reliable. However, Inkblot is one of the popularly implemented projective test that can provide an incisive perspective into the creative mind of the subjects.

During the beginning of competency movement, these tests are used for assessment. However, vague evidence in favour of projective test as reliable method of predicting managerial behaviour has discouraged their application in recent times. Projective tests can be administered and interpreted only by well-trained psychologists. These tests are also time-consuming and difficult to extend to a large number of population. However, projective tests have their own importance in personality assessments due to their imaginative and unstructured approach. Despite the subjective approach and cumbersomeness in using these tests, they continued to be effective tests in diagnosing the underlying assumptions and motives.

BOX 4.3 Thematic Apperception Test

TAT is used to analyze a person's pattern of thought, attitude, observational capacity and emotional responses. This is also known as Picture Interpretation Technique. The test had been developed by Christiana Morgan and Henry Murray in 1930s. It is widely used as a personality assessment test. Though it is also a projective technique, here unlike in inkblot test, unambiguous and structured material is used to evoke responses from the participants. In this study, 31 different pictures depicting a variety of social and cultural situations is shown inviting the participant to come up with an explanation of the situation in a story/narration form. These 31 pictures are classified into two types. The first type consisting 10 pictures are gender-specific and remaining 21 pictures are unisex.

The test can also be used to assess the achievement motivation, problem-solving skills, interpersonal relationships, and need for power. The test which basically had been used as a tool of psychoanalytic evaluation found favour with competency assessors in early 20th century. However, TAT as a technique of competency assessment is fraught with many limitations. Firstly, there is no standard form of implementing and interpreting this test. Secondly, the interpretation of picture cards varies significantly. Thirdly, the imaginary explanations narrated by participants in response to the pictures not necessarily correlated to the real life world. Fourthly, it is practically difficult to derive the relevant inferences using the narration style, content and situation explained by the participants of TAT for the purpose of competency assessment. TAT can be effectively used as a tool of competency assessment only when pictures are customized to the requirement of managerial positions identified for assessment. However, TAT is used more as a generic assessment tool rather than a competency assessment tool in an organizational context.

Personality Tests

Personality tests and inventories are widely used in competency assessment programme. MMPI (Minnesota Multi Phasic Personality Inventory), MBTI (Myers-Briggs Type Indicator), PF-16, Thomas personality profiling system (Box 4.4) are the most popular personality tests. Skill inventory tests, communication and value testing scales are also used to measure the personality characteristics. Personality tests found to have reasonable reliability and content validity. They are also found to be reasonable predictors of managerial behaviour. The success of using personality assessment test in competency assessment programmes is moderate. The role of personality traits in competency of any managerial job is profound.

BOX 4.4 Thomas Personality Profiling System

Dr. William Marston developed Thomas personality profiling system in 1928 to assess a person's ability to handle a job. Unlike projective techniques, this is developed especially keeping in view the requirement of business organizations and working environment. According to the author of instrument, people would display four basic behavioural characteristics in working environment. These are: dominance, influence over others, steadiness and compliance, popularly known as DISC.

The instrument called as 'The Personality Profile Analysis' contains 24 boxes each consisting four descriptive words/phrases. Respondent is expected to choose one word which is most descriptive and one word least descriptive of self out of four words in each box. The instrument uses forced choice distribution. Therefore, respondent has no choice, but to tick the most and least applicable words of the self. The administration of the instrument takes about 7 to 9 minutes and about another 7 minutes for interpretation using standardized software. The instrument generates variety of reports that include personality profile analysis. The reliability and content validity of the instrument found to be significantly high. It is used as one of the key instruments in competency assessment.

Leaderless Group Discussion

Leaderless group discussion is employed to assess the social and influential skills of assesses apart from communication and analytical abilities. In a typical leaderless group discussion, participants are given a problem/topic to identify solution in collaboration with the group. Generally, the problem is giving in a written form. Group may be asked to find out the solution either in competitive or cooperative means with the other participants. There would be one or more observers who are well-trained on small group activity make observation and study the behaviour of participants. They record the proceedings and their observations. Based on this record, they interpret the results for each of the participants. Leaderless group discussion is one of the techniques used in competency assessment programme. The technique of leaderless group discussion would be more effective when a problem relevant to the work situation is given and when the group membership is homogenous in experience and work profile. However, their abilities should not be very homogenous. It tends to be ineffective and poor predictor of behaviour when the task given is irrelevant to the group. Tailor made leaderless group discussion is one of the popularly used techniques in competency assessments. It is found that specifically developed leaderless group discussion in the context of organization would be more useful than generic leaderless group discussion. The reliability and content validity of tailor-made leaderless group discussion is believed to be fairly high.

There are some potential problems with leaderless group discussion. Much of the effectiveness of this technique depends on the verbal ability of participants. Unless, participants are very communicative, it becomes difficult to measure anything meaningful. The desired results may not come forth if the group is either too heterogeneous or too homogeneous. This technique, in order to be effective in a competency assessment programme, the expectations: what behaviour and responses are expected from the participants must be pre-defined which can be compared with actual observations for a meaningful analysis. Research on leaderless group discussion as a technique of competency assessment found that observers tend to be swayed by verbal forcefulness rather than real leadership quality. This technique is also not much useful for assessing the first level employees but can be very effective for middle and senior level employees' assessment.

Cooperative Discussions

The said technique is highly useful to elicit collaborative spirit and related competencies required in some roles. In this technique, participants are encouraged to share their views and compliment their perspectives in order to build a scenario of solution to a stated problem. Cooperative discussion can be used as a competency assessment method. Here participants are presented with a problem and they are suggested to discuss and bring out a solution, participant's collaborative and persuasive skills and communication style is explored by observers and assessment on related competencies is carried out.

Competitive Discussions

This technique is similar to cooperative discussion with a difference that here conflicting views/scenarios are presented which a participant will chose one over the other and convince his/her choice of preference. Group tends to pick up contrary view to that of participant and push back. In this competitive environment how a participant handles the pressure while pursuing others to appreciate his/her view point and seek espousal for the same or at least win point of argument convincingly. Competitive discussion can be used as a competency assessment technique to measure pressure and persuasive profile of a role incumbent.

BOX 4.5 Bespoken vs Off-the-shelf Exercises

It is highly debated issue in assessment circles: whether customized assessment tools are good for reliable measure of competencies or commercial tools available over the counter are sufficient. Bespoken or customized instruments consume time, resources and fraught with challenges of reliability and validity. However, such instruments since developed against a clearly-defined requirement and purpose tend to produce results with great accuracy and precision. Often these results also will be free from any dilution or pitfalls in their findings and inferences. Hence, managerial actions to bridge the gaps of competencies or other human resource actions become worthy. In contrast, commercial tools tend to be highly sophisticated and consume much lesser time in their administration and analysis of results. Reliability and validity may not be an issue. Limitation comes from the fact that they are built for multi-purpose without understating the specific need of an assessment exercise in an organization. The fact is every competency assessment exercise is unique and operational definition of competency can be different. Sometime such difference can be substantial. In such unique situation, results obtained using generic assessment tools and exercises have formidable limitations. Their reliability and validity, in general sense, may be established but in a particular situation the same may not withstand. One way to overcome such limitation is to initially test the commercial tools on a sample as pilot project and results can be tested. Necessary modifications can be carried out based on the results. It is suggested that large organizations ideally must explore implementation of customized assessment exercises and tools development and deployment where there is a possibility of continual competency assessment on a sizeable population. At least, these organizations must make attempts to suitably modify assessment tools or opted for commercial way. Medium and small organizations can opt for commercial tools for generic and common competencies, and can opt bespoken method for specific competencies.

Oral Presentations

It is very common to use oral presentation as a competency assessment exercise, especially for the roles like sales, marketing, consulting and leadership roles. In fact most of leadership roles pre-suppose a good deal of presentation work as a part of job. A number of topics and issues are identified as a part of this exercise, wherein participants will be given a particular topic relevant to the profile and will be asked to make a presentations driving a message or solution or highlighting certain key insights. Here a participant will be asked to make a presentation to either a group or to the observers. Communication, connect, languages, persuasion, influence are some of the competencies which can be assessed using this particular technique.

Interview

In some contexts, interview is also used as a competency assessment technique. However, this is found to be bearing high degree of subjectivity. Therefore, in order to minimize subjectivity, it is important to develop a specific format, statements and inquiries and their interpretation be standardized. Interview is easy to use and highly flexible, but alone it cannot provide definite results. It is advisable that interview method can be used along with other competency assessment techniques for cross verification of assessment findings.

Analysis and Decision-making Exercises

This is to an extent similar to role, but different in its approach and complexity of the problem. Here the participant is provided with unorganized data content, but a clear theme. Participant is expected to read the pattern and analyze the theme and expected to organize the data content in logical form around the theme. Also, participant will be given a problem and data to arrive into a decision. Typically, data and content can drive the participant towards multiple directions for decision-making, but a smart participant is expected to chose a path which is efficient, and has the high probability of success. These tests can measure competencies related to analytical and decision-making capability. These tests cannot measure behavioural competencies, and they are more apt for managerial decision-making capability analysis.

Management Games

Management game is used for a variety of human resource assessments. In competency assessment too, this technique is widely used to assess the decision-making skills, influencing abilities, communication abilities, analytical skills, leadership potential and approach to the team activity. In this method, a team of six to eight participants would be given a management problem to generate solutions. The problem presented to the team generally would be representative in nature to the work profile and experience of the team members. Physical tasks/ activities are also used to design the management game. In this approach, team members are expected to assemble a few related parts presented in a disconnected manner or resources are given to the team to create a finished material.

Unlike in leaderless group discussion, where the team members may or may not work in cooperation, here team members work together in cooperation to identify the most appropriate solution to the problem assigned to them. Assessors who are well-trained on using the technique of management game would assume the responsibility of observing the group members. Assessors observe the behaviour of group members, specifically the manner they approach the problem, alternatives considered in identifying the solutions, inter personal behaviour, communication style, etc. Observers also make note on assertiveness, dominance, cooperativeness of the participants. Generally, measurement scales are developed for apprising participants' abilities on such dimensions. At the end, based on their report of observation, assessment for the total team and also for each member would be made. Management games found to be reliable methods in assessing the competency level of assesses. Management games similar to leaderless group discussion suffer a few limitations like it is difficult for observers to keep observation on all the members and make objective assessment. Management games also consume long hours, sometimes three to four hours.

In-basket Exercises

In-basket exercises which have fairly high face validity are one of the reliable techniques of competency assessment. The evidence accumulated across many organizations which have used in-basket method reveals that the predictive value of the test is high. Therefore, in-basket exercise is generally seen with all assessment exercises. This technique can be effectively used in competency assessment of junior, middle and senior level executives. In this method of assessment, an assessee is given a simulated work role to perform. The assessee would be given brief description of the organization, its policies, products, financials, and other related data apart from the description of the role to be performed. Assessee is expected to deal with various documents such as reports, memorandums, inter office memos, correspondence and take decisions based on the data. The assessee also can delegate certain tasks either hypothetically or in real sense to others. Also, need to dispose the papers, record the observations and schedule meetings with others. All these tasks are to be completed in a given time-frame.

All the tasks and activities in an in-basket exercise are to be developed simulating the actual role (Box 4.6). The correlation between the real role and simulated role determines the content validity of the in-basket exercise. The participant of in-basket exercise would be asked to peruse the documents and perform the tasks as defined. Once, the participant through with the

BOX 4.6 Developing an in-basket Exercise

It is not very difficult to develop an in-basket exercise. In-basket exercise, as a technique of competency assessment, must be very specific to the job and should not be generic. Person who is involved in developing this exercise should have comprehensive knowledge about the job, organization and preferably about the industry and also knowledge about in-basket exercise.

1. The initial step in designing an in-basket exercise is determining the performance/competency dimensions to be assessed. This involves precisely defining what an in-basket exercise is expected to measure. For example, in-basket exercise can be designed to assess the decision-making skills, time management, analytical abilities, approach to the problem, ability to plan, perspective, reasoning,

communication ability and so on. Depending on the number and intensity of dimensions, the volume of in-basket exercise is decided. Job analysis, description, Key result area documents of a job need to be studied to identify the typical nature of tasks of a job. Interview with current incumbents and observation while incumbents performing the job would also provide the job-related information. This information must be used to identify the competency requirements of a job.

2. Further, developing the in-basket exercise components such as office memos, notes, telephonic messages, policy papers, description of problems, data, strategy plans, future plans, etc. The in-basket components must be developed in such a way that they are adequate enough to assess the competency of a particular dimension. The exercise also must provide brief about the organization, working environment, products, human resource, financials, competitors, etc. depending on the type of in-basket exercise.
3. In the next step, guidelines for participants must be drafted. The guidelines must contain instructions, dos and don'ts, time allowed and guide-lines for performing the in-basket exercise.
4. After this, there must be an assessor manual. This manual must illustrate how the assessment is to be carried out, the description about dimensions of competency and the procedure to be followed for evaluation of the participant's performance on these competency dimensions. The observations to be made, the manner the recording to be done and common pitfalls must be dealt with. The manual must be drafted in order to ensure objective and uniform interpretation of results.
5. Finally, there must be a standard format (reckoner) which can be used to assess the competency of a participant based on performance scores in an in-basket exercise. In other words, there must be a kind of key to translate the performance scores of in-basket into competency scores. It is also possible to develop scales for each of the competency dimensions. Evaluators can use the scale while assessing. The scores awarded to each of the competency can be consolidated to derive a cumulative score for in-basket exercise.

In order to ensure reliability of the exercise and also enhance the predictability as a tool of competency assessment, the in-basket exercise must be subjected to pilot runs before using it for the regular assessments.

exercise would be asked to answer a few questions in written or oral form mainly revolving around justification for the actions. In a few cases, participants would be interviewed by assessors to gather more information about the various actions taken and tasks performed by the participant. Assessors review the paper work carried out, recordings, observations and the decisions taken and the duration for completing the work. All the reviews and reviews of interview form as assessment.

Self-concept Centric Tools

Based on the theory of self concept, a questionnaire-based tool can be developed which will be greatly useful in competency assessment. The theory of self-concept emphasizes that human being as early as two or three months old would start recognizing that self is very distinctive and different from other beings and objects which is known as existential self. They also soon start recognizing that the self has distinctive strengths and abilities which are known as categorical self. The theory of self-concept is also organized into three parts for greater understanding.

First one is known as self-image which deals with one's own understating of the self. It is an idea how is one's personality, values, interest, disinterest, perspectives and how one sees into self and classifies. The second component is known as self-esteem, which deals with how much one believes in the self about what one is and what one is not This also speaks about self-worth and how one values self. This is the corner stone for personality traits like self-confidence, inferiority and superiority and for accurate self assessment. The third component in the self-concept is known as ideal self. This is what one wish to be and day dreams about it or makes efforts to be like that.

Based on the above discussed theory of self-concept, instruments can be developed to capture the self-concept through the three dimensions of self-image, self-worth and ideal self, which can contribute for a systematic competency assessment of employees. In order to make the data obtained using self-concept based tools reliable, employees shall be made aware of this concept and encourage them to articulate in a manner that captures the self-concept. It is advised to use an essay writing kind of descriptive tool which would help to collect the data in a meaningful manner seeking inputs for each of dimensions of self-concept. Such data can be analyzed in order to identify the competencies and also the competencies which a person wish to have in the course of time.

Career Anchor Assessment Tools

Based on Edger Schein career anchor theoretical framework, assessment tools can be developed to measure and understand the career preferences of participants. Often what some employees believe they are interested can be different from what actually they seek in their careers. Career anchors can include technical, managerial, and secretarial, and each of the careers require a set of specific related competencies. Career anchor assessment tools can provide amazing data not only for career preferences of participants, but also whether they possess required competencies. As per Schein, generally people tend to chose careers those provide opportunities for deployment of their competencies. Development and usage of career anchor-centric assessment tools to measure competencies is complex and involve high intensity of work. However, they can provide amazing results and findings facilitating job fitment related competency assessment. Here a participant is provided with a set of questions and simulations those elicit their underlying or active interest in various fields and disciplines. Based on the score, a participant gain can be used to interpret the career preference of concerned participant.

Culture Assessment Tools

It is vividly clear that culture fit and cultural agility are important competencies for many employees to succeed in their roles, given globalization of operations and workforce. Culture sensitivity, culture adoptability, culture socialization and culture values are some of the sub-competencies which fall under this category. Effectiveness of managerial decisions, roll out of organizational programmes and initiatives largely dependent on their cultural amicability. Questionnaires, oral presentations and team plays can be used as instruments to assess culture quotient in employees. However, culture as a competency can have distinct definition in every organization. Based on operational elements of such definition the assessment tools need to be developed and administered. Culture as a competency has assumed greater significance in contemporary organizations despite of failures of some employees in meeting competency requirement, because of their low proficiency in culture adoptability and sensitivity.

Validating Assessment Exercises

Before the assessment exercises are actually used for assessing the competencies of employees, these must be subjected to reliability and validation tests. Pilot tests need to be conducted using representative sample of employees. Each of these exercises described above and also any new test created must follow this protocol for robustness. The pilot tests are required to be put in place as if they are the real ones. However, communication to employees and administrators must be clear that they are indeed pilots. Relevant statistical and qualitative techniques must be used for testing the reliability. The results can also be discussed in the context of perception of physical reality involving a few resource persons. Based on the pilot results, the assessment tools and exercises need to be modified/improved or adopted as it they are found fit. The results of pilot studies must be carefully documented. The experience of administrators/assessors/raters with pilot study also must be documented for drawing relevant lessons which would be immensely useful when actually implementation is kicked-off. It must be noted with utmost care that the assessment exercises should not be used for competency assessment unless their reliability and validity are established in clear terms through well-conducted studies.

Preparing Competency Assessment Reports

Method(s) to be followed for preparing competency assessment reports need to be defined. The report generally would be individual employee-wise. However, if required a group report also can be prepared. The format must be pre-defined for a meaningful and structured presentation of assessment results. There must be a single cumulative score for each of the tests. Again, a consolidated score combining the results of all the tests administered for each of the employees must be developed. However, a difficulty arises when weightage are to be ascribed to these individual tests. This is a dynamic issue since the importance of a particular test differs from job-to-job. For example, decision-making skills related exercise is extremely significant to a particular job over others and for other jobs, it may be communication skills and still for others both can have equal importance. Therefore, the methodology for arriving into a combined assessment score need to be built for each of the jobs targeted for competency assessment. In this context, Clifton's Strength Finder is illustrated in Box 4.7.

BOX 4.7 Clifton's Strength Finder 2.0

Clifton in collaboration with Gallup through their research over a period of four decades had developed a framework called strength finder. The basic premise of this framework is every human-being has immense talent within them which when identified and used properly can do wonders. This is an online instrument which has gained immense popularity in corporate organizations. However, the findings emanated out of strength finder are not suggested to be used for selection and career related decisions. Despite this limitation, this assessment can be greatly helpful in development of competencies. This is a comprehensive assessment covering 34 themes such as: achiever, activator, adaptability, analytical, arranger. belief, command, communication, competition, connectedness, consistency, context, deliberation, developer. Empathy, focus, futuristic, harmony, ideation, includer, individualization. Input, intellection, learner, maximizer, positivity, realtor, responsibility, restorative, self-assurance, significance, strategic and woo. Strength finder consists of 177 stimuli inviting 177 responses around these 34 themes. It can generate a report highlighting strengths of a respond on all the 34 themes. Advantage of strength finder instrument is it is comprehensive and based on a philosophy that strengths are important and enhancement of strengths is much beneficial and easier as compared to weakness correction. Strength finder may or may not be useful in competency assessment depending upon competency framework and purpose of such an assessment. Nevertheless, strength finder is definitely an important tool to cross check the competency assessment findings and also its framework can be inspirational in design and deployment of competency assessment tools.

Developing Assessor Manual and Assessor Training

It is very important that once assessment exercises are developed customizing to the requirement of organization and needs of various jobs identified for the purpose of competency assessment, a full fledged assessor's manual should be developed. The manual must contain comprehensive details about the concept, history and technologies of competency assessment, greater details about assessment exercise developed in the context of organization and the interpretation method along with specimen schedules, reports and case studies. The manual can help significantly in maintaining the reliable and uniform administration and interpretation of competency assessment activity. The manual must be very specific to the organization and the details of assessment exercises especially need to be discussed in a detailed manner. The other important aspect that an assessor manual must contain are: role of assessor, dos and don'ts while implementing competency assessment programme, common pitfalls and traps in competency assessment, code of conduct for assessors, purpose of assessment, assessment exercises and interpretation method, method of consolidating the assessment results for each individual wherever multi rater assessment is used and selective case studies of competency assessment. The manual can be developed in-house, if expertise is available or with the help of outside experts on the subject. In any case, it would be useful to forward copies of draft manual for critical evaluation. Based on the evaluation and comments, the manual can be finalized. The quality of manual determines the effectiveness of implementation of an assessment programme and it would also serves as a standard for auditing the assessment programme.

The assessors need to be trained based on the assessor's manual. All assessors should be well-informed about various assessment exercises, method of administration, interpretation, etc. The assessors' course must be intensive and interaction-based. They must be supplied reading material prior to class room kind of training. They also need to be imparted report writing skills, interview skills, feedback skills apart from in-depth technology of assessment exercises. Assessors need to be fully-equipped and be encouraged to conduct dry runs of assessment before proceeding to the actual assessment. The dry runs give them an experience and confidence to administer the assessment in the most systematic manner. Unless, the assessors are trained to the perfect position, assessment exercise should not be initiated since much of the effectiveness comes from the performance of the assessors.

An important aspect that should be address is how these assessors are selected/whether they are drawn from inside the organization or from external sources. Answers to these questions entirely depend on the internal environment of the organization and of course the nature of competency assessment programme. It is imperative that internal people are drawn as assessors wherever technical competency assessment is also involved. Internal people expected to possess the knowledge of technology, products, business strategies and finances. The real challenge is setting the criteria for selecting the assessors from the internal source. A rational approach must be followed that repose confidence in the competency assessment system rather than merely adhering to the conventional system of opting senior hierarchical level persons. In addition to the knowledge, it must be ensured that persons to be identified as assessors must be truly willing to contribute. They must be perceived as unbiased, having knowledge of organization and job, able communicator, a good analyst, an incisive observer, a good listener and a person deeply interested in human development. However, most of organizations in India are on hierarchy oriented, making it difficult to obtain acceptance if assessors are drawn from the junior levels to that of assessees. Selecting assessors merely following seniority principle also can cause havoc. Therefore, these aspects need to be balanced to the effectiveness of assessment programme.

If external source is drawn for this purpose, they would be first of all required to be exposed to all these aspects of organization. Organization can opt for external source for choosing the assessors without much difficulty wherever only behavioural and managerial competencies are to be assessed. The other alternative is combining both the internal and external source for building a team of assessors. External source can be utilized for managerial and behavioural competency and internal source for technical competency assessment. At the end of this, sub-step in the long journey of competency assessment is putting in place a team of competency assessors who are trained on assessment technology based on specially developed and customized competency assessment manual.

Another important question that needs to be addressed is how many assessors are to be trained. Generally, there must be one assessor for every two assessees. However, keeping in view the last minute drop outs and to maintain the standards, 50% more than the required (estimated) number of assessors should be trained.

Assessment Centers

Assessment center is one of the most popularly used methods in identifying and mapping competency. Though the primary use of assessment center is for selection, placement and promotional decisions of employees, this method can be effectively used to map the competencies of employees. Assessing managerial competencies has never been an easy task since the profile of a manager's role is constantly evolving. Adding to it, no single technique invented so far is self-sufficient on its own to assess a person's competencies with good reliability and validity. This has paved a way for origin of assessment center that allows use of combination of techniques by multiple assessors to predict multi-dimensional competencies. All these techniques yield reliable information on various dimensions of a person's competencies, which when integrated can be used to predict potential of that person to perform a role effectively.

Description of assessment center

Assessment center is a method that lasts for three to four days in which a combination of well-integrated exercises, tests, simulations, observation by professional assessors and psychometric tools are applied to identify and evaluate the competencies of employees. According to Thornton III and Byham (1982) an assessment center is defined as 'a procedure that uses multiple assessment techniques to evaluate employees for a variety of manpower purposes and decisions'. An assessment center must comprise the following elements:

1. Multiple dimensions of assessment
2. Multiple exercises/instruments/tools/techniques
3. Multiple assessors

There are many myths surrounding assessment centre especially in the context of what constitutes an assessment centre.

Mere use of following methods/techniques cannot be treated as assessment center since they do not confirm to the basic standards and requirements of assessment center:

1. *Mere use of work simulations:* Using work simulations alone to assess competencies are not tantamount to assessment center. This is one of the techniques used in the center. Even when an organization deploys more than one assessor to conduct these simulations, it cannot be qualified as assessment center.
2. *Interview alone:* Interview whether structured or unstructured and whether single or multiple cannot substitute the assessment center. It is one of the methods used in assessment center.
3. *Pencil-paper tests:* Use of paper and pencil tests or use of a battery of psychometric tests is not sufficient to make them as assessment centers or equivalent to it.
4. *Single assessor assessment:* A single assessor conducting all the assessment even when all the assessment techniques are used is not treated as assessment centre. Use of multiple assessors is a pre-requisite in assessment center.
5. *Unintegrated assessment data:* Mere using of multiple assessors and deploying multiple techniques still cannot qualify the process as assessment center unless such observations of multiple assessors and data obtained using such multiple methods is integrated.
6. *Instruments/techniques without predictable value:* Instruments and techniques that are to be used in assessment center should possess the reliability and validity and must have predictable properties.

Background of assessment center

Concept and practice of assessment center is first introduced by Armed Forces of Germany in selection of military officers during the Second World War. They did use a combination of complex exercises, situational tests, and multiple assessment methods and deployed multiple assessors to identify the leadership competencies. German Army had even appointed assessment officers for this purpose. The credit for making advancements in assessment center technique goes to The British War Office Selection Board (WOSB). Advancements made are more in the nature of bringing scientific sanctity to assessment centers through development of empirical evaluation methods, reliability and validity testing of assessment center operations. British army has extensively used assessment center in selection and training of army officers and popularized the technique worldwide. Countries like Canada and Australia had also adapted the British model of assessment center in the selection of army officers with a few modifications to suit their requirements.

Assessment center approach which confined to the use of army selection boards in several countries was first experimented in selection of civil officers in United Kingdom. Significant changes were brought about in exercises and techniques developed by army boards to suit the civil setting. AT&T is the first corporate that has effectively tapped the benefits of assessment center in assessing the competencies of its managerial employees. AT&T had innovated a good number of methods beginning from identification of desirable managerial competencies assessment techniques, exercises to training of assessors. Success of AT&T with assessment center approach has contributed for popularizing this method in a number of corporate organizations like IBM, XEROX, General Electric in the following years.

Ten common pitfalls with assessment centers

Currently, assessment center is one of the most popular and preferred techniques in management of human resource. Different organizations ascribe different reasons for adoption of assessment center technique. These reasons range from no specific reason to specific reason such as utilizing the outcome of assessment center for recruitment/development/reward/career planning purposes and combination of all these purposes. There is no denying the fact that assessment center is certainly a very powerful and comprehensive instrument that can objectively assess the potential of human resource. The data that assessment center implementation yields are very valuable and can be used for variety of human resource related decisions. Handling assessment center is a specialist function because its implementation and application of results for human resource decisions calls for adequate knowledge and experience in management of assessment center. It is also a fact that mismanaging an assessment center can cause organizational catastrophe. The bigger fact in this is organizations that are successful in execution of assessment center are far less in number in comparison to organizations that failed. Therefore, in my opinion it makes sense in analyzing and understanding the reasons that cause assessment center to fail rather than basking in the glory of two or three successful case studies. With this view, the ten common reasons that are accountable for assessment center downfall in a number of organizations are described as follows:

1. *Unclear objectives:* Often managers and organizations hurry up with new techniques like assessment center without clearly defining how, why and what they intended to do with such an exercise. Firstly, planning, implementation and application of assessment tend to be ambiguous when objectives are not clear. Secondly, the exercise lacks a clear direction. Thirdly, and most importantly, assessment center is likely to end up as an end in itself implying that the results of assessment center may and may not be utilized. Fourthly, and finally assessment center implementation is likely to be abandoned mid way on the face of few challenges that generally arise during the course. Therefore, one of the dominant reasons for failure of assessment center is absence of clear objectives. Many organizations messed up assessment center on account of these unclear objectives.
2. *Measuring linguistics:* There is a Hyderabad-based organization that messed up assessment center technique due to this linguistic issue. This case goes like this: All instruments and methods used as a part of assessment center were in English. Consultants who implemented assessment center came from another part of the country who had no knowledge of the language (Telugu) spoken in that organization. This language barrier played a significant role in assessing potential of employees. For example, employees whose English language ability is

good scored over those whose knowledge is poor. It means, assessment center had ended up in assessing English language potential of employees rather than functional and managerial potential. Therefore, managers must understand the implications of language in assessment center before implementing the same. After all, assessment center is much more than mere jargon and smart talking.

3. *Measuring intelligence:* Great danger with some of the instruments used as a part of assessment center can be that they are intelligence-centric rather than competency-centric. Hence, these are susceptible to manipulation by a few smart people. Intelligence measures make assessment center as any other general knowledge/awareness test. However, some managers whose understanding about assessment center is dominated by testing obsessions blend intelligence measures. This contributes for testing intelligence and not performance/potential of employees. Therefore, this mess-up provides organizations with data of generic intelligent employees and not about performers and development needs or information on any such related human resource issues. Assessment center experiences fail when such intelligent things happen.

4. *Measuring perceptions/intentions:* It is hard to come across any employee without good intentions. It is equally hard to find a person who puts in efforts to translate these good intentions into reality. Further, assessment center is much superior and sophisticated technique than that of normal behavioural instruments that measure perceptions alone. Tragedy is that quite a few instruments, techniques, tools and methods used on the name of assessment center are either perceptions or intentions oriented and seldom factual and realistic oriented. These instruments also rarely take adequate care in eliminating social desirability factor resulting in assessing all the good intentions and general perceptions than actual performance and exact potential that exist within human resource.

5. *Adopting generic instruments/methods:* This is classic example of how assessment center can be messed up

through treating it like an assembly product. In many cases, managers engage consultants to conduct assessment center whose knowledge about organization is far from satisfactory. These consultants tend to deploy a range of questionnaires/check lists/schedules/tools/techniques/ methods that are very generic in nature like Omni bus. The fact, however, is that every organization is unique in it's own way even within the same industry, location and cultural context. This requires an assessment center method conceptualized, developed, tested and validated in that organizational context. In other words, the techniques must be organization-specific and should possess absolute compatibility. Due to negligence of this fact, many organizations contribute towards messing up assessment center.

6. *Implementing without preparing ground:* Implementation of assessment center involves preparing organization and employees well in advance. It implies that all employees must be communicated regarding objective of assessment center intervention, how it is proposed to implement and benefits with such an intervention and what will be done with the results assessment center provides. Secondly, suggestions of employees also must be invited in regard to implementation and post-assessment scenario. Unfortunately, this non-preparation is cited as one of the significant reasons for messing up assessment center. It is because when employees are not warmed up before hand, it results in distrust and spreads adverse remarks and negative stories about assessment center intervention that dents the whole exercise.

7. *No top-down implementation:* Assessment center ideally must be implemented adopting top-down approach. This means, managers at the higher levels of organization needs to be covered in the first instance. It serves the purpose of expelling all apprehensions about assessment center. In many cases, organizations start or apply assessment center limited to few cadres and levels. This breeds suspicions in the minds of people culminating in failure of assessment center. We must remember that absolute commitment and wholehearted participation of

employees is mandatory for effectiveness of assessment center. Haphazard coverage of assessment center in terms of employees is a reason for mess up of assessment center.

8. *No judicious blend of objective-subjective measures:* Assessment center must be designed combining objective and subjective measures in a judicious and scientific manner. This is because each one of them alone falls inadequate in assessing employees. Human being is an emotional entity, and therefore, all traits/characteristics are not accessible for objective measures. At the same time, there should not be too much of subjective measures, because ensuring their objectivity becomes a major challenge. In a significant number of cases, consultants comfortable with psychometrics apply their expertise in increasing the dosage of objective (statistical) measures beyond a rational limitation. This contributes for assessment center producing dispassionate results. The over usage of quantitative measurement science is cited as one of the reasons for assessment center not living up to the expectation.

9. *Assessment center as independent intervention:* Lack of integration of assessment center intervention with overall human resource policy and practice framework is another factor that is responsible for ineffectiveness. In a considerable number of cases, assessment center is implemented as an independent exercise that has no relation with ongoing or planned human resource activities like training, appraisal, career planning and so on, Therefore, the whole effort ends up as an academic exercise or just to gain a feeling of in the company of modern human resource practices organizations. An assessment center that has no connection with people related issues is just an effort in futility.

10. *Linking assessment center results with rewards:* Linking assessment center results with grant of rewards like determining compensation, career upgradations, and assignments allocation before maturing the same can cause chaos in organizations. There are cases where assessment results have not matched with reality on the ground like

actual performance of people. Therefore, organizations must restrain themselves using this data for critical decisions in the first stage itself. Preferably, assessment center results must be utilized for developmental purposes followed by allocation of assignments. Results can be used for other purposes like compensation, recruitment, and promotions when it is conclusively proved and validated that assessment center results are absolutely reliable. This suggests that organizations must allow a reasonable gestation period for experiencing the assessment results before it is considered for going over the board.

Assessment center is certainly a complex and composite intervention among other Organization Development interventions. This complexity and comprehensiveness provides both: great challenge and great opportunity. Assessment center can create powerful impact and redefine the human resource strategy if conceptualized, developed, executed, analyzed and evaluated systematically and strictly in adherence to fundamental tenets and ground reality. Implementation that is devoid of these factors can dilute the intervention and adds up to the list of organizations that contributed for messing up assessment center.

Process of Assessment Center

There is no hard and fast rule in the method of designing and executing assessment center. Process or steps followed in assessment center can vary from organization to organization depending on its requirement and objective. However, all organizations need to go through the following stages in design and implementation of assessment center:

Stage 1: *Deciding for assessment center:* It is not easy for an organization to simply decide for setting up and running assessment centers. A host of factors need to be considered before a decision is taken such as objective of assessment center exercise, resource commitment, need of organization and employees and employees to be covered under this exercise.

Stage 2: *Identification of competency dimensions/development of competency dictionary:* An organization must define the type and standards of competencies at various levels of organization in order to assess employees against these standards. This in itself is a comprehensive exercise involving job analysis and competency-based studies. This issue is discussed in a detailed fashion in chapter three.

Stage 3: *Development of assessment exercises:* Assessment exercises, work simulations, interview schedules, role play, business games, psychometric tests, etc., are to be designed at this stage with the competencies identified at the Stage 2 as basis. The competency dictionary and competency definitions work as key for these exercises.

Stage 4: *Defining measurement methods:* This is corollary to the factor discussed at stage three above. Appropriate measurement methods must be developed to assess the competencies. Measurement is key for ensuring good reliability and validity of the assessment exercises.

Stage 5: *Validation of assessment exercises:* Exercises, various testing instruments and schedules developed at Stage 3 need to be subjected to reliability and validity tests before these are actually used to assess the competencies of employees. This may require an organization to conduct a pilot study and analyze the results.

Stage 6: *Development of assessor's manual:* It is of utmost important that an organization intending to run assessment centers must develop its own assessment center manual to ensure objectivity and system approach. This manual deals with all implementation issues and helps as a handbook not only for assessors but also for assessment administrators. The assessor's manual must contain the competency dictionary, assessment center design, schedule, all exercises along with instructions, sample rating and analysis sheets, guidelines for conducting interviews, role plays and business games and a specimen final report.

Stage 7: *Training of assessors:* Resource persons need to be identified through internal and external sources and must be imparted adequate training in conducting assessment centers and on the methodological aspects. The manual developed at

Stage 6 above can be of significant help in this regard. However, the original manual copy should not be handed over at the stage of training due to confidentiality reasons as this manual should not fall in the hands of participant employees.

Stage 8: *Implementation of assessment centers:* Participants of assessment center (assesses) preferably should be drawn from a group of employees who can be assigned a role/position that is significantly different from the presently they are holding. Assessment center is best implemented in a group situation where in about 12 assesses take part with 6 assessors and 1 assessment administrator facilitating the entire process at a venue away from work place setting. The group situation can provide opportunities for observing inter personal and team building skills of assesses.

Stage 9: *Report writing:* Individual assessment reports should be generated based on the results obtained using different assessment techniques and observations made by multiple assessors. All the data should be integrated and inferences shall be drawn.

Stage 10: *Review of assessment design* (Assessment exercises and methods of assessment): The final stage in establishing assessment centers is reviewing the results of implementation of assessment center especially various assessment exercises, tools, simulations that were developed and used to assess the competencies of assessees. Keeping in view the experiences and insights gained from implementation, future assessment centers can be improved upon.

Assessment Center vs Development Center

Assessment center is not same that of development center. They mainly differ in their purpose: assessment center is used to assess competencies of assessees for human resource related decisions such as selection, promotion and allocation of assignments where as development center is used for training and developmental purpose of assessees. Though, there are no well defined definitions or rules that differentiate both these, they differ in their purpose, aim, focus, methodology and report writing style as shown in Table 4.2 The differences discussed here are not meant to be understood in a rigid manner since enough of flexibility exists in adopting the procedure of each other.

TABLE 4.2 Assessment Center vs Development Center: Compare and Contrast

Aspect	*Assessment center*	*Development center*
Purpose	To enable organization to take decision in regard to recruitment, reward, career and succession planning and allocation of assignments, etc.	To enable organization identify developmental needs of employees
Methodology	Uses a combination of assessment methods such as work simulations, role play, critical incident technique, repertory grid, interview, observation by team of assessors etc., in assessment of employees' competence	Though, flexible to use the methods employed in assessment centers, development center uses self-assessment and peer assessment to a large extent
Aim	To provide organization with accurate information on employees' current and potential competence	Do
Duration	Involves a minimum of two to three days	Takes about a day
Participation	Assessors are used at a ratio of one assessor for every two assessees. The methodology, type of tests and implementation of method are pre-decided by assessors. Self-assessment is given low emphasis	Development center is employee-driven though a ratio of 1:1 (assessor and employee) is suggested. Employees generally have freedom to suggest their own method of assessing developmental needs
Focus	Focuses on the immediate needs of organization by providing the assessment of competencies	Addresses the organizational needs on medium and long terms by providing the assessment of developmental needs of employees
Role of assessor	Judgmental	Facilitation

Preparatory briefing	Limited briefing is given about the assessment activities	Exhaustive details are provided about the assessment method and consequences
Feedback report	Chiefly contains assessed employees' ratings of analytical and interpersonal competencies and generally submitted to management at the end of the assessment exercise for human resource related decisions	Primarily highlights the developmental issues/ concerns of employees and the report is available to employees instantly
Control	Management of organization possesses total control over the information obtained using the center	Individual employee possesses substantial control over the information

Assessment centers: Problems and challenges

Designing and implementing assessment centers is not free from problems and challenges as shown in Tables 4.3 and 4.4. However, all the problems illustrated here can be avoided if

TABLE 4.3 Problems of Assessment Centers

Problem	*Description*
Subjectivity/ bias	Assessment center though is a highly reliable method of assessing the competencies is not absolutely free from subjectivity. The methods used in the center such as interview, observation by assessors are susceptible for subjectivity and bias.
Distrust	In some cases, there is a possibility of employees distrusting the process. Unless, this distrust is dealt effectively prior to implementing assessment center, it can result in creating barriers for objective assessment.
Ineffective communication	This is very sensitive issue. There should not be over or under communication. Open communication is basic necessity for success of the centers. Employees need to have a proper communication not only about the assessment center being implemented but also general communication in organization must be effective.

TABLE 4.3 Problems of Assessment Centers (Contd.)

Problem	*Description*
Time consuming	Assessment centers are time consuming and takes about 3 to 4 days to cover about a dozen employees with the involvement of not less than 6 assessors and 1 assessment administrator.
Resource intensive	Assessment centers involve allocation of substantial resource in terms of money, effort and manpower.

TABLE 4.4 Challenges of Assessment Centers

Challenge	*Description*
Model competencies	Assessment center instruments are to be designed based on the desirable competencies to perform a position successfully. Generally, model competencies developed/available in the organization are used for this purpose. Therefore, the key for choosing type of assessment testing is the model competencies. The challenge is—a manager's job is tend to be dynamic and highly evolving making it difficult to predict what kind of competencies are essential and desirable.
Identification and selection of assessment techniques	Effectiveness of assessment center is largely dependent on the appropriateness of assessment techniques used, their combination, reliability and validity. Therefore, it is a significant challenge to identify/develop and use right techniques in right combination.
Development of testing exercises and manuals	Assessment is organization specific. Therefore, often off-the-shelve commercially available exercises may not be of significant help. Every organization may have to design its own exercises and assessors manuals which can be time and cost-intensive.
Availability of competent assessors	Assessors perform vital role in assessment. Well trained, professional and experienced assessors are in shortage. Organizations intending to implement assessment centers often encounter a problem in hiring/engaging competent assessors.

Report writing and feedback	Assessment report needs to be developed participant-wise. Essential aspect is there must be a clear integration of the data obtained using a combination of assessment techniques also there must be integration of observations made by different assessors. This is a time consuming and challenging issue. Feedback must be offered to participants in a non threatening, objective and positive manner.

assessment centers are designed and executed professionally. These problems and challenges highlight that launching assessment center should be preceded by ensuring an effective communication and foolproof pre-assessment center preparations. Though, assessment centers are resource intensive, but the benefits they offer outweigh the cost factor. Handling assessment centers is certainly a specialized function that pre supposes taking care a range of aspects such as developing assessment instruments, exercises, establishing reliability and validity of them, developing assessor's manual and assessors training and report writing. These are the natural challenges which can be converted into sources of opportunities for demonstrating the authenticity of assessment center approach.

Experiences with Assessment Centers

Experiences with assessment centers so far are mixed. There are assessees whose feedback supports the view that assessment centers are very useful and reliable methods in assessing the competency profile and there are also people who negate such a view. Organizations' experiences also show the similar divergence. As Dodd quoted by Thornton III and Byham (1982) had conducted a comprehensive research exploring attitudes of the participants of assessment centers implemented in organizations such as AT&T, IBM and found that:

1. About 37% of participants believe that some participants have prior information about the assessment center programme, and its various exercises that gives them undue advantage.
2. About 58% to 93% of participants believe that the programme measures important managerial qualities.

However, 41% report that their performance in assessment center was different from real life situations.

3. About 80% to 85% report that they understand the feed-back given but anywhere from 10% to 30% believe that the assessment center did not accurately identify strengths and weaknesses.
4. Though, a good percentage of employees endorse that assessment center result can be used for promotion decisions, but majority of them favours its usage for identifying developmental needs of employees.

Though a few organizations in India have implemented assessment centers, the experiences are yet to be systematically evaluated. Experiences of PricewaterHouse Coopers, a management consultancy which had established assessment centers in a few Delhi and Mumbai-based organizations is shown in Box 4.8.

BOX 4.8 PricewaterHouse Cooper's Experience of Assessment Centers in India

PricewaterHouse Cooper's, a management consultancy now taken over by IBM have conducted assessment centers in a few organizations based in Delhi and Mumbai. They have used customized instruments and exercise to assess the competencies. Their experience with Indian organizations reveals that:

1. Assessment center in Indian context can work best when used for developmental purpose
2. Assessment centers should be used only subsequent to a systematic evaluation of the need, objective and the resource availability of an organization
3. Participants tend to seek instant feedback, i.e., immediately after the application of tests and exercises which is difficult to fulfill as it involves detailed discussion among the assessors.
4. Assessment techniques and exercises should be developed and selected with utmost care and strategic consideration
5. Group composition should be worked out sensitively and also strategically
6. Implementation of assessment centers must be transparent, its objectives and aim must be clear to the employees. Participant employees must be given adequate briefing to remove apprehensions failing which they tend to develop threatening feeling.
7. Improper design and implementation of assessment center can lead to low employee morale and enhances employee attrition rate.

Assessment centre techniques

A wide range of techniques are employed in assessment centers to identify and appraise variety of competencies as shown in Table 4.5.

TABLE 4.5 Techniques Used in Assessment Centres

Organization	*Techniques used in Assessment Centers*
Gujarat Heavy Chemicals Limited	Position clarification, Objective setting, Performance review, Position evaluation, Self-appraisal, Competency mapping, MAP (Multi-Dimensional Personality assessment Scale) and MBTI (Myers Briggs Type Indicator), FIRO-B (Fundamental interpersonal relationship Orientation Behavior).
JK Corporation Limited	Presentation, Written report, Personal interview, Business game, Case study, Team role audit, SPIRO-M profile, role play, In-Basket exercise, Managerial style diagnosis.
PricewaterHouse Coopers	Customized instruments suiting to organizational context comprising, Personal interview, Role play, Business game, Psychometric testing, work simulation and Case study.
SmithKline Beecham Consumer Healthcare	Structured interviews, Case study, Scenario discussion and portfolio presentation.

360 Degree Feedback as a Competency Assessment Method

360 degree feedback which is a multi rater system can also be used as competency assessment method. Of course, many organizations also consider 360 degree feedback system as an alternative method for assessment of people competencies. The 360 degree system has become popular and vogue with most of contemporary organizations as this can provide a kind of quick snapshot on the effectiveness of leaders/managers based on perceptions of the stakeholders. Interestingly 360 degree system, as a competency assessment method, can be used to assess competency effectiveness of an incumbent in a role as well as on a department/function. The 360 degree assessment

involves all the stakeholders like: boss, team members, peers, reportees, customers as well as self. Use of 360 degree feedback system has immense benefit for competency assessment, because many competencies like empowerment, ability to motivate others, coaching, mentoring, communication, empathy, intuition etc. are very observable rather than physically measurable competencies which can be assessed by the stakeholders, because of their continual observation of a role holder. However, 360 degree feedback system as a competency assessment method is not free from pitfalls. Sometimes, the feedback may lack quality, sometimes it can be more than perceptual, but politically motivated and role holders may not take the feedback in a constructive manner as the same can be threatening. Despite the said pitfalls, 360 degree feedback system is one of the most powerful methods that can be used in competency assessment especially of behavioural and emotional competencies. The following steps are involved in developing a customized 360 degree feedback system as a competency assessment method:

1. *Defining objective:* As a first step, the objective of 360 degree feedback process shall be defined clearly: how the assessment outcomes will be used. For example, the assessment results will be used only for development or it can be used for reward or it can be used for multiple human resource decisions. It needs to be noted that many studies have found that the results of the assessment were taken seriously when used only for developmental purpose and the same tend to be disagreed or contested more frequently when the results are applied for other human resource decisions like compensation, promotions or role adjustments. Potential of such disagreements shall not dampen an organization's plan to utilize the findings for multiple purposes though it is advisable to start the usage of assessment results for developmental purpose, before the same is extended for other purposes.

2. *Identify roles/Role holders:* Second key step in this process is identifying a set of roles as well as role holders who would be covered under the 360 degree assessment. Usually, leadership roles and role holders are given priority given their impact and relevance to organizations.

It is also important to inform the role holders about the assessment process and the purpose of assessment. Efforts shall be made to mitigate any anxieties, if exist, which can cause dilution of assessment exercise.

3. *Identify competencies for assessment:* It is important to identify whether all competencies or some competencies related to a role or set of roles will be assessed using the 360 degree feedback system. The 360 degree feedback system can be an effective method for competencies especially behavioural and may not be apt for functional and technical competencies. The competencies shall be identified drawing from competency model of the role/ roles under assessment project.
4. *Understand the operational measures:* Operational measures or behaviours associated with each of the competencies must be clearly understood. For example, what nuances are expected out of a competency like communication? Is it language, expression, medium, connect, terminology, language etiquette, cultural aspects of communication? Operational measures significantly help in understating the nature of competency. It is also important to understand the levels of proficiency as applicable to the role, and how they differ in their scale and definition.
5. *Understand stated outcomes:* Both role outcomes and outcomes expected out of each competency in the context of a role shall be dwelled upon as it is highly relevant in formulating 360 degree feedback as a part of competency assessment. Operational measures shall reflect the outcomes directly or indirectly. Therefore, a cross verification shall also be dealt in order to ensure the validation between measures and outcomes.
6. *Build questionnaire:* Based on the steps as discussed above, questionnaire need to be developed capturing statements. Questionnaire can consist direct statements or perceptual surrogate statements both in positive and negative perspective. Scale development also shall be implemented in order to measure responses on the

statements. Questionnaire shall be subjected to pilot study before the final use and output of pilot study must be validated and reliability needs to be carried out. Based on reliability and validity test, the questionnaire can be refined.

7. *Administration of questionnaire:* All stakeholders can use the questionnaire to provide their feedback on the role holder. All care must be exercised to brief respondents. Most importantly assurances need to be made that all responses will be dealt with utmost confidentiality since the same is important for objective feedback. Depending on an organization and convenience of respondents, the questionnaire can be administered using paper-pencil or electronic medium. Establishing trust and credibility is imperative for a health assessment.

8. *Collection of data:* Data gathered using the questionnaire need be meaningfully collated and analyzed competency-wise. The data further shall be maintained either role-wise or role holder-wise in consonance with the purpose of the exercise. Ensuring error-free data input and analysis is highly critical. Statistical tool can be used wherever the data is large enough. Data is also required to be organized stakeholder group-wise like peer group, staff, customers so on and so forth. A cursory check is advised to see if there are any apparent inconsistencies or incompleteness in the data either competency-wise or whole data profile.

9. *Formatting report:* Report can be generated based on classification and analysis of data with the necessary interpretation. Report can be role-wise or incumbent-wise be generated. The typical report presents how an incumbent is doing competency-wise. Typically report must focus on positives to begin with on each of the competencies of a subject/role holder/incumbent for whom 360 degree method is used as assessment and development tool. In the second part, the report must clearly define and reason out the limitations and development needs on each of the competencies. It is important that languages

and presentation of the report must be clear and free from ambiguity and freewheeling interpretations. Report can be presented competency-wise and as well as in a cluster mode to draw meaningful inferences which can be auctioned upon. Report also must eliminate or avoid any technical jargon that constrains easy comprehension. Report should be non threatening yet factual driving the clear message. Report also must deal how the assessment was carried out, detailing steps in a manner that build confidence and credibility of the assessment report.

10. *Communication/sharing report:* Once the 360 degree report is developed the next sequential critical step is sharing the report with concerned role holder/incumbent. It is advisable to communicate the report in person. Wherever it is not feasible due to spread of employees, a dialogue with them must be held before the report reaches them. Such dialogue should cover aspects like objective of assessment, methodology followed, and competencies covered for assessment and how positively and directly they are related to effective performance of the role. Advantages and limitations of 360 degree method as an assessment tool also need to be explained. How the findings of the report can be actioned for development and other managerial actions must be dealt. Often absence of a positive dialogue creates lack of confidence among recipients of the report and eventually they resist implementation of the findings. This opportunity also must focus on clarifying the doubts of employees both on 360 degree assessment method and usage of this method for competency assessment. Subsequent to the said dialogue, the report can be presented to the concerned employees and allowing them adequate time to read through the report and develop their understanding. It is also of paramount importance that questions, comments and doubts of employees to whom the report is sent are invited on reading the report. Such a session will contribute to greater understating and acceptance of the report findings.

Part II: Executing Competency Assessment Programme

As discussed above, the following are the prerequisite for executing a competency assessment programme:

1. Competency models are created or adopted with suitable modification in respect of job incumbents to be assessed.
2. Competency assessment exercises are developed on the basis of competency models and their reliability and validity is established through appropriate studies.
3. Assessors manual is developed and assessors are trained on the use of manual.

Execution is twice the challenge of designing a competency assessment programme. Challenges arise during execution stage mainly due to two factors. One, a few problems and ambiguities may arise while competency assessment project is implemented which are not thought of earlier. These issues need to be resolved on time and keeping in view the core objective of competency assessment programme. Two, the number of people to be involved during execution stage would be considerable calling for administrative and emotional management. A few suggestive steps that enable a good execution programme are discussed as follows:

Step 1: Making Administrative Arrangements

A few competency assessment exercises do require that participants be away from their usual work place. Also, group exercise presupposes that all participants must be gathered at a place. Therefore, it may be desirable that all participants are taken away to a remote location like hill station or holiday resort. This needs that necessary arrangements are made well in advance. Especially, execution of assessment and development centers require that participants are away from work location and must be in a group. Carrying out the assessment activity outside the office also provide participants a relaxed environment, and free them from botheration of usual work responsibilities. The assessment exercise may require two to three days for their completion. Therefore, boarding and lodging arrangement would be required to be made accordingly. In addition to these, assessment aids like stationary, television, pens, pads, white board, markers, flip charts, etc., are required to be arranged.

The due importance must be given for these arrangements since laxity in this aspect can create dissatisfaction and also inconveniences to participants and assessors. Such dissatisfaction can sometimes have an adverse impact on the overall administration of assessment programme. Therefore, competency project management must take personal care in reviewing all these arrangements.

Step 2: Identifying Job Incumbents

An objective and transparent criteria must be set for identifying the job incumbents, who are to be covered under competency assessment programme. As much as possible, efforts shall be made to cover all employees working in a particular job. For example, if competency assessment is being conducted for finance executives, all such executives working in finance must be covered. Wherever it would not be possible, based on the seniority or any such easily demonstrable criteria, the participants shall be identified. The objective should be two fold: the first is identification process of participants for assessment should not create any controversy or perception of discrimination since it can cause apprehensions in the minds of people, and also loss of confidence in the assessment programme. Second is, the identification need to be done in such a manner that can help deriving maximum benefit out of such elaborate exercise. In any case, the process of selecting employees for assessment should be open and transparent so as to bring credibility to the exercise.

Step 3: Communicating Identified Employees

The employees who are identified to be covered under competency assessment programme should be communicated about all relevant details. In addition to the formal written communication, it would be effective to assemble them within the premises of organization to have a personal dialogue with them in order to address their concerns and queries. Competency project manager accompanied by one or two project members can have a personal discussion with these employees. They must be informed of the objective, method and purpose of assessment. They must be ensured of the confidentiality of the results and assessment. All efforts should be made to remove apprehensions and communication gaps. The introduction needs to be done in such a way that employees must look forward towards the day of competency assessment that give them information about their capabilities and developmental assessments. The participants also must be given details of venue, board and lodging arrangements and details of contact. If it is possible at this stage itself, the whole schedule of competency assessment can be handed over. The schedule must consist of participant-wise details like the type of exercises, their sequence, details of assessors and timings.

Step 4: Executing Competency Assessment Programme

The fourth and final step is getting down to actual execution of competency assessment programme. The execution would be carried out as per the laid down schedule. The adherence to schedule by assesses and assessors will be monitored by competency project manager. The following sub-steps will be involved in execution:

1. The participants on their arrival to the venue of competency assessment programme would be given a briefing on how they are going to spend the coming two/three days participating in various assessment events. They also would be given guidelines and details of various facilities and persons involved in the event. The briefing event must be used to relive the participants from stress and also to build rapport among all the participants and assessors and administrators.
2. The assessment exercises would be conducted as scheduled. It is important that assessment exercises should be sequenced in a logical manner. The exercises which are light and can be finished quickly must be started first and intensive ones can be applied once the seriousness is built into the group.
3. Assessors need to meet and integrate the results of all the assessment exercises and observations towards the end of the assessment. Each of the assessors should present the results together with working sheets and their observations.

They are needed to substantiate their interpretations. There would be two more assesses involved for assessment of a single participant in certain type of assessments. Therefore, they need to reconcile their test results and individual observations before drafting the final report. The final report must present the integrated result/score for each of the participants on various competencies. There can be a trap with internal assessors that they may try to use their prior knowledge about an assessee. This trap need to be managed failing which results can be contaminated. There can be two reports where the competency assessment is comprehensive comprising technical, managerial and behavioural competencies. One report may be devoted to technical competencies and the other dealing with managerial and behavioural competencies.

4. The assessment report which starts with description of personal profile of assessee can be structured into four parts. The executive summary of an employee's competency assessment can be provided in the first part. This part essentially provides the snapshot of participants' performance in various assessment exercises dealing with various technical, managerial and behavioural competencies. The second part is a detailed one, illustrating the performance of an assessee in each of exercises along with working sheets, rating sheets and interpretation. For example, the performance of an assessee in a communication-related assessment exercise results would be discussed under the heading of communication ability and under the broad head of behavioural and managerial competency. The observations and basis for particular interpretation of the assessee would be provided in the third part, and the possible implication of assessment results for various human resource and developmental plans would be discussed in the fourth part of the report. The limitations of the study, if any, can be annexed with the report.
5. The report must be written soon after completion of assessment exercise. Care needs to be taken to avoid delay in writing the report as it can cause dilution, and

also assessors tend to forget some observations. The competency assessment report also needs to be dealt in terms of strengths and areas of developmental concern in respect of each assessee. While doing so, assessor/ interpreter must diligently avoid using adjectives and highly judgmental statements. Similarly, the use of negative and discouraging/ critical language should be avoided.

6. The competency assessment report should be written in easily comprehensive language. Use of technical jargon must be avoided as much as possible. The report must convey the competency profile of the assessee. It must be noted that the report is written for the perusal of two people. The first purpose is to provide feedback to the individual concerned and the second to the management. Therefore, the report must facilitate easy understanding enabling them to initiate necessary developmental action. This is not a research report, but a managerial report. Therefore, the format of report also must follow as a digest rather than a research document.
7. The last but very important sub-step in execution of competency development programme is providing a feedback and counselling to the participants. It is a sensitive exercise so that enough care and preparations should be taken. The feedback must be given in private and in a confidential manner. The participant must be made comfortable, received warmly, and no interruption should be allowed while feedback session is in progress. The feedback of assessment must be given in the context of organization and competencies related to the job. Throughout the feedback, the sensitivity, esteem and dignity of the participant should be given a due consideration. The feedback session must focus on strengths of the employee, areas of developmental concern, effective and ineffective behavioural elements of the participant. The feedback contents must be supported by examples and incidents of performance demonstrated by participants during competency assessment. Details of results obtained by the participant in each of the exercises can be presented, and wherever required, their relevance

must be explained lucidly. Often, employees would be in doubt how an exercise can measure a particular competency. This doubt must be cleared with suitable examples demonstrating the exercise as a reliable indicator of a competency. The participant also must be given adequate opportunity to explain why such performance and circumstances were given for that. The participant's explanation should not be rejected. Rather, alternative behaviours of effective behaviour must be illustrated. The feedback must be dealt in the context of job competencies only, and no generic statement must be made. Though the assessors are not well-trained counsellors, they can make an attempt to counsel the employees. Sometimes, employees may get upset with their results. A few of them may find it difficult to accept them. They should not be insisted to bow down to the assessment. Instead they must be advised to introspect calmly and think over it after a break.

It is important that at the beginning of the feedback session, the employee must be given a brief about objective of the feedback session and how he/she can utilize the opportunity to seek clarifications and express the concerns. Assessors also must invite employee's opinion/views about the assessment center and the experience in order to gather the opinion.

Part III: Cost Benefit Analysis of Competency Assessment Programmes

Often competency assessment programmes run into controversy, because of lack of direct evidence that such programmes add business value. Ironically, some of the programmes even fail to create impact at employees' level who are primary beneficiaries of such initiatives. Further application of competency assessment programmes are expensive on all fronts—time, money and emotional overload in organizations. Hence, it is important that competency assessment initiatives shall be evaluated for their cost-benefit.

Usually competency assessment programmes, which are drawn from organizational business needs, tend to provide business value. It is equally important that competency assessment programmes are also implemented systematically since programmes derived from business needs can also fail to yield results, if execution is ineffective and unsystematic. The following process is advisable to establish the cost-benefit analysis of competency assessment programmes in organizations:

Step 1: Understand Organizational Needs

First step is to understand organizational needs, vision, mission and business plans. An evaluation can be carried out to understand whether competency building efforts can contribute to address such organizational need, thus identified. If it is so, the beginning for competency assessment can be launched.

Step 2: Define Competency Assessment Goals in Business Language

How launch of competency assessment programme and its outcome can positively influence organizational growth in monetary and non-monetary mode shall be clearly defined in measurable terms. This is the most critical phase in cost-benefit analysis. How the assessment can lead to diagnose the competency gap challenge, and how the same can lead to helping business growth and averting placing wrong employees to wrong positions or hiring right people to right positions, and how assessment can lead to alter of existing human resource applications must be dealt. Cumulative effect of all these can be summed up and cost benefit analysis from a monetary perspective shall be stated. There can be many non-monetary gains for organizations like good governance, improvement of morale and employee satisfaction with careers. These benefits shall be articulated in the form of competency assessment benefit objectives. Such benefits shall be compared with cost budgets and net value can be interpreted. Limitations of such cost-benefit analysis must be scrutinized objectively before the benefits of competency assessment are presented. For example, biggest limitation is how well the competency assessment objectives and programme details have worked out. It may not yield desired results if excellence in execution is not achieved.

Step 3: State Cost and Benefit Goals for each Competency Assessment Programme

The cost and the benefit it is expected to accrue for a systematic monitoring and to achieve precision, shall be stated. Based on this, every programme on its roll out can be measured for benefits and also mid-term corrections can be carried out.

Questions for Discussion

4.1 Write objectives and purpose of competency assessment programme? How it can benefit organizations in competency-based Human Resource Management?

4.2 What are essential requirements for launching a competency assessment proagrmme? How and why organizations shall decide upon implementing competency assessment programme?

4.3 What is the cost benefit analysis model of competency assessment progarmme? Does this really help in improving the bottom line for organizations? How does it help employees in enhancing their competencies?

4.4 How a competency assessment programme is developed and planned? Does it depend on type and size of organizations?

4.5 Write short notes on the following:

(a) Signs and samples
(b) Paper and pencil tests
(c) Case study method
(d) Critical incident technique
(e) Leaderless group discussion
(f) Projective tests
(g) Personality tests
(h) Career anchor assessment tests
(i) Bespoken vs off-the-shelf exercises
(j) Management games
(k) Rorschach inkblot test
(l) Murray's thematic test
(m) In-basket exercises

4.6 Discuss assessment center and various techniques and methods of assessment center.

4.7 Compare and contrast assessment center and development center.

4.8 What are the pitfalls of assessment center?

4.9 Define the process of assessment center.

4.10 Discuss experiences of organizations with assessment center as a popular method of competency assessment technique.

4.11 Write short notes on Clifton's strength finder as a competency assessment tool.

4.12 Discuss different approaches to competency assessment?

4.13 Write on 360 degree feedback as competency assessment technique?

4.14 Write on assessor manual development?

Case Studies for Discussion

1. ABC Corporation is an automobile manufacturing company and market leader in mid size passenger cars. It has over 1200 employees on the rolls working in a variety of departments including assembly plant, R&D, marketing and logistics. The corporation has well-defined competency framework which has been developed on careful mapping and modelling of competencies. However, the corporation is yet to apply the said competency model for any human resource applications including using it for assessing competency proficiencies of current incumbents of different roles. The corporation is hesitant to use it for competency assessment with a fear that it may demoralize employees especially those who may discover that their competency gaps are significant. However, there is also realization that unless competency assessment is conducted it is not feasible to approach Human Resource Management in a systematic manner. Discuss if you are human resource manager how will you approach this problem in the given situation? Will you advise the corporation to implement competency assessment progarmme? If yes, why do you recommend and what precautions you initiate to remove employee anxieties?

2. SoftTeq is an information technology product company engaged in data warehousing tools creation, development and maintenance. The company which had seen aggressive growth has started experiencing slow down though market is growing at a rapid speed. A key challenge factor for its inability to catch up with customer expectation and declining market growth is due to shortage of human resource competencies. The company had re-evaluated the business strategy, various processes and innovation and sales performance and found that the challenge lies in poor innovation and sales capabilities. The consultant's report show that the cost of launch of competency assessment is about USD 3 million given the global spread of the human resources. However, it is not clear what are the monetory benefits of such programme to the organization. There is an argument voiced by one section of leaders in the company that such initiatives do not benefit the company's financial condition, and rather they divert attention. Discuss how and what methods you can use to show the cost benefits of competency assessment progarmme? How can you convince the leadership team that competency assessment initiative can create a strategic focus rather than diverting the attention apart from generating a substantial growth fillip?

3. NMR Group is an infrastructure company having interests in irrigation, power plants and roads and buildings construction. The competency model of the company comprises a variety of competencies like strategic, leadership, functional, technical, behavioural and culture-related competencies. These competencies are also defined at different proficiency levels like fundamental, intermediate and advanced. The proficiencies are also linked to the grade structure of organization as well as nature of roles. The competency architecture show that need for higher proficiency in a competency if the grade of employee is higher. The complexity of the framework is the number of competencies and proficiency levels differ not only based on grade and nature of roles employees perform, but also depends on which group of company like power or irrigation the employee works for. The group management has taken a decision to use the competency model for competency assessment of employees. Human resource department has been asked to develop competency assessment manual, assessment tools and plan for implementing the assessment over 180 managers. Based on competency model it can be stated that a variety of competency assessment tools, techniques and methods are required to be deployed in order extract scores of employees on each of the competencies. For example, assessment tools required to assess strategic competencies like envisioning and decision-making can be different from the tools required to identify proficiency in behavioural competencies like positivity and cultural agility. The mandate and reading of the need suggests that assessment techniques like assessment center, 360 degree feedback, management games like role play, critical incident technique and projective techniques that glean underlying beliefs, personality techniques and also analytical methods are required for effective assessment of competencies.

You are given the role and responsibility of building assessment manual comprising methodology and techniques of competencies assessment. Explain what techniques and tools you suggest for building exercises for what kind of competencies? Do you see the need to establish the compatibility between a particular assessment technique with a particular type of competency? What are the essential elements of a competency assessment exercise tool kit? What are the merits and demerits of having to build such a manual? How do you validate the competency assessment exercises?

Reference

Thornton, G.C. III and W.C. Byham (1982): *Assessment Centres and Managerial Performance*, New York: Academic Press.

CHAPTER 5

Competency-Based HRM Applications

Organizations can and must make progress towards deploying competency orientation to other important Human Resource Management applications like talent hiring, development, compensation, performance and career management systems. Such a journey can begin only when human resource competencies are mapped, modelled and assessment technologies are developed. It is not apt for organizations to jump start with competency-based Human Resource Management applications without going through successful completion of three dimensions of competency management: mapping, modelling and assessing as discussed in the foregoing chapters.

Objective of this chapter is to discuss how competency-based human resource applications can be developed and implemented in organizations for greater talent and business gains. The chapter is organized into five parts: Part I deals with competency-based talent hiring practices like competency-based job descriptions, specifications, resource planning, candidate evaluation, interviews and selection and induction (see Figure 5.1). The sole purpose and outcome of any training and development effort hinges on competency development. However, many organizations undertake training and development efforts more as knowledge imparting exercise rather than as means to create and build well-defined competencies those can significantly contribute for employee and business growth. How a competency approach can help and catapult an organization into a truly competency-based learning organization and their essential features are vividly discussed in Part II.

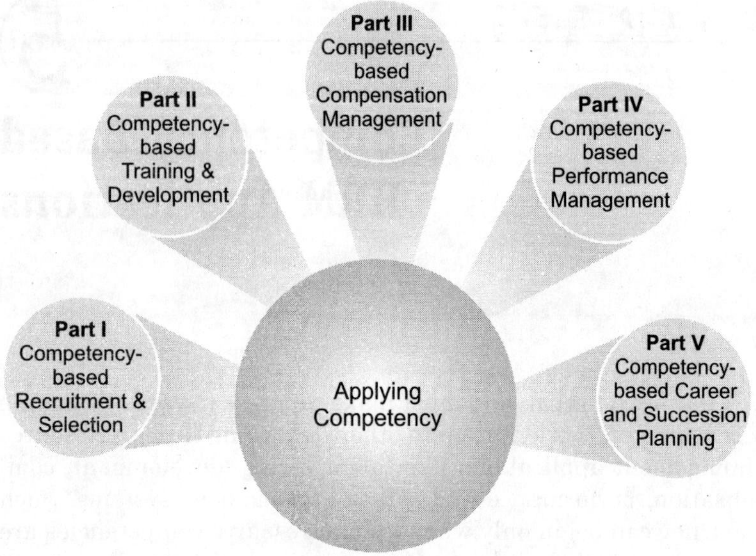

FIGURE 5.1 Competency-based HRM Application.

Part III presents how competency management can be used to define and re-define compensation and reward structure, where in higher competencies and higher proficiencies are valued higher in the compensation value chain. Also, how competency-based approach can create rational equity and work effectively to remove compensation anomalies are described in this part of the chapter. Part IV is dedicated to present competency-based performance management on the premise that competency excellence and lack of excellence as a reliable predictor of how an organization will perform and how well employees individually and collectively can perform. Competency-based goal setting, competency-based performance appraisal and feedback system are some of the key themes this part captures. Part V deals with careers in the context of competency management. Competency-based career management explodes the myth of career planning as a mere vertical growth which is centered around promotions and grades and titles. More importantly, career planning systems of organizations designed to provide vertical growth have shown formidable limitation in providing career opportunities to all employees and also quite a few of career systems have led employees to chose career paths which are not meant for their interests and capabilities. Such systems have given fillip to aspirations to attain titles and power and have not any appreciation to capabilities resulting in poor leadership mettle and low innovation literacy in organizations. In contrast, competency-based career planning system discussed how each and every employee can gain unlimited opportunities to grow in career in line with their proficiency and clarity of competencies they possess. At the end, the chapter summary provide a bird's view of competency-based Human Resource Management applications and their background.

Part I: Competency-based Recruitment and Selection

Competency-based recruitment and selection can be defined as a process in which every candidate is assessed for competency proficiency related to a job/position through a well defined set of action-oriented assessment tools. Importantly, they are less tested for intelligence and tested more for their understating and application capability. This is not as simple as applying one or two process steps to understand superficial attitude flavour of a candidate, but a comprehensive method to understand the natural and acquired competency strengths of a person. For many years, recruitment and selection process is solely drawn from testing of intelligence with heavy bias to assess information the candidate holds rather than their interpretation and decision capability. As a result, even top class selection tests have failed to yield desired results in establishing correlation between successes of a recruitee on the job to that of test scores that person had scored. In other words, the traditional selection test could not prove that candidates who score better in these selection tests could perform better on jobs comparing to other candidates who scored less in the same tests. In contrast, competency-based recruitment and selection process can hugely help hiring right candidates to right jobs at right level. Organizational competency framework and competency models can be used to develop selection tests. Especially competency assessment tools which are developed to identify and assess competencies of employees already employed in the organization can be extended to recruitment and selection. The art and practice of competency-based recruitment and selection can be developed by set of ten steps discussed as follows:

Step 1: Developing Competency-based Resource Planning

Human resource planning is often highly neglected area though it is of strategic importance to all organizations without exception. Right from the time of time and motion study perpetuated by Taylor's scientific management, human resource planning has been more of an approximate estimate of quality and quantity of human resources a particular operation require instead of an assessment with high precision. Human resource planning is often practiced on what people manning the roles and their managers say, and is seldom based on scientific assessment of requirement. Therefore, human resource planning in many organizations has been the victim of Parkinson principle or mythical man month (Brook's law). If human resources are precious and success of organizations largely dependent on the quality of such human resource, it is ironical that organizations do not pay required attention and commit themselves for a quality human resource planning study and exercise. One of the most scientific ways to approach to assess human resource requirements of an organization is drawing competency-based approach. In a competency-based approach, the thrust is on what kind of competencies and at what proficiency each level is required to man and manage a particular operation in highly optimized manner. A competency chart comprising type of competencies and their cumulative score is drawn. For example, to manage a paint shop in an automobile plant, as a first step, different competencies required and their proficiency level required is need to be mapped. Based on such mapping, other human resource applications like hiring, training and appraising can be done.

There are two essential components in a standard human resource planning process. These are: work load analysis and work force analysis. As the title suggest in order to successfully complete an operation, tasks are involved and their sequence and nature are studied as a part of work load analysis. The type of human resource competencies and their depth (proficiency requirements) are studied as a part of workforce analysis. There are multiple techniques that organizations use in human resource planning ranging from simply observing and studying the people performing a particular operation and coming up with quantity and quality of human resources required to systematically conduct time and motion studies to map automation needs.

BOX 5.1 Mythical Man Month

This is also known as Brook's law. Mythical Man month is an excellent book authored by Frederick P. Brooks J. Kenan Professor of Computer Science at University of North Carolina in 1975. The book deals with different aspects of software engineering and programming that include importantly human resource planning aspects in managing software projects. Frederick asserts that adding manpower to a software project late, further delays the completion of a project. This finding, now known as Brook's law in software and management circles, had shaken and continues to serve as a caution to information technology companies worldwide. According to the author, the man-month as a unit for measuring size of job is a dangerous and deceptive myth, hence the name—the mythical man month. What is mythical about the man-month based human resource planning? An example may help to drive home the point here. Consider a moderately complex software application from the early microcomputer era, such as the Lotus 1-2-3 or word star. Assume that such a program might take one very smart, highly motivated, expert programmer approximately for a year to design, code, debug, and document. Imagine that market pressures are such that we want to get the program finished in a month, rather than in a year. What is the solution? All probability you might say, get 12 experienced and smart coders, divide the work and project can be completed in a month. But Brook states that time cannot be wraped up so easily because 12 months does not equal to 12 programmers based on his experience as team leader managing the development of operating system (OS/360) at IBM. Why it is so? Because more the team members, more are the communication and coordination challenges. They tend to over-spend time on meetings, drafting project plans, negotiating inter faces and in this process progress can be adversely impacted due to the said group dynamics. Further, training requirements and performance speed of programmers also vary. In a nutshell, ancillary tasks will go up as size of team increases that include keeping one member of team as a leader, one for coordinating the team members' schedules, and another for housekeeping and one more for updating progress charts and so on. Many of the human resource problems in organizations can be

BOX 5.1 Mythical Man Month (*Contd.*)

attributed to the traditional method of assessing human resource requirements and adhering to time elapsed human resource planning techniques. Many conventional techniques of human resource planning do not augur well since the world of work has got completely transformed in the contemporary organizations. Unless human resource planning is systematic and accurate protecting value of human capital is far-fetched. Competency-based human resource planning has the potential to remove these obstacles and ensure the right people with right competencies for right roles are planned well. Indeed good competency-based human resource applications start with competency-based human resource planning practice.

BOX 5.2 Parkinson Principle

Parkinson principle has an important role in understanding and managing human resource planning in organizations. Cyril Northcote Parkinson, Professor at University of Malaya was the one who had propounded this remarkable principle in his book titled 'The Parkinson Principle'. There are two vital elements within Parkinson Principle. These are:

1. Work tends to expand to fill the time available for its completion. In other words, the task to be completed increases in its perceived importance and complexity in a direct ratio with the time to be spent on its completion. For instance, an architect who generally requires a week's time to complete a building plan would tend to spend two weeks for the same task if the time given is two weeks.
2. The number of employees in any working group tends to increase regardless of the amount of work to be done. An official has to multiply subordinates and not rivals and officials have to work for each other. For example, a firm having 100 employees' takes a decision to set up a time keeping office and employs a junior assistant to look after the same. After a couple of years, the said employee makes an appeal to the management that lack of career growth is de-motivating him. On consideration, management promotes him as senior assistant. After a few months, this employee pursues management to add a junior assistant to work along with him and this junior assistant becomes senior assistant and the existing senior assistant becomes chief assistant and both of them add another junior assistant.

Any organization when it grows big and start employing hundreds of people, it becomes a self perpetuating empire creating so much internal work that it no longer needs any contract with outside world. Parkinson principle has important teachings for human resource planning. The most important lesson is that when human resource planning is based on people rather than on competencies it tend to breed inefficiencies and lead to adding more people and bringing down the efficiencies, whereas when done based on competencies the same can contribute for significant enhancement and optimization of human resources.

In this process, the approach of competency-based human resource planning plays a pivotal role. The major difference between competency-based human resource planning practice to that of conventional models of human resource planning process are: competencies are considered as cardinal in assessing requirements of human resources rather than just number of people required with particular academic qualifications. What technical, functional, strategic, leadership, cultural and behavioural competencies are required and at what proficiency are they required in reference to successful execution and completion of a task/operation/project/activity will be studied as a part of competency-based human resource planning. The competency framework of an organization will be extensively used for this purpose. In fact, human resource planning is the first HR application in a competency-based HRM management. A typical competency-based human resource planning ends the activity with an inventory of number of competencies required. This inventory will be translated into number of people required who possess these competencies. For example, when this translation is done, the competency-based human resource planning would stipulate that a specific number of people required with the prescribed competencies and at prescribed proficient levels for a defined duration.

Step 2: Developing Competency Descriptions and Specifications

In a traditional recruitment and selection process, job descriptions and specifications are developed which can be used for hiring and placing people, whereas in a competency-based approach, competency descriptions and specifications are developed. A successful competency-based human resource planning would provide an inventory of competencies required, their sequence and cluster. Based on the outcome of such planning exercise, the competency descriptions are developed. For example, competency Set-I may require a combination of technical and analytical competencies and Set-II may require leadership, strategic and cultural competencies and Set-III may require a combination of functional and behavioural competencies and Set-IV may require combination of the three sets. Once such cluster-based job descriptions are developed, the same can lead for competency specification statement creation. The specification statement is nothing, but a minimum acceptable proficiency requirement in a given cluster. It means the set of competencies will be arranged in a hierarchical manner classifying them into 2, 3 or 4 levels or as appropriate facilitating to use in a particular competency specification for a particular role. Each of the set can be called as competency description statement and the levels can be defined as competency specification. The competency description document will bear properties like the nature of activities, tasks, responsibilities, decision-making areas on one side and competency requirement against each of such tasks/decision-making on the other side. An organization can create as many competency descriptions as it may need depending on the purpose. However, it may need to create and make available role-based competency descriptions for every role or set of similar roles for the purpose of competency-based recruitment and selection. Such competency descriptions also can be used for a variety of human resource applications like compensation management, career planning, succession planning and so on.

Step 3: Developing Competency-based Hiring Plan

An effective recruitment and selection process is a prerequisite to a good competency-based hiring plan for attraction and selection of talented human resource. The hiring plan must contain details such as the kind of competencies required to be hired, the target date by when such competencies are necessary and location and the purpose of hiring. The plan also can provide details of value addition to the business due to such hiring, details of hiring managers and sequence of hiring like what shall be hired on priority and what can be brought on board over the course of time. Often organizations neglect the significance of creating a competency-based hiring plan and leave it partially defined resulting in unsystematic hiring and loss of attracting real talent. Such competency-based hiring plan must have a direct linkage and correlation with business plans. Usually organizations have hiring plans in the form on number of people required and the cost associated with it and not number of competencies required and their business value to organization. Therefore, from a critical perspective, it is a huge change management since organizations need to think of a competency mode and not in number of people perspective and from a value perspective rather than from a cost point of view. Competency-based hiring plan also give a positive touch to organizations efforts in hiring talents. The plan also preferably should deal with where and at what concentration the competencies are available in various geographies and the market value and price of such competencies. This is also called as market mapping of competency availability/supply. Market competency mapping can hugely help in cutting down the turnaround time for recruitment and selection and also can save hiring financial budgets for organizations. Preferably hiring plans also must deal with talent attraction mechanisms in reference to type and nature of competencies. For example, what media and talent pool source shall be used to attract telecom technology competency professionals and what media shall be used to attract finance competency professionals likewise, because the media and source of talent must be apt in line with kind of competencies being planned to be hired.

Building mutual attraction in the place of merely organizations trying to attract candidates (one sided attraction) should be the priority. One-sided attraction will definitely fail to accrue the real benefits. Competency-based hiring plan must also reckon certain practical aspects of how to build brand image not only for the organization, but also to the practice of competency-based hiring process. The process itself has the potential to arouse interest among the candidates especially those seeking to make meaningful impact through their performance. Using competency-based hiring as an instrument of building a good brand in the employment market is a practical idea. Putting competency-based employment advertisements and making competency-based recruitment presentation in engineering and business schools and job fairs are some of the avenues. An organization should identify, chose and position its key competency focus, for example, innovation or execution excellence or transition or solution building as the central theme for the competency-based recruitment branding.

Developing competency-based employment applications and resumes is another important milestone in developing competency-based hiring plans. Qualifications and experience based employment applications generally create an impression that all candidates responding to vacant positions are homogeneous, whereas the competency-based application formats can throw a clear light on the heterogeneity in the light of competencies. Shortlisting and identifying suitable profiles for positions become easy and less administrative overload for organizations. It also becomes easy as well as logical to explain candidates why some are listed and some are rejected. Creation of competency codes and automation of short listing process in particular and resume uploading in general can help organizations significantly.

Step 4: Developing Competency-based Assessment Tools/Tests

This step is not intended to start developing competency assessment tools and tests since it presupposes that such tests must have been developed as a part of competency assessment methods discussed in Chapter 4 of this book. The objective of this step is to leverage competency assessment methods those have already been established in an organization. As a part of this step, assessment methods available must be validated in the context of hiring plans and objectives, especially what kind of competencies and at what proficiency levels are to be hired. It is imperative that there must be sharply relevant and correlated assessment tests and tools identified for each of the competency and also for a set of competencies together. Those candidates which are shortlisted based on their competency profiles against competency descriptions of the company need to be subjected to these assessment tests. The tests can be self-administered or administered by trained professionals depending on the design and implementation mechanism of such tests. The tests also can be paper-pencil based on online tests. Often there may be competency assessment tests and tools readily available in organizations, but largely they might have been styled for internal assessments. In such scenario, the methodology and preparation for implementation tend to be different, because when such tests are administered on new candidates the type of preparation required can be potentially different. This is essentially true when considering various guidelines and introductory mechanism. Potential job seekers can be wary and may be hesitant to take the tests as method of assessing their competencies and fitness to perform the job, because traditional methods largely reply upon their qualifications and chronological experience including type of organizations they have worked for both (currently and in the past). It also may not be legal to expose the potential future employees to these tests as assessments for selection decision without clearly establishing their reliability and validity and establishing ethical and social standards of such tests. Therefore, every organization applying competency assessment tools as methods of selection must upfront brief and educate the candidates the nature and purpose of these tests.

This step is primarily intended to shape-up and transform the existing competency assessment tools and tests as recruitment and selection competency assessment tools. Also developing suitable ice breakers and guidelines those can ensure that candidates are at ease and willing to take up these tests in right spirit. This involves change in mental makeup of candidates too since they must have been largely used to traditional methods of testing for selection. Especially experienced and aged candidates tend to be apprehensive of this process and would be keen to understand their implications before they accept to subject themselves through this process. This step particular shall be geared to address such concerns and facilitate to remove the apprehensions in a positive and constructive manner. Sometimes, regardless of reliability and validity and relevance of such assessment tests, the cultural issues involved on administering the tests if is not addressed satisfactory the testing can be a failure and may not yield desired results to the organizations. Hence catalytic aspects of assessment tests administration is the most important step in customizing and applying competency assessment over the potential employees as a part of recruitment and selection.

Step 5: Developing Competency-based Interviewing

Interview method as a technique of recruitment and selection is ubiquitous and used by almost all organizations across the globe. Competency-based interview process is qualitatively different from that of traditional interview process used in organizations. In traditional form, the structured interview process is used and many candidates are used to it, experienced with it and make shadow practices to present themselves in the manner that can guarantee them success in interview rather than in the job. Seldom unstructured interview technique is leveraged in traditional hiring process. Competency-based interview technique largely use situational-based and unstructured approach exploring the competency proficiency and passion of the candidates and their linkage to positions on hiring plan. In a competency based interview technique the candidates are expected to explain what competencies they use on regular basis in their jobs and how they have impacted their work and outcomes given to organizations in a story and descriptive form. Candidates also can use not only work settings but also personal and social settings in driving home the point that how they use their competencies to pursue, convince, win, collaborate and create ideas or achieve something. Box 5.3 shows types of interviews.

BOX 5.3 Types of Interviews

Though researchers have come up identifying different methods of interviews as variant as almost 50 types, primarily there are three types of interviews. These are:

1. *Biological interview:* Discussion between interviewer and interviewee centers on the facts stated in employment application or popularly known as curriculum vitae or biodata. Candidates spend considerable time to explain their academic background, work experience, personal details, and hobbies in a chronological order. Such an explanation provides the journey, background and evolutions in a candidate's life. Though this is very important part of any interview, it often sounds repetitive as the information is already available to the interviewer in written form at much before meeting the candidate in person. The benefit of personal meeting is limited since rarely any unknown or key insights are gathered in a biological

interview which is not stated on the paper. However, still biological interview is an important part of interview technique as it creates an opportunity to validate and understand a candidate's real biodata and seek any additional information that may be needed. Competency-based interviewing cares for this element as much as in traditional interviews with a differencc that such an interview is essentially focused on linking the biological information to establish link or lack of link with competency descriptions of the role or roles for which a candidate is being considered.

2. *Backward looking interview:* Encouraging a candidate to talk about past successes and failures and what they mean to that person, how learning occurred and how it probably altered the perspective are some of the topics which are discussed as a part of backward looking interview. Backward looking interview substantially improves the chances of understating a candidate's competencies in areas like, analysis, reflection, approach of learning, positivity, negativity and presentation style and focus. Adding unstructured questions in flow with situation can yield fertile information about the candidate. Definitely backward looking interview can help interviewer to understand a candidate much more powerfully and validate against the competency description of a role. Diagnosis of behavioural patterns and exploring a candidate's competency in areas such as decision-making, conflict resolution, collaboration, confrontation, openness, trust, authenticity, proactiveness, creativeness, self-awareness are some of the competencies those can be discovered with reasonable reliability.
3. *Forward looking interview:* While backward looking interview capture the past and how it shaped a candidate's behavioural and value system, forward looking interview tries to capture the aspirations and goals of a candidate. This method is also based on situational and unstructured interview category. There are no hard and fast rules in raising topics for discussion within the purview of interview ethics. Information gathered as a part of this discussion can be cross validated against biological and backward looking interview information to draw pertinent inferences in deciding a candidate's fitness to a role and confirming against competency description of a role. It is desirable to bring to the attention of a candidate if any contrary information or views are noticed among these interviews for a clarification and remove anomaly in assessment.

In traditional interview form, the technique is just confined to gather some preliminary information and do the routine intelligence testing which may not be very relevant for predicting fitness and success of a candidate in a role. Further, intelligence testing-oriented interviews are nothing, but a type of cognitive ability tests in oral format. Studies show that interview as recruitment and selection technique has least reliability among variety of assessment tests, and especially, the traditional form is fraught with many limitations like bias and halo effect. Competency-based interview comprise biological, backward and forward looking discussion to some extent can gather information which can be relevant and useful for selection decision. In order to be successful, it is highly advisable that interview objectives are set clearly, competency descriptions are translated into interview discussion format, interviewers are trained on competency descriptions and cues that they should look for in candidates, and candidates guidelines are clearly defined describing cultural aspects and interpretation directions are set for use. Cultural aspects also gain prominence since the same influences how a candidate approaches interview and behaves. For example, Asian candidates try to please and would not like to provide no confronting answer though sometimes they may not believe in what an interviewer may be stating. Competency-based interviewing can be used in combination with other testing mechanisms for discovering strengths and limitations of candidates seeking roles.

Step 6: Developing Competency-based Selection Decision Criteria

Making sure that managers who are given responsibility and authority to take selection decisions are well trained is important in competency-based recruitment and selection. Organizations need to develop selection decision-making criteria, and also need to ensure those standards are applied to all candidates in equitable manner. Never a selection decision can be drawn based on results of one method/tool/test as most of the techniques we use in selection testing are not necessarily exact science. Therefore, it is rationale approach choosing multiple sources of information like, psychometrics; paper pencil based tests, aptitude tests, cognitive ability tests and interview results and cross reference the information for arriving into final decision. Often test administrators and interviewers, due to lack of concentration or due to prejudice, may omit some vital information or get influenced by recent experiences. All such limitations can be overcome when multiple techniques and their results are used for decision-making. However, comparing, contrasting and consolidating results of multiple tests are easier said than done. It is because sometime results may come in conflict with each other. Guidelines to deal with such situations and methods of analysis should be standardized. Such standardization can be done around competency descriptions. The results need to be classified and factored against each of competency drawing evidence and test results from all the assessment tests that a candidate must have undergone. Some organizations also develop equations to sum up the results and achieve objectivity in drawing predictive scores. Weightage for a competency may also differ based on the nature of a role. Negotiation may the most important competency for sales role and compliance may the most important competency for a taxation role. Taking into account all these realities, it is necessary that organizations have equation formula and benchmark predictive score for each role or set of roles for facilitating a selection decision. Guidelines would help to ensure quality of hiring and also uniformity.

Step 7: Developing Competency-based Selection Fitment Criteria

Not only identifying right candidates with right competencies is important but also placing them into right levels within an organizational structure is important too. Sometimes after going through all the selection exercise, organizations tend to lose candidate, because of fitment issues. Developing and implementing a systematic fitment is an integral part of competency-based recruitment and selection. Fitment criteria should include details like competency description of a role, various proficiency levels, benchmark scores and how predictive competency score of a candidate can be evaluated and compared against these standards in order to arrive into a fitment. If an organization has applied competency framework to compensation management too, then it becomes easier for an organization to fix compensation and benefits in commensurate with competency quotient. The same principle applies for grade fitment too. If an organization is already implementing competency-based organizational structure and career planning system, then it becomes logical to extend the same principle for fixing the grades for new hires based on their competencies and proficiencies. If the grade fitment is not on competency criteria, but based on conventional mode of years of experience and academic background alone, it tends to nullify the objective of competency-based human resource applications. Also, such conventional fitments can cause disparities and defeat competency approach. Organizations those practice competency based Human Resource Management clearly laid down competency and compensation matrix and compensation and grade matrix clearly for uniform implementation.

Step 8: Developing Competency-based Offer Management

Making appointment offer and rolling out to the selected candidate is a normal activity in any hiring process, but the terms and format of it can substantially be different when the selection and hiring is based on competency approach. In an employment market of conventional human resource practices, wherein appointment offers and employment terms are based on hierarchical grades and designation titles, it is important to effectively communicate the candidates how the competency-based fitments and competency-based compensation works. Entry and exit clauses, compensation/increments/performance based variable pay/bonus, career planning practices, performance appraisals, training etc. will be in consonance with competency expectations and meeting stipulated requirements of competency descriptions of a role from time-to-time. These all can be, to an extent, new to quite a few candidates. Therefore, preceding the roll out of an offer with a good educational communication about the content of offer is a pre-requisite for better understanding. This can be done in person meeting or through media. An offer issued without an oral brief to candidates can meet only with partial success that too at the expense of candidates creating their own understanding.

Step 9: Developing Competency-based on Boarding Process

Organizations usually utilize the first day of people joining them to fill up various forms and to set up the administrative and logistical aids like setting up an e-mail account, allotment of work station, opening of bank account, healthcare insurance, so on and so forth. Undoubtedly, all these are important activities but the on boarding process also can be leveraged for driving competency culture and behaviour in organizations. Day one provides good opportunity to capture the competency history of candidates and validating them against employment applications and tagging the information into competency inventory of an organization. In order to fulfill this, organizations need to look at their forms and day 1 on boarding process and re-orient them towards competency architecture and even having information forms to be filled by the candidate competency-ladder wise. Though on boarding is meant to be more of administrative in nature, it is important as this process is used to drive the competency behaviour in organizations.

Step 10: Developing Competency-based Induction Process

The last and the most critical step in competency-based recruitment and selection is developing and implementing competency based induction programme. Often induction programmes in organizations are confined to introducing company information like vision, mission and objectives, organizational structure and departments and customers so on and so forth. Undoubtedly all these are important, but what is more important is gaining this opportunity to impress upon on the new employees about competency-based human resource management approaches and how it will positively impact their work-life and career. It is desirable that organizations draw induction process curriculum around organizational and human resource competencies and how they lead to what they produce and deliver to customers. This is also an opportunity to take all the new employees through the entire width and breadth of competency framework. The essence of competency-based Human Resource Management applications start with right induction into competency movement.

When induction progarmmes largely focus on company information and designed to prepare employees just to settle down at work place will not be able to contribute to lasting impact on employees. Such process can fulfill only hygiene factors, but definitely will not create excitement and motivation. Well-established fact is that organizations face infant mortality (early attrition) due to ineffective induction programmes where employees do not see much difference or avenues to realize their potential. In a competency-based induction process, the emphasis is how competency is at the center of training, performance, career and succession planning and compensation management in organizations. How competencies can be reliable predictors of effective performance and the need for employees to develop a personal competency enhancement plan for which organization would render all the support. Induction process should be utilized to encourage new employees to develop personal vision statements for themselves how they would achieve their career goals through building competencies and how such competency building can be detailed with organizational competencies and business growth. It would provide immense clarity and direction to employees when they build a competency-based personal vision statements. Such statements can be linked to an employee training, career and compensation systems in all logical manner. Through this approach, employees will be able to see not only how they are approaching their work in a new organization, but also see a long-term working and career for them, This will provide stability to the employees as well as to organizations. Objective of a competency-based induction process must be to inspire new joines to look at their work and career from a new perspective—a perspective where competency and proficiency matters more than titles and designations and a perspective where they are masters of their careers and not dependent on organization to provide them some vertical career movements which give short-term fulfilment and debilitate in a long-term, because it is competency that sustains long and not the titles.

Part II: Competency-based Training and Development

Training and development is the king pin of competency-based Human Resource Management applications. Competency approach has direct and strong positive correlation between competency approach and training and development practices. How the training needs are identified, classified and consolidated, how training efforts are evaluated, how training initiatives are executed—all have immense value to competency movements in organizations. Competency-based training is qualitatively different from traditional pedagogical training methods especially when it comes to imparting the training. These aspects however will be discussed in detail in the following content. The advantage with applying competency approach to training efforts is unlike other human resource systems where the gestation period tend to be longer for yielding the results, here the results can come forth sooner and straighter manner. Another important advantage is the competency movement which can begin with training and development arena, unlike other functions where unless and until a basic competency framework is in place it is difficult to make a beginning on those areas of Human Resource Management. A scientific competency-based training and development application follow the following key steps:

Step 1: Developing Competency-based Training and Development Plan

The maiden step in extending competency approach to training and development is building a serious business case. Why, what and how the training is intended to support employee and organizational growth must be evaluated and a credible description shall be appended. Such a training and development plan should be seen and establish a clear linkage at every stage of business plan in a way that can be qualified as strategic training plan. While achieving such an objective, it shall bear in mind that training effort need not be a dependent variable reckoning business as independent variable. This is because in a competency-based training and development approach, training has the potential to perform an independent role and influence the journey and shape the business growth especially in a knowledge economy. After all in a knowledge economy, it is the competency and competency proficiency of people that is going to determine whether an organization can be successful or not. There are many organizations which have aspirations and plans for business growth, but there are very few organizations that have a salutary operational plan especially from people competency building perspective how they want to achieve. A good competency building plan in the form of training and development is as useful as a good strategic business plan for a company. Developing competency-based training and development plan would involve understating customers and markets of the company business, organizational growth plans, technology, marketing and investments and also competencies associated with such dimensions of the business. How competencies would be build through training and development, investment thesis, infrastructure requirements and facilities, curriculum aspects, faculty and courses and so on need to be detailed in the plan both in strategic and at operational mode. It is not necessary that all the trainings would take place in the class room, a few of it may be on the job or using simulation or special projects or long-term coaching: so based on nature of competency and methodology that would be appropriate can be planned and described in the training and development plan. The plan also should aspire to create own IP (intellectual property) in the form of course curriculum, reading and reference material, instruction methodologies suiting to its set of competencies. A typical competency-based training and development plan starts with articulating its objective, operational plan and milestones apart from investments and beneficiaries of the plan as discussed. The presence of such plan immensely helps organizations to pursue the training and developmental plans in a logical and sustainable fashion and accrue valuable benefits to organizations and employees. Absence of such plans pave the way for haphazard and piece meal efforts not creating proportionate benefits and impact in organizations. It is also desirable that the plan also briefly focus on philosophical underpinning of competency based training and developmental approach: this is dealing with aspects like whether competency building among employees is based on strength enhancement paradigm or weakness correction or combination of both. Ultimately the plan should be capable of helping all concerned to clarify and provide them a direction in their role as a participant or a contributor or a leader or a trainer or an auditor. In order to develop the plan, all these role holders must be consulted and be involved under the guidance of experts and majority views shall reflect in the plan for a successful roll out.

Step 2: Developing a Competency-based Training and Development Needs Assessment

This is an optional step for organizations which already have competency models and assessment tools and use them extensively to identify and define training and development needs. Organizations which have a basic competency framework in place, but not converted them into assessment tools and even when converted not applied to individual or a group of employees to identify the needs, it is important that such organizations need to take up the needs assessment study in a formal way. The training needs assessment study can be at three levels—organization, department/function and individual employee level. Again the same can be for a year (immediate term) mid-term (3 years) and long-term (5 years). Training needs assessment must flow from training and development plan of organizations. The needs shall be identified against the pronounced competencies of organizations in the same way those competencies are defined in organizations. In case if an organization does not have a defined competency framework then the immediate step should be to use the opportunity of training needs assessment study to define the competency framework. The basic difference between traditional training needs assessment and competency-based training needs assessment is to identify and plot the needs in the light of required competencies and their proficiency level rather than at a generic aptitude and base skill level. Therefore, the need to have a well-defined competency framework is fundamental for competency based training needs assessment exercise.

Competency-based training needs assessment prerequisites two more key aspects. These are individual employee-based training needs assessment and approach of continuous training needs assessment. Traditional training needs assessment studies also cover the training needs at individual employee level, however often when it comes to utilizing them they depend on group level classification. It is essential in competency-based training and development system that the data of training needs collected at each employee level need to be given higher importance and need to be preserved as a master data record. Secondly, training needs assessment approach should clearly articulate how this need assessment is a continuous process providing live data on developmental needs rather than one time initiative.

Training need assessment should be conducted once a year covering all the employees and all competencies. Methods of assessment can include: formal testing, self assessments using standard inventories, manager evaluations, committee evaluations, performance appraisals, critical assignments and simulation exercises, competency descriptions and interviews. The data obtained using all these methods must be consolidated and competency needs should be plotted for each employee, department and organizational level. The consolidated training needs can be published as competency needs by appropriately aligning them to organizational competency framework. Competency based training needs assessment need to be a systematic activity and shall be comprehensive for greater results. Often organizations chose one or two methods to identify training needs which may not give robust results, because sometimes job incumbents believe their training needs tend to be imaginary and actual needs may stay in sideways in such studies. The effectiveness of competency-based training and development largely comes from the health and reliability of the training needs data collected using training needs assessment. If this step goes wrong, or is incorrectly or partially executed can leave a lot more than what is desired. A good awareness among employees and pre education in organizations is vital for launching training needs assessment, because sometimes employees can be apprehensive and duly concerned with the consequences of such assessment. They may not be clear whether outcome of such training needs assessment would lead to development or redundancies or role changes. Hence, administrators of training needs study shall undertake a positive educational campaign presenting how the study will benefit them to enhance their competencies, and how data obtained at individual employee level will be maintained confidentially, and how their privacy and related rights will not be compromised, and most importantly how such data will be utilized for other human resource decisions like reward and punishment mechanisms.

It is also important that manager and employees who are assigned with the responsibility of training needs assessment are trained and have acceptability and credibility among large section of employees. Especially in global organizations it also assume importance under whose supervision and guidance such study is being conducted and whether it targeted at one group or multiple groups or regions. All such issues can be addressed if there is a good pre-training needs assessment awareness and communication campaign. Training needs assessment ought to be centered on strengths exploration rather than on weakness identification as an approach if it had to meet standards of competency-based training needs assessment approach. Also every employee shall have the opportunity to go through training needs assessment report of the self and validate the same. It it spirited agreement that go long way in building competency-based Human Resource Management. Training needs also shall be identified and defined at proficiency level as captured in the competency framework standards of an organization. It is generally seen and evidenced in organizations that though training needs are identified, but their proficiency levels remain undefined leading to huge gap in competency building exercise despite of good efforts.

Step 3: Developing Competency-based Training and Development Calendar

Once competency-based training and development process is completed successfully and published various competency needs of an organization, the next sequential step is defining competency-based training and development calendar at multiple levels. The calendar is nothing but publishing various courses in consonance with competency needs thus identified. This may be called as competency building and enhancement calendar, wherein details such as: nature of courses and how it is useful to build a particular competency, curriculum, sub themes, pre-training study requirements, eligibility criteria and dates and venue, faculty details and previous batch history is provided in the most useful manner. It is not unusual for some calendars to contain feedback reports provided by earlier participants' independent to its nature whether they are positive or negative, but essentially aimed at giving 360 degree view of the course. Competency-based training and development calendar should not be designed and understood like the normal training calendars published across organizations and training institutions; here the objective and concept of calendar is, it shall rise to the level to guide an employee who is seeking to build or enhance a particular competency, the advantages and disadvantages or appropriateness of choosing that particular course in their journey of competency building. A competency-based training and development calendar also addresses each employee what courses that employee shall undergo in reference to such calendar in the light of training needs identified for that employee. The number of courses offered and their frequency shall be proportionate to the need percentage identified in a particular organization. A competency based training calendar would never carry training courses/programmes those are not related to competency needs and is merely based on wish or feel good factor. No employee would ever be encouraged to seek participation in a course that is not related to that employee cluster of competencies and need so identified for that person. The calendar also shall help as self guiding document to an employee to plan their participation in a course in order to fulfill their developmental needs. No participation is automatic, but needs to go through something like statement of purpose and pre-course readings and adherence to reading requirements.

The single most use of a competency-based training calendar is to create awareness of the development opportunity available within the organizations for honing competencies. The calendar shall not be understood merely containing class room courses, but also shall be inclusive of project works, simulations, role plays, long-term on-the-job trainings, seminars, thesis presentations, paper presentations and so on. The calendar shall be used as a single source of information for all developmental activities rather than a mere ritual calendar containing a few traditional courses. It is also advisable that competency-based training calendar carry evaluation and feedback mechanism that is deployed in competency building programmes. The calendar shall drive a clear linkage between competency needs identified at each competency and proficiency level to training programmes thus incorporated. One should not lose sight of an important objective of a calendar that is the calendar itself must be capable of motivating employees to seek participation in competency building efforts rather than as a mundane task or something like better to do kind of attitude. Timeliness of publication of such calendar is important as it is seen with some of the organizations that calendars appearing in the middle of the year rendering what happened in the last few months as no relevant.

The calendar can be organized into as many parts as meaningful like technical, functional, leadership, behavioural sections and also programmes offered organization-wide, department-wise and a group of employees-wise or individual-based programmes. Most importantly, the calendar presents developmental programmes and initiatives in a competency-wise and proficiency-wise manner and useful methodological brief of instruction is also described.

Step 4: Developing Competency Compatible Training Infrastructure

It is often not about budgets and money alone how effective infrastructure can be developed paving way for competency building programmes in organizations. Many times, organizations spend disproportionate budgets and accrue poor benefits as the focus is on constructing building and creating and least on maintenance and sustainability. Also infrastructure is mostly synonymous with class rooms and simulations and less on technology and suitability of development aids for a particular competency. Therefore, in a competency-based approach, the training infrastructure creation hinges on what is required for each competency, because the aids and ambience required for imparting a technical competency like designing will be different from a behavioural competency like communication or empathy. Organizations unwillingness to give cognizance to such subtle variations can lead to greater ineffectiveness in competency building efforts. Ergonomics and adult learning imperatives shall be reckoned while designing training infrastructure. It is not about opulence or richness, but it is about compatibility and soul in the infrastructure that would create right ambience for harmonious learning. The infrastructure itself can reflect the type of competencies those are imparted at such place. The size and capacity would depend on the competency agenda and training and development plan developed at organizational level in short and long terms. There is no doubt that this will be a strategic investment for organizations especially to those which are knowledge-driven where competencies are nothing but prime drivers of growth.

The location of such infrastructure and multiplicity requirements should depend on competency enhancement requirements and not necessarily depend on size of an organization. In brief, this shall be the place where employees are motivated to come and transform themselves and a place where learning is religion and is sheer competency-centric. When organizations cannot create such infrastructure requirements which is competency-centric over a single effort can also plan in a phased manner, but the focus has to be on sustainability and longevity. Freedom from distractions such as noise, unpleasant temperatures, separation from the actual workplace, sufficient space for carrying out certain type of exercises, training aids like computers, over head projects, flip charts, white boards and so on fall under this category.

Step 5: Developing Competency Specialized Faculty

A high quality competency-based training and development cannot exist in any form without having a faculty which is highly competent in their respective areas of competency—both in subject matter and methodology of imparting. It is not uncommon with organizations spending efforts and focus more on infrastructure and structures and less on faculty and creation of conductive conditions where high quality faculty would like to stay and work. Organizations, especially large ones, are governed using stability, order, control and command principles which would be barriers for freedom seeking faculty who thrive in conditions like flexibility, discretion and ideation.

Faculty hiring methods, career and performance management also need to be defined clearly as the existing systems applicable to regular employees may not go down well for the faculty positions. Attempt shall be to blend some of the advantages of corporate organizations with advantages of top class educational institutions for better results rather than adopting one over the other. Competency building efforts suffer due to lack of quality faculty than anything else. Hence, there shall be a rigorous programme dedicated to build sound faculty. Job rotations and combining practising managers with academicians and consultants will greatly help to build the good faculty base. Apart from teaching responsibilities faculty when they have opportunities to do research and especially action research drawing from the organization would be a definite encouragement for a quality faculty.

It is desirable that for each of competency there shall be chair to promote advanced learning and research in that competency. A competency-based training effort shall aspire to establish a world class identity for each of competency through high quality training faculty and demonstration of their knowledge. Collaborations with similar institutes especially from faculty point of view and institutionalizing visiting faculty and exchange programmes also will go a long way in favour of faculty improvement. The general malady of executives who are ineffective at workplace being moved to faculty positions or merely some executives being highly successful in their positions cannot be understood as right people for faculty. Being good in subject knowledge at work place is one thing and ability to impart it something a different skill and not necessarily being good in subject will grant a skill of imparting. It is important that these maladies are factored while articulating and developing competency-based faculty who are truly specialized.

Step 6: Developing Competency Centric Courseware and Reading and Reference Material

Not many organizations give adequate emphasis on developing and making available customized courseware and reading material to employees. The core of competency-based training and development rests with the intellectual content. However, knowing very well that their value and usefulness is very high, organizations make efforts without much success. This is because developing courseware involves years of work, intellectual skills and deep understanding of competency which cannot be created through normal managerial reviews and cannot be produced through normal faculty and managers. The coursewares available to the employees are generally seen either very generic or not specially created for the competency and proficiency. Some organizations confine themselves making available off-the-shelf books, which may be useful, but may not fulfill the needs of competency requirements. The main difference between traditional training and developmental approach to that of competency approach is that the emphasis for building customized material is very high in competency approach. The material shall be organized competency-wise and also proficiency-wise, and all presentation material, case studies and analytical tools shall be standardized for optimal learning.

Availability of online libraries and journals and books is of great help, but the real value will come from customized reading and reference material. Organizations need to make consistent and continuous efforts to build the courseware in a work setting on adult learning, orientation, which would help to understand and appreciate the problems and solutions. It is not uncommon that employees become critical about reading material quoting them as very theoretical and conceptual texts, which reminds them of their school days rather than giving a hands on orientation. What courseware required in organizations for employees is mostly like manuals and handbooks, and less of textbooks and the manuals too presented in their world of work. There shall be atleast one courseware for each of the competencies, and each courseware shall have separate parts dealing with each of the proficiency levels of competency. This courseware shall give a look and feel of highly structured reading material suiting to requirements of employees undergoing the competency training. It shall cover concepts, case studies, problems, solutions, analysis and comments. Courseware developed for dissemination through online versions will also help significantly. Sometimes, classroom instructions or workshops may limit themselves creating awareness among participants, but courseware and reference material can substantially help employees who continue with their learning and keen to pursue further. Maturity of competency-based training and development practices of an organization can easily be understood when we go through the courseware preparation and their standards rather than through any other indicator. Organizations which have done serious efforts have always focused on a high quality reading and reference material for competencies. That would leave a long lasting impact and would truly create an IP kind of authenticity to competency-based approach. Case studies, games, role plays, critical incident history, action plays, and theme skits and videos, all should be the integral part of the courseware.

Step 7: Developing Competency-based Nomination and Participation System

Quality of competency-based training and development programmes come from quality of participants. Though the approach is not intended to carry a heavy filtration, but need to have intake quality control, because irrelevant participation would gradually weaken the rigour and quality standards of training programmes. Nomination and participation to competency-based training programme is expected based on competency assessment scores of employees. Employees who are found to have gaps (the gap between desirable standards/proficiency vs. actual proficiency of employee) will qualify to participate in a competency programme that is targeted at addressing fulfilling such gaps. These are called competency certification programmes. Many-a-time, organizations and managers encourage employees who are idle or employees to whom they want to reward are nominated to participate in training programmes in traditional approach, because there would be no selection process. In contrast, in a competency-based approach, there is a clearly defined and measured admission criteria for participation in any competency-based training programmes. Unless an employee fulfills the certification requirements of a particular level he/she will not be permitted to pursue higher level certification. It is a rational expectation that every organization pursuing competency-based training and development approach shall put in place an admission and participation criteria and publish it widely creating awareness among employees. The systematic admission process would give a fillip to enhancement of quality of programmes. Nomination to training programmes shall precede the announcement and with target dates facilitating completion of pre-course requirements. This is especially important where re-training course requirements are laid down which would become integral part of admission criteria. Batch size and blend of participation should depend on the demographics and competency type and methodology of training. Every participant would be expected to receive clear instruction before they come to participate in competency certification courses about the dos and don'ts and benefits of the programme.

Step 8: Developing Delivery of Competency-based Training Programmes

Wherever step 1 to 7 are practiced well, the delivery of competency-based training programmes is largely assured. Session plan, duration, breaks, faculty introductions, venue familiarization and facilities, welcome of participants all play their own little role in effectiveness of training programmes. All these arrangements, though appear small, have importance in the overall delivery of programmes. It must be ensured that the training programme should deliver what it had assured during pre-training communications and the implementation should be as planned without failure. Faculty drop outs, session cancellation, over runs and uncalled free time breaks all play dampening role so need to be cautious during implementation stage. The gap between schedule and actual implementation should be same for authenticity and faith in the programmes. From implementation perspective, it is good to have version and edition titles for each of competency programme for easy identification. The real success of competency-based training and development is in its implementation spirit. Therefore, execution of programmes shall be handled by the people whose competency for administration and implementation of learning activities is very high.

Step 9: Competency-based Training System Feedback and Post Programme Follow-up

Feedback plays an important role in competency-based training and development approach, wherein the feedback is mainly focused not mere on transfer of learning, but what participants feel about the actual competency building effectiveness. The feedback system needs to be created where the measurement of actual competency enhancement can be achieved. Seeking a new descriptive feedback would not help much, both in improving the programme as well as methodology. Generally, it is seen regardless of actual impact; participants tend to provide feedback which is highly range-bound leaving little that can be used. It is desirable that there shall be a kind of measurement or testing at the entry of competency-based training programme and repeat of which at the end of programme can provide the quotient of actual gain. Acceptable quotient or scores can be arrived for declaring a participant as successfully completed the participation. The average scores and trends can be used for analysis in order to understand the effectiveness of a particular competency certification programme. Feedback system in the context of competency-based approach has multiple items—general opinion to actual learning, testing to recommendations on what need to undergo a change or what improvement shall be done. So it is critical for organizations to allocate adequate time and pay required attention to this activity rather than rushing on the last day as a ritual for ending the programme. It is also an integral part of competency-based approach that post programme follow up and curriculum is created to keep competency certification holder update and refreshment reading is provided. It cannot be construed that once certification is given, it is done, like a one-time activity. Since competency assessment is continuous, the participation in a competency certification programmes also shall be continuous. Post programme follow up also can include tracking what participants reflect upon the programme over a period of time.

Step 10: Competency-based Training Evaluation

Indeed very important step in competency-based training and development human resource applications is—valuation of competency certification courses and their utility and value to organization and employees in highly measurable manner. This evaluation is beyond what organizations collect, collate and analyze the training feedback data. This step is intended to test and establish how competency certification programmes can result in business value at bottom line and how it can change the competency mix and proficiency of employees reflecting in enrichment of human capital. Competency-based training evaluation can be done at various levels—at transfer of learning level, competency enhancement level and business value level. The tools and methods required at each level may differ.

At a first level, the valuation must be done using pre and post training evaluation on participants. All participants can be taken through a sample testing before the competency certification programme, and the same test can be repeated after the programme and scores can be compared to see what kind of impact it has. The second method is to use the competency assessment tools of that particular competency, and obtain the scores to establish competency proficiency of participants. Also, participants can be subjected re-assessment of competency to see how the scores are emerging post-training. All these exercises help how much employees have learned, but they may not necessarily help whether there is an impact at work place. Therefore at second level, assessment need to carry out whether employees are able to transfer their learning at work place and are they solving more problems or they optimizing or they become productive or they become more innovative so on and so forth. Essentially what is evaluated here are the benefits a work place gains out of competency certification and proving that such participation is not mere an academic endeavour, but a practical competency enhancement that gives edge at work place. Therefore, the overall productivity or visible positive work place changes need to be tracked. Managers and customers feedback apart from actual productive measures can be sources for this evaluation. This is the most important level of evaluation for competency-based training.

The final and ultimate test of competency certification programme emanates from their business results. Whether enhancement of competencies has helped organizational business to grow or whether competencies lead to more success? Whether competencies lead to defect reduction? Whether they have helped in reduction of accidents? Whether it helped to enhance retention of employees? Whether it contributed for harmonious employee relations and reduction in unrest? Depending on the nature of business, the results measures can be developed and can be measured in relation to competency certification programmes. The intermediate or intervening variables have impact on the business need to be controlled while trying to establish the contribution of competency certification programmes over the business. Effectiveness of a competency programme at learning and transfer of learning to work place are positive, there is a clear chance for obtaining the positive business results. In that sense, need for obtaining positive results at initial levels is almost mandatory for training programmes to establish their contribution to business.

Return on investment is another scientific method that shall be deployed for establishing contribution of competency-based training approach, in general, and competency certification programmes, in particular. The direct investment (training budget both capital expenditure and running expenditure) and indirect investment (working days wages of employees and managers) need to be compared with competency training programmes have yielded in terms of monetary and non-monetary terms so to establish return on investment. Any good competency based training and development efforts must accrue benefits at least more than its investment by five times. The return can be in the form of productivity improvements, enhanced performance, optimization of resources, decline in input cost or increase in revenue or lesser number of people requirement for the same operation, innovation in processes resulting in efficiencies, increased customer satisfaction etc. Organizations shall establish a well defined criterion for carrying out such studies at regular intervals for establishing return on investment.

Part III: Competency-based Compensation Management System

If competency approach is applied for recruitment and training, the next logical step is extending the same approach for the employees the way they are compensated for their work and performance. Compensation system has remarkable impact and influence on employees, and if competency approach is applied to the compensation management system, the same can go a long way in institutionalizing competency-based culture in organizations. For several decades, compensation management is caught in the web of macro principles like cost of living and compensation structures, forever, are expanded to accommodate variety of benefits. Compensation is also mostly understood to be tied up with grades and designation titles, and years of experience, and are seldom based on competencies and proficiency of competencies that the employees hold. Since such traditional compensation models are not able to take cognizance of competency, organizations have come up with the models like performance-centric variables pay and skill incentives. These short-term measures like skill incentives and special allowances really could not address the issue that employee face or expect organizations to address. There are many organizations which face no success in attracting competent people or retaining competent employees, because their compensation method and structure tend to be far away from competency approach. It is extremely challenging for the organizations to create a competency-based compensation management on many accounts. Firstly, there is a huge cultural change involved since for many years organizations have never used competency as the central principle for compensation management. So when an organization which has been in existence for years and followed different model for compensation management like seniority, grade and performance, and moving it to competency-based compensation management can upset the fundamental structure that is in place all these years. It will be definitely easier to implement in organizations which are start ups or smaller in size. For big organizations or organizations in existence for years, the choice is not whether they will do or not, the choice is how they can do because Competency-based Human Resource Management can remain a pipe dream if the approach is not extended to compensation management which is at the root for institutionalization of competency-based approach. Apart from cultural issues, technical challenges do arise in creating a competency-based compensation management, because how do we decide which competency is higher and which competency is lower? Is it based on supply and demand of such competencies in the talent market or should it be based on pure complexity and depth of such competencies or criticality of particular competency to business and such criticality is by presence or by their absence? Since these questions are complex and difficult to develop plausible answers organizations fall back on traditional methods of compensation management, thus by weakening competency approach. However, organizations if committed, can make sustainable efforts which will take them to the goal of competency-based compensation management. For that, organizations need to take logical actions as discussed below in steps:

Step 1: Developing Competency-based Compensation Strategy

Compensation strategy in many organizations is not managed by conscious efforts, but is based on affordability of organizations and by market forces such as supply and demand of talent and also cost of living and wages of local labour markets. All these forces play their own role to influence the compensation approach. Many times organizations become susceptible to these forces and do not see through what factors and how they are playing a significant role. In such a scenario, organizations tend to be on defensive mode all the time and just respond to pressures either from employees or business. It would be ironical since compensation management which can give a strategic edge to organizations becomes something that ought to be defended. Therefore, it is important that enough thought is given where options are debated, and a particular approach is chosen for compensation management after a deliberate thought rather than an accidental management system. An organization need to consider the factors like what is the overall objective of compensation management? Is this simply paying for effort or would like to consider as an instrument to motivate and retain high performing employees? Would compensation be socialistic or differentiator? Whether an organization wants to be a great paymaster of the industry or just want to confine to the average like 50th percentile? Whether compensation levels are dependent on grades/levels? Whether it is dependent on seniority or performance? Whether it is dependent on location? Whether will it be dependent on person and person's background like qualification? Is it based on competency? Or is it based on host of all these factors? These questions shall be answered in compensation strategy document.

Competency-based compensation approach has the potential to answer all these questions. The strategy document just need to explicitly define and explain how the competency-based compensation management will be designed, and what is the objective it will achieve. How compensation equity and the approach to weigh and allocate credits to competencies will be achieved, and how such credit points will determine the compensation management need to be decided. Whether compensation level will be dropped if competency of an employee is downgraded through assessment and at what frequency the compensation level will be reviewed. The document can be used as a guiding principle to clarify the conflicting situations or divergent views. The document can be helpful to ensure consistency and continuity in approach. Absence of such strategy document can lead to managers to manage compensation in a piecemeal manner, sometimes conflicting their own decisions and operational approaches. Especially in a competency-based compensation management, it is more important to have strategy document in place.

Step 2: Developing Criteria for Relative Worth of Competencies

In a traditional compensation management, relative worth of jobs is evaluated using job evaluation methods, and sometimes position description methods. In the case of competency-based compensation management, it is ought to be competencies and their relative worth. Therefore, an organization which is aspiring to drive competency-based compensation management must have cleanly laid down and measurable competency model. It may be unusual for the organizations to have quantifiable and measurable competencies in organizations since mostly organizations even when they have competency frameworks those are mostly used for training and recruitment and seldom is such practice extended to arena of compensation management given the sensitivity and complexity. In order to apply the competency framework to compensation management, the first and foremost thing is competencies shall be given numerical value or relative value-based on a rational criterion. The criteria most recommended is to establish how each of the competencies in the framework can contribute to organizational objectives and bottom line. So the criteria can consist of:

1. *Monetary value measures:* Revenue, profits, cost-efficiencies, cost reduction, cost optimization, debt reduction, cash flow, DSO, productivity enhancement.
2. *Non-monetary value measures:* Employee satisfaction, customer satisfaction, industrial peace, credibility, authenticity, culture, employee retention, company branding, decision-making effectiveness.
3. *Combined value measures:* Innovation, breakthrough, leadership effectiveness.

Each of the competencies needs to be tested on how they contribute to value measures and at what level they contribute. Do they have a direct impact or indirect impact on these measures, and how the presence of each of these competencies alters the value an organization can accrue?

Some statistical tools like analysis of variance, chi-square may be necessary and control of intervening variable like external factors those possibly can influence the value measures need to be controlled in order to understand the contribution of each of competencies. Based on the level of contribution established, a quantifiable value can be assigned which in turn can be used for determining compensation level. Also, results obtained (competency numerical value) can be cross-validated with other measures like survey and position evaluation scores. For example, all relevant stakeholders like incumbents of positions, customers and mangers can be invited to rank the competencies in order of their importance to organizational value measures. Based on such survey, competencies can be arranged in an ascending or descending manner the way it is deem fit. Such survey results shall be cross-verified and referenced with statistical study.

Establishing competency value in relation to each other is more complex than traditional job evaluation methods, because of two prime reasons. One is effectiveness and contribution of each competency tend to vary depending on the person demonstrating the competency implying person has a significant role in competency-based approach comparing to position per se. Secondly, each competency can vary substantially in their contribution to organizational measures depending on the proficiency being used. Logically at higher proficiency, the same competency can contribute differently, also depending on the life cycle of an organization, and supply and demand of such competencies in the talent market can have profound impact on the relative worth of competencies. At the end of this step, organizations must come up clearly articulated criteria using one or more above ideas for establishing relative worth of competencies.

Step 3: Developing Socialization of Criteria for Broader Acceptance

Often, regardless of how robust and scientific the criteria may be for determining the worth of competencies, the same may or may not be acceptable to all stakeholders. If the acceptance is medium, resistance can create hurdles for rolling out competency-based compensation management system. There are experiences especially with corporate organizations that began undertaking competency-based approach for compensation management, but abandoned half way through because of strong resistance. This is due to variety of reasons. Understandably employees whose competencies are likely to fare below average in their importance would like to challenge the approach and employees whose competencies are faring at average also may join the group and sometimes competencies may be important, but people manning them may not be at the top of performance curve so the initiative is likely to get dampened because of the issues of these nature. Especially organizations and employees are used to compensation management on a different criterion like job/grades/designations for a long time and switching it to competency-based involves a good change management programme, and good change Management pre supposes effective involvement of all stakeholders. Therefore, once criteria is identified and developed, the same shall be presented to all stakeholders and debated. Any feedback received and suggestions made shall be valued and reckoned and incorporated in a rational manner. It is also advisable that competency-based approach shall be applied to compensation management only when such application to recruitment, selection, training and development are extended, and experience with such approach has been successful. Compensation area cannot be the area to start with for applying competency-based approach. Consensus and acceptance becomes easy when the approach has been successful in other areas. The probability of success with competency-based compensation management is high whenever the criteria for establishing relative worth of competencies is well known and accepted by all stakeholders.

Step 4: Implementing Competency-based Compensation Management

Once the criteria are successfully set and awareness is created among all stakeholders, an organization can approach with actual implementation. Implementation ideally should be in a phased manner rather than organization wide one shot implementation. It is better to pilot and test and proceed with large scale implementation based on ground reality. Any large scale implementation will fraught with a challenge of overwhelm if a mid-course correction is required. Compensation structure, and components need to be understood fully before competency-based structure is introduced. It is also seen that in many organizations, the compensation structure is influenced by taxation and other saving mechanisms. Though the basic value of compensation is determined by other factors. There are two critical decisions involved in implementing competency-based compensation roll-out. First is what percentage of total compensation shall be drawn from competency and what other components of compensation structure, and on what basis these are formed as a part of structure. An important aspect that shall be noted here is skill-based compensation qualitatively different from competency-based compensation roll out. A small part of compensation or one of the components can be skill-based compensation, whereas the lion share of compensation of employee come from competency in competency-based compensation structure. Other factors like grade/title/designation/location will remain important elements in skill-based pay. Competency-based compensation replaces the traditional base pay in terms of percentage of total salary pay out, and in terms of its importance in the total pay package of an employee. Competency-based compensation can be clustered implying a group of competencies at a given proficiency level and can lead to particular rate of compensation. Or broad bands of competency clusters can be developed in organizations in order to determine compensation levels. It is desirable that there shall be no more than 8 to 12 slabs of compensation-based competency and there shall be no more than 4 slabs within the same competency cluster both from administration and equity perspective. Also, care shall be taken while designing compensation package of employees that no less than 60 per cent of total compensation shall emerge from competency and proficiency of competency. If it is less than 60 per cent on the overall compensation value, competency tends to have no great influence on the competency behaviour of employees. Remaining compensation can be relating to factors like cost of living, retiral and other benefits. The 60 per cent compensation also can vary depending on importance of competency and its contribution on continuous basis against the criteria, thus finalized. All the competencies either can be ranked from 1 to whatever the number in order of their importance or sum of points can be assigned to each competency in consonance with their importance based on the criteria that has been set. Accordingly, either ranks or points can be translated into financial value for arriving into competency-based compensation value in the overall pay package of an employee. The explanation and rationale to an employee has to be very transparent or the formula must be made available to all employees to calculate their competency points and their financial value to arrive at the total competency-based pay. For example, every point can be valued at, say USD 100 and every employee will know how many points they can accrue based on the self competencies score and their contribution to business credit. When they calculate their points and convert them into total dollars, it will be clear for them how much they are paid and what basis they are aid.

Wherever proficiency of competency also has bearing in their contribution against set performance criteria, each proficiency level also shall be assigned the point value. For example, each competency can be defined at proficiency level like fundamental to mastery; each of these levels may carry points like—fundamental can be 10 points, whereas mastery may fetch 100 points. Again each of these points can be assigned financial value like 1 point may carry USD 100 and 10 points can carry USD 1000 likewise for determining the value of proficiency in each of these competencies. Therefore, sum of employee competency compensation comprises type of competencies, number of competencies and proficiency levels and the cumulative score obtained for each employee can be converted into financial value as per the formula and made easily understandable to all employees. When all these calculations and conversion formulae are published and made aware, the implementation of competency-based compensation management can be effective.

Step 5: Review and Renewal of Competency-based Compensation Management

An important question that arises is how often and at what interval and frequency, the competency-based management shall be reviewed and revised. It cannot be understood that the compensation system will remain static since the value of competency is arrived on. We need to be realistic that with changing business scenario and changing talent market dynamics and also sometimes based on the kind of talent emerging for particular competency clusters, the value and contribution level of competency tend to undergo change. So it is realistic expectation that compensation levels thus arrived and competency points thus finalized shall be reviewed, and this may involve reassessment of competency hierarchical architecture or competency significance using the established criteria. Such review and renewal sometimes will result in change of value points of competencies, and as a consequence competency-based compensation level also may change either upward or downward for some or more competencies. This frequency of review can be fixed like once in two years or as necessitated by business and market changes or technological changes in an organization. This has to be dynamic system where changes are captured in real time failing which the real value of competency-based compensation management will be lost. Also, individual employees now well aware of implications and importance of honing competencies will work probably hard to acquire either new competencies relevant to their work or make efforts to obtain higher proficiency. Therefore, even from such a perspective, it is a necessary that review shall happen regularly and constantly so that it works as a motivation for employees to acquire competencies and demonstrate utility and get rewarded appropriately. Competency-based compensation management could not gain popularity as it deserves and in fact the acceptance has seen decline, because of organizations inability to respond to changes quickly, and conduct assessment and compensation revisions as required timely. The success of competency-based compensation management at employee level definitely is dependent on timely reviews and revisions. In a traditional compensation model, there is an established system of reviews and revisions based on cost of living or industry practice of doing it at a particular time. Such established procedures may not be seen since competency application to competency management is new. Therefore it is critical that this issue is resolved and a framework for review and revision is created with an objective to make competency-based compensation management successful and valuable and to ensure employee get what aspire to see in competency-based compensation management. In circumstances wherever it is required there ought to be mechanism to review the established criteria that is used to determining the worth of competencies and point system to make the criteria methodology as dynamic and receptive.

Often administrators are in quandary whether such competency-based compensation management system is susceptible to traditional negotiation or bargaining as happens in wage revisions especially in brick and mortar companies. The solution is the framework that can be subjected to debate and negotiations and consensus, but once the methodology is fixed the actual financial values shall not be subjected to negotiations as that will undermine the competency movement. Competency-based management provide enough opportunity and flexibility even at an individual employee level, to earn higher wages by acquiring competencies and enhancing proficiency in competency, thus by contributing. The objective of competency-based management is not only to provide systematic method for arriving compensation but also to provide focus to employees growth and also to link employee to organizational work in highly constructive manner. Renewal framework shall factor all these realities.

Part IV: Competency-based Performance Management

One of the center pieces of competency-based Human Resource Management is performance management. The competency approach has unique proposition and potential to transform the way performance management is administered in organizations. It can be a total revolution in its approach and perspective. The traditional performance management models like goal setting even at its best form often is confined to task performance, leaving the crucial contextual performance unattended. Goal appraisal tend to be reduced to farce. Ineffective feedback sessions can rendered to be ritualistic in most organizations more often than seldom. Several studies clearly show that the most controversial and abused human resource system in organization is performance appraisal. It has created more despondency and loss of hope and confidence than it has given a direction, morale and learning to employees. Several organizations have many times made attempts to revise or change their performance appraisal system in their quest to bring in something that would help rather than harming the employee morale while attaining the objective of performance measurement. Even those organizations claim moderate success with their performance appraisal, fail to answer how their system helps in enhancing the performance rather than mere limiting itself to assessing and understanding the performance level of employees. Systems like bell curve and key result area dictionary and frequent interval appraisals too have not yielded the desired results, because all of them have looked performance management from a narrow perspective to extracting work from employees rather than making them passionate about their work. In contrast, competency-based performance management can offer an integrated approach where performance measurement is a minor factor and building high performance and transforming employees to aim and achieve self-actualization is the key. Competency-based performance management comprises following steps to introduce and institutionalize competency-based approach:

Step 1: Developing Growth Approach to Performance Management

Many performance management systems in organizations lack wholeness, sanctity and consonance. This is because, generally speaking, performance management system is understood as nothing but involving three dimensions of goal setting, apprising and feedback. The essence is lost because the real purpose and sense of performance management lies in enhancing performance and altering mediocre performance into great performances. Most of the times performance appraisal practices in organizations have imposed greater limitations in order to capture the performance rather unleashing the passion within the individuals. Performance appraisal has become sources of negative energy and breed greater distrust and unhealthy competition and comparisons rather than collaborations. Therefore, great deal of change management is involved to extend competency approach to performance management, moving performance management more of a regulatory, policing and pushing employees to encouraging, guiding, motivating and instilling a sense of growth and harmony. Quite a few organizations, realizing the importance of growth paradigm have tried to blend competency appraisal with performance of tasks. This approach cannot give them full success because of it is half-hearted attempt. The underlying approach and assumptions are very important to drive any initiative. Either organizations shall be committed to growth approach, where focus shall be building competency of employees with a trust and commitment that well competent employees produce great performance or they have to confine themselves to transactional performance which is limiting both from organization and employee point-of-view. This is called as growth approach to performance management, wherein organizations are willing to be patient and invest in building in competencies of employees with a belief that competencies are reliable predictors of good performance. It is a common sense to understand and interpret that how an incompetent or moderately competent person can ever deliver great performance, and how one may play their game well. Organizations have no choice, but to singularly focus on building competencies in order to achieve peak performance in a sustainable manner. The only difference is competency approach takes more time to provide results, but the results it can produce can be outstanding and last long comparing to transactional performance management where results can be quick, but focused on short-term and performances can be very elementary. Organizations need to free themselves from this short-sighted approach and seeking temporary gains.

Competency approach involves investment and growth building approach. The approach is nothing but focusing more on creating fundamental strength. However, competency approach do not discourage having focus on key result areas and goal setting, but it only emphasizes the importance of juxtaposing it with competency building in more pronounced manner. This means organizations start giving a new meaning and blend to their existing performance management, and sometimes, it may involve total overhaul of their performance management system.

Employee and organizational growth orientation shall be the cornerstone for performance management. Therefore, a performance management shall strive to create a practice where employee see that by adhering to it, they will be able to translate their potential into performance and organizations should see the possibilities of achieving targets and growth mandate. It calls for going beyond the traditional way of managing performance and performance plans.

Step 2: Developing Competency-based Performance Management Framework

Once at philosophical or strategic level, it is reconciled that performance management does require a growth orientation, the sequential step will be building competency-based performance management model in organizations. This may involve total revamp of existing process and practice. Many organizations tend to have an annual goal-setting and appraisal process. Some organizations might also have progressed to cascading down the organizational goals to individual employee level. What essentially the traditional performance management system misses is the precedents or contributors for good performance. Mere setting goals—whether stringent or stretch or moderate goals and leaving it to employees to achieve them is just believing that whatever is binding through a mutual arrangement is bound to happen. But in reality, many times many employees fail to achieve the agreed goals, because they realize during the course that they are not fully equipped to deal with those tasks and achieve whatever has been agreed upon. Any system or process including performance management tends to create antagonism when experience with such process is more of negative and less of success. Therefore, the first task is understanding the existing performance management system in organizations and plotting its strengths and weaknesses. A detailed assessment need to be carried out to see how the competencies required carrying out the typical tasks of that role is tied in the performance management system.

In order to approach performance management with a competency perspective, it is mandatory that an organization should have a matured and well-evolved competency model and the same must have already been tested and extended to other Human Resource Management practises like recruitment and selection and training and development. Absence of competency model will not augur well when an organization wants to create a competency-based performance management system. That will be a mere rhetoric as employees will not take it serious as the same may not possess the logical relation to the role and competencies associated with such role. Competency model and competency descriptions form the core basis of performance management system. Competencies applicable to each role as defined in competency descriptions shall be translated into key goals for employees. The proficiency levels of competencies can be used as rating and measurement standards to assess the competencies at the end of appraisal cycle. Also, a system should be created where the competencies requirement of a role is also associated with development opportunities available to build and enhance such competencies. This means an employee will not only have competencies as key goals, but development process is also defined. Managers also need to take responsibility for investing time and guidance to help employees in building competencies. In essence, the goal setting revolves around competency targets and proficiency levels and all in work context. The assumption is greater learning for competency building would automatically result in greater performance, because competency building initiatives here are not academic endeavours, but practical applications. There shall be either quarterly or half-yearly appraisal of competency assessment and should take mid-term correction to sustain the direction and efforts. The assessment also must involve how competency building and proficiency enhancement efforts are impacting performance of employees at work. The feedback sessions will be focusing on developmental feedback on learning efforts and progress of employees. The process of cascade shall be maintained for rational linkage between organizational goals and individual employee goals. Therefore, it is advisable that organizations shall identify competencies required to achieve its business goals and mission both for short-term and long-term. Those competency goals can be cascaded down by linking them to competency descriptions and tricking down it to role competencies, and to the individual employee competency goal sheets. First time organizations before introducing competency-based performance goals setting must undertake a comprehensive educational programme aimed at creating awareness among employees; how the entire system will work; and how it will help to transform them as competency based human resources; and how it can unleash their strengths and passion. Competency-based performance management has the power of creating huge positive energy in the place of traditional performance appraisals which are to some extent perceived as retrograde and coercive to employees.

Step 3: Setting Competency-based Performance Goals

As briefly discussed in Step 2, there shall be systematic flow and connection between organizational business goals and competency goals. Organizations shall use annual business planning sessions to identify what competencies and at what intensity and proficiency would be required to achieve such goals. A document describing the competency needs aligned with business goals shall be published. The organizational competency goals shall be further broken into function or department-wise or even inter-functional. From this level, these competencies can be tested against competency model of organizations especially to understand whether competency model is adequate in this context or does it need revisions. After the verification of competency model, the competency needs shall be incorporated into competency descriptions of various roles in organizations as a kind of competency standardization dictionary. The role-based competency descriptions form the basis for identifying and setting competency goals for each and every employee in organization. Mid and large sized organizations invariably need to automate this process to ensure efficiencies and avoid manual errors, and also such automation can help in analysis and monitoring of the entire competency goals setting process in a scientific manner. Once competency goals are set, it is important for the administrators to draw the dump of entire data in detailed as well as random to check the quality and consistency of competency goals and the process followed by employees and managers. How part is very important in competency-based performance management. How employees will be supported and opportunities will be provided shall be dealt, and also likewise how employees will acquire these competencies and how they will make efforts need to clearly be captured as performance targets. The basic difference between traditional performance management and competency-based performance management is—past performance of an employee is the consideration in traditional perspective, and future is the key for competency approach.

Step 4: Competency-based Performance Appraisal

The process that may be followed for appraising the competency acquisition, enhancement and utilization is to a great extent similar to that of traditional performance appraisal except that there can be some objective testing possible on competencies by way of testing. Like the standard form of a good appraisal, employee shall be given an opportunity to do the self-assessment on competencies and indicate rating on a scale. The manager can go through the self-assessment and validate all the details given there and apply own objective appraisal on competencies of employee while arriving onto the rating. Managers need to consider the achievements and contribution of employee and how over the appraisal duration, he or she had put in efforts to demonstrate competencies in work setting through application and impact of work processes. Any testing that might have happened and scores or performance indicators obtained using such testing also can be considered. The competency descriptions available to each role can also be used as standards especially the behavioural indicators in assessment of employee competencies. In a competency-based performance appraisals, the practises like bell curve will not be applicable as employees cannot be artificially pushed into categories of bell curve regardless of their proficiency. It is desirable from a governance perspective that there shall be a committee comprised of experts though in house to appraise the competencies at highest proficiency level. There shall be opportunities to employees to appeal if they are in disagreements with their competency appraisal as a part of the system. The appeal can be through respective reviewing managers as we deal in the standard traditional model of performance appraisal or through a specially formed group to go through all such disagreements and to recommend correction actions based on facts. The system should be open and transparent providing freedom for dissent and reason. Also, managers must bear in mind that there shall be a clear correlation between competency proficiency and their impact on the productivity/performance/outcome/contribution, and need to cite such relationships elaborately. Wherever there are dissonances between proficiency levels and actual level of performance, there must be an addendum with a clear analysis why such discrepancy existing. Is it due to lack of opportunities to employee to actually deploy the competency, or the relationship between that competency, and performance in reality doesn't exist? Findings of this nature are important not only for the objective assessment of competency-based performance but also to renew the competency framework in the real-work context.

Step 5: Competency-based Performance Feedback System

One of the most critical steps in institutionalizing competency-based performance management system is to religiously implement competency-based feedback system. In many organizations, despite of a decent awareness about the significance of feedback, it is neglected, when it comes to actual action. It is ironical that everybody feel that it is important for them to have feedback from their managers and peer group and also sometimes from reportees, but when it comes to them giving feedback most of them procrastinate. Even when they offer feedback, it is haphazard and momentary, mostly initiated in extra ordinary temperamental conditions and commenting on some performances rather than offering systematic feedback. Therefore, feedback ought to be formalized and a standard practice must be followed. Give the importance of feedback system in competency approach, managers shall be trained to offer feedback and a process must be defined for adherence across the organization. Feedback offered especially on competency of employees tends to be well-received. Managers shall maintain a kind of log book which will be helpful to them when the times come to offer feedback to employees. Based on log book or book of critical incidents, managers can offer feedback with evidence to employees. Feedback can be both on strengths and limitations and must be given in a friendly environment. We need to learn that any feedback given in antagonistic situations, employees tend to be defensive and would never work on it. Feedback also must be given at regular intervals, like at least once in three months in a detailed fashion. The feedback session also can be sued to identify action items for correcting or improving the situation or sustaining the good work. The objective of competency-based feedback system is to capture an early opportunity to provide objective view on competency status and growth of an employee and help in improvement rather than in the traditional method where the feedback system ends serving as a critical reporting event in which employees non-performance and weaknesses are highlighted as a reprimand. As a process for individuals who are in middle and senior level leadership positions, it is required that feedback is organized not only with immediate managers, but involving all stakeholders like reportees, peer group and customers. This can be a kind of 360 degree feedback system. Unlike normal 360 degree feedback system, here the feedback on competency related behaviours and linking them to performance. Feedback providers also feel positive and tend to be more objective when feedback is on competencies rather than judgments on performance of employees. Feedback records and data must form the basis for further competency building of employees, and in particular, such data should work as basis for training and development efforts. Mere seeking and providing feedback without acting on it will reduce the entire feedback system as a farce. Therefore, feedback system records should be directly linked to competency-based training and development administration.

Part V: Competency-based Career and Succession Planning System

Often career planning systems are confined to defining the path how employees can grow in vertical grade structures and carry fancy titles. This is because mostly organizational structures and processes are created based on hierarchical system of superiors and subordinates. Per se, hierarchy is not something less valuable, but the way it is structured give fillip to dysfunctional syndrome in organizations since it is assumed that whosoever is in a particular grade tend to have certain powers to decide course of things regardless of their competency. There is an implicit naïve assumption that whosoever is at senior levels can be understood to have the desired competencies. When promotions and career escalations are done on years of experience and task performance appraisals such an assumption that whosoever at senior level will automatically possess the required competencies is definitely an unscientific assumption. Many leadership failures or poor leadership quotient in organizations can be attributed to lack of focus on competencies and mere handling careers and succession planning based on some vague seniority and years of experience principle, coupled with lop-sided performance appraisal ratings. Therefore, it is an important task as well as challenging to move an organization from traditional form of promotion-oriented career planning to competency-based career planning systems. This will upset quite a few employees in organizations who have got used to a particular way of career planning which is more certain and less dynamic. Competency-based career and succession planning system is very dynamic and unsettle quite a few aspects since the career movements are based on competency acquisition and enhancement. It is a complete shift of reality for some, as moderately experiences employees sometime sue to their higher competency proficient may have righter chances to move up in the career much faster than some of other employees who might have been considered as seniors in the past. The chief advantage with competency-based career planning system is there is no constraint on opportunities which are popularly known as vacancies in organizational parlance. Some employees though considered technical fit cases for promotion do not get promoted, because of lack of vacancies. Career planning system need to be designed in such a way that each performing employee creates their own opportunities for growth, because employee growth cannot be separated from organizational growth. Unfortunately in traditional form, these two are de-linked so regardless of organizational growth most of the times, some employees do get elevated only to experience job erosion in the role. A competency-based career planning system can overcome this malady as a highly competency employee would contribute for significant growth in organization and a growing organization would generate opportunities for career upliftment. In that sense, competency-based career planning system is a self-sustaining process, where employees would create their own opportunities through the competency enhancement. A competency-based career and succession planning system can be created by adhering to the following steps:

Step 1: Setting Objectives for Competency-based Career Planning System

When an organization is planning to introduce competency-based career planning system as a fist step, it must spell out objectives of such career planning system. It also must decide whether such planning is targeted only career planning or intending to include succession planning also. Both these systems can go hand-in-hand as career planning at some point can take the shape of succession planning in order meet employee aspirations and organizational risk protection in terms of leadership pipeline. The objectives of career planning system typically can be to address career concerns of employees to meet organizational objectives to build a good career planning system that augment well with organizational growth plans. Career planning system objectives should have consistency with overall organizational Human Resource Management approach, especially focussing on competency orientation. Unless there is an overall competency framework, competency modelling and assessing tools and such competency approach is extended to other Human Resource Management application, it may not give the desired results if an organization wants to restrict application of competency approach merely to career systems.

In case where organizations have already have the existing practice of competency applications in other human resource practises, it ought to be studied and integrated with career planning system while drafting the objectives. The objectives will guide the entire journey of design and implementation of career management system. It is typical that organizations provide growth philosophy to both from employee and organizational front as career planning objective. Also it can address how competency-based career planning can provide unlimited career opportunities to employees and how employees can take control of their career themselves. It is empowering employees in many ways since they can decide themselves where they want to reach in their career by attaining competencies and proficiencies in proportionate to their ambition. Organizations can benefit through competencies those provide growth and innovation. Objectives of career planning system must be clear to all employees and enough of awareness needs to be created among employees how the competency-based career planning system works.

Step 2: Designing Competency-based Career Planning System

Number of competencies and proficiency of competencies play a crucial role in designing competency-based career planning system. Competency framework and descriptions shall be studied for defining levels of competencies, and they need to be pegged at levels of careers in the organization. For example, competency architecture of an organization can be classified into a minimum of three levels and a maximum of six levels. At the minimum level, there can be again a minimum of two and maximum of four competencies with fundamental proficiency level. That can be called for example as level one of the organizations. At the second level, there can be a minimum of four and maximum of six competencies with moderate proficiency levels and at the third level of career ladder, there shall be a requirement of minimum of six and maximum of eight competencies with a mastery in proficiency level. At the final level or senior most level of the company employees shall be expected to possess a minimum of eight and a maximum of ten competencies with highest proficiency, and they are like champions of those competencies within and outside of an organization. It does not mean that competency-based career planning do not give room for achieving highest standards in one or two competencies and climbing up the career ladder. It does, in technical and functional ladder, but may not be in leadership ladder of the company where the requirement is multiple competencies with varied proficiency levels. Based on objectives, different competency-based career ladders can be designed with defined criteria that may prescribe even a single competency championship or multiple competencies with different proficiency levels. Such opportunities can exist organization both depending on the kind of employee, an organization has and their aspirations to grow in particular ladders and organizational growth plans which generate number of opportunities for employees to grow in competency ladders.

When such competency-based career planning system is designed, initially there can be lot of apprehensions as it may appear as radical and creating an intellectual class in the company in the place of hierarchies. So, whenever a competency career planning system is designed it should have consensus among employees and such approach should be open and transparent. The design should have strong fundamentals and principles behind it. Without rationale, organizations merely in order to introduce a new system cannot get into designing competency-based career planning system. A design which is not well-thoughtout can create more challenges than the challenges an organization may have with the current system. Design shall be consistent with competency framework and competency descriptions shall form the basis for career ladders. Depending on the objectives and philosophy of organization duration as a pre-condition in the criteria from moving up in the career ladder can be defined. This is because quite a few experts and practitioners believe even when employees possess competencies it is ideal to prescribe a minimum time limit for moving up employees in order to establish the competency proficiency of employees on a reasonable time frame on a sustainable fashion.

Step 3: Implementing Competency-based Career Planning System

It is a formidable challenge to roll out a competency-based career planning system replacing the traditional promotion policy and process in any organization. This may involve protracted negotiations and persuasions and draft and redraft of implementation strategy. Unless most of the employees are bought into the new system, there is no way a competency-based career planning system can be successful how well the system might have been designed. Hence, it is important that the system is designed by taking inputs from employees and involving them at design stage itself. The actual roll out should be preceded by good communication and clear plan for sun setting the existing system. It is also advisable that implementation can be in a phased manner where the senior-most layers is brought under the purview of competency-based system at the first place and gradually extending it to other layers of organization. Of course, sometimes it is also a fact that rolling out the new competency-based career system is better to start with junior layers where the acceptance and resistance is lower with relatively younger workforce where such resistance can be higher at senior level. It is a paradoxical situation, since at junior level the impact of such change may not be much for organization, and where the impact can be powerful the resistance also can be significant. Hence, organizations shall choose an implementation approach that is conducive to its reality and prevailing work culture.

It is also possible that competency-based career planning process is deployed in combination with traditional and existing promotion process to begin with, and gradually the traditional promotion process can be weaned away in order to manage the shock of change in a way that can be coped easily. The implementation road map should be thoroughly analyzed and scenario mapping should be done detailing how the competency-based career planning is implemented, how the impact on the ground in terms of leadership pipeline building, opportunities created and contribution to attainment of organizational goals and any other significant benefits it might likely to accrue. Once the situation looks comfortable and the resistance levels are managed positively that may be the strategic time for organization to push through the competency-based career planning system agenda. It is ideal for mid- and large-sized organizations to opt for automation of competency-based career planning process which can be helpful for employees to do the self-assessment on regular basis and also managers can collaborate in such assessment. This way an organization can be successful in institutionalizing the competency-based career planning process.

Step 4: Implementing Competency-based Succession Planning

If the competency-based career planning system is rolled-out, and if the results of such roll-out is positive, an organization can contemplate of driving competency approach towards succession planning. Independent to competency-based approach; many organizations tend to indulge in competency assessment for the purpose of succession planning as a risk mitigation strategy for leadership levels. Such standalone and piece meal measures may help temporarily to address the situation, but the same may not provide long-term solution and sustainability. Further, the competencies used for assessment either as part of assessment center or development center not necessarily, sharply aligned and emanated from organizational need or they may be more of generic competencies. Such assessments will not give objective results and will not help conclusively in succession planning. Therefore, it is advisable that organization take up succession planning only when they have well-defined competency framework and such framework is used for career planning and experience with such roll-out is definitely positive. Because without establishing proper competency-based career planning jumping into succession planning is unscientific and will not provide a good succession plan at all. The career planning, which is in implementation, can be automatically extended to succession planning when it comes to senior layer of an organization. Competency-based career panning assessments can always provide the view and pipeline of employees with competencies required at highest level with highest proficiencies. That is the core advantage of competency-based career planning where there will be the adequate number of employees with such highest competency levels who can take up bigger responsibilities. So in that sense, succession planning is nothing but extension of competency-based career planning. The planning and assessment carried out can generate a reliable data on who is ready to perform in the top-most layer of organization based on competency ratings, but also can provide who can be ready in future with a clear timelines. Therefore, organizations that follow competency-based career planning need to have a separate activity as succession planning assessment and can separately generate the data for this purpose from an administrative point of view.

Step 5: Review and Renewal of Competency-based Career Planning System

Once a competency-based career planning system is drafted and rolled-out, it is desirable that the practice shall remain in force for a reasonable duration without being outdated and becoming non-relevant. It should be designed keeping in view not only immediate term, but also mid-term needs of the workforce and organization. However, no system can be rigid and insensitive to the changes as especially business organizations tend to experience changes more often. Therefore, while protecting the stability and sustainability of the career planning system, it should also leave enough room for flexibility and changes. In normal course, a competency-based career planning system shall be reviewed and renewed in consonance with findings once in every four years. However, such stipulation can be relaxed in conditions where cease of changes can be retrograde. Such flexibility shall be given strictly based on merits and value of changes. Mere to accommodate certain demands and relax the conditions, no change shall be accommodated or contemplated. Governance of a human resource system also hinges on how tightly a process is managed without giving levy to unhealthy pressures and demands. When changes occur particularly the major ones, it is again repeat of the cycle of change management. An organization shall take consensus in view while effecting changes and also should launch awareness programme on the changes. The changes shall not impact adversely a group of employees and should only accommodate changes if they are furthering the career planning objectives and competencies of employees. Administrators must note an important aspect: Review is meant for renewal of the career planning system and not merely review is just for taking the stock of stock or situation. Review must involve a systematic assessment of design process, implementation phase, and change management assessment, benefits out of roll-out, barriers experienced, facilitators noticed and overall perception of employees. A detailed report can be generated based on the data by correlating the findings obtained using various methods. There is no doubt that any system requires timely changes, and competency-based career planning system is no exception. This step only suggests that changes and renewal should not be done for the sake of giving a new look and feel, but should be done based on change of reality.

Questions for Discussion

5.1 Describe what a competency-based Human Resource Management application is? What are the pre-requisites for an organization to choose competency-based Human Resource Management application?

5.2 Discuss how an organization can use existing competency framework to transform their recruitment and selection function into competency-based hiring method? What are the various steps involved?

5.3 What is competency-based human resource planning process? Write short notes on mythical man month?

5.4 Why an organization should introduce competency-based training and development? Will it transform an organization into competency-based learning organization? What measures it should take to achieve this goal?

5.5 Often traditional form of compensation management leaves employees dissatisfied with their compensation! Can a competency-based compensation system create an acceptable equity? If yes, how it can create?

5.6 Create an operational plan for implementation of competency-based compensation management?

5.7 How different is competency-based performance management from KRA-based performance management system? What are the benefits in extending competency approach to performance management system?

5.8 Will competency-based career planning system be able to solve career related problems of employees? If no, please write why it cannot address the problem, and if yes, defend how it can resolve?

Case Studies for Discussion

1. ESR Global Corporation is a conglomerate of nine companies engaged in automobile spare parts, steam coal power station equipment manufacturing, steel manufacturing, office furniture, hotels and real estate. It has well-defined competency framework applicable to middle and senior level management of the conglomerate. However, no one has ever done a study how appropriately suited this competency framework for each of companies in the conglomerate. Despite this, the company's management board decided to extend the competency framework to their executive compensation administration. Assume that you are the HR manager who is given this responsibility of designing competency-based compensation management system. Discuss how you would approach the issue and what steps you will take to create what management desires without causing failure of disturbing the existing value of compensation management practice? Discuss how do you ensure that competency framework which is designed for entire conglomerate is apt for one of the companies?

2. Sys Info system is in existence for the last two decades offering enterprise solutions to its clientele headquartered in San Jose, California. It has over 2000 employees spread across six counties. The workforce profile is mainly engineering graduates, who have work experience ranging from 2 to 18 years. The company has a performance management system which has a well-defined criterion of goal setting, appraisal and feedback. An analysis of previous three year appraisal data show that about 80 per cent of employees either meet or exceeding their goals thus set for them by their managers. However, as an organization Sys Info could not meet its organizational goals in the last three years. Further, the assessment has shown that organization really lack competent resources who can steer the organization towards growth. It is a paradoxical situation for the organization where its workforce meets the goals, but organization fails. Is it cascading problem? Is it a problem of task-based performance appraisal? Whether competency-based performance management can help this organization? Discuss the possibilities?

Suggested Reading

Bartram, D. (2005): "The Great Eight Competencies: A Criterion-Centric Approach to Validation," *Journal of Applied Psychology*, **90**, pp. 1185–1203.

Catano, V., Darr, M., and Campbell, C. (2007): "Performance Appraisal of Behaviour-based Competencies: A Reliable and Valid Procedure," *Personnel Psychology*, **60**, pp. 201–230.

Cheng, M.I. and Dainty, R.I.J. (2005): "Toward a Multidimensional Competency-based Managerial Performance Framework: A Hybrid Approach," *Journal of Managerial Psychology*, **20**, pp. 380–396.

Draganidis, F. and G. Mentzas (2006): "Competency-based Management: A Review of Systems and Approaches," *Information Management and Computer Security*, **14**, pp. 51–64.

Dubois, D. and Rothwell, W. (2000): *The Competency Toolkit*, Vols. **1** & **2**, HRM Press.

Dubois, D. and Rothwell, W. (2004): *Competency-Based Human Resource Management*, Davies-Black Publishing.

Homer, M. (2001): Skills and Competency Management: Industrial and Commercial Training, **33**:2, pp. 59–62.

Horton, S. (2000): "Introduction—The Competency-based Movement: Its Origins and Impact on the Public Sector," *The International Journal of Public Sector Management*, **13**, pp. 306–318.

Kochanski, J.T. and Ruse, D.H. (1996): "Designing a Competency-based Human Resources Organization," *Human Resource Management*, **35**, pp. 19–34.

Lucia, A.D. and Lepsinger, R. (1999): *The Art and Science of Competency Models: Pinpointing Critical Success Factors in Organizations*, San Francisco: Jossey-Bass.

McEvoy, G., Hayton, J., Wrnick, A., Mumford, T., Hanks, S., and Blahna, M. (2005): "A Competency-based Model for Developing Human Resource Professionals," *Journal of Management Education*, **29**, pp. 383–402.

Rausch, E., Sherman, H., and Washbush, J.B. (2002): "Defining and Assessing Competencies for Competency-based, Outcome-Focused Management Development," *The Journal of Management Development*, **21**, pp. 184–200.

Sanchez, J.I. and Levine, E.L. (2009): "What is (or should be) the Difference between Competency Modelling and Traditional Job Analysis?" *Human Resource Management Review*, **19**, pp. 53–63.

Schmidt, F.L. and Hunter, J.E. (1998): "The Validity and Utility of Selection Methods in Personnel Psychology: Practice and Theoretical Implications of Research Findings," *Psychological Bulletin*, **124**, pp. 262–274.

Shandler, D. (2000): *Competency and the Learning Organization*, Crisp Learning.

Shippmann, J.S., Ash, R.A., Battista, M., Carr, L., Eyde, L.D., Hesketh, B., Kehoe, J., Pearlman, K., and Sanchez, J.I. (2000): "The Practice of Competency Modeling," *Personnel Psychology*, **53**, pp. 703–740.

Spencer, L.M. in Cherniss, C. and Goleman, D. (Eds) (2001): "The Economic Value of Emotional Intelligence Competencies and EIC-based HR Programs," *in The Emotionally Intelligent Workplace: How to Select for, Measure, and Improve Emotional Intelligence in Individuals*, Groups and Organizations. San Francisco, CA: Jossey-Bass/Wiley.

Spencer, L.M. (2004): Competency Model Statistical Validation and Business Case Development, HR Technologies White Paper.

Spencer, L. and Spencer, S. (1993): *Competence at Work: Models for Superior Performance*. Wiley, New Jersey.

Ulrich, D. and Brockbank, W. (2005): *The HR Value Proposition*, Boston: Harvard Business School Press.

Wood, R. and Payne, T. (1998): *Competency-Based Recruitment and Selection*, Wiley, New Jersey.

Author Index

Subject Index